WHITMAN
THE POET

Wadsworth Guides to Literary Study
Maurice Beebe, General Editor

WHITMAN
THE POET

Materials for Study

EDITED BY

John C. Broderick
WAKE FOREST COLLEGE

WADSWORTH PUBLISHING COMPANY, INC.

BELMONT, CALIFORNIA

To Floyd Stovall

Second printing, December 1964

L.C. Cat. Card No.: 62–13200
Printed in the United States of
America

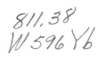

CONTENTS

Part Two
Writings about Whitman

5 Contemporary Critical Estimates (1855–1892)

6 Whitman's Form and Technique

7 Whitman's Prosody

8 Whitman's Style and Language

PREFACE

Despite his undeniable interest as a person, as a force for freedom in life and letters, and even, for some readers, as a psychological, biographical, or bibliographical puzzle, Walt Whitman is fundamentally a poet. As a poet, his achievement has been sometimes obscured by his own utterances, by intemperate attacks on the man because of alleged indecency in the writing, and by extravagant counterclaims by Whitman's partisans. Nevertheless, as the selections in this volume show, Whitman's poetry has been the subject of comment and debate ever since the publication of *Leaves of Grass* in 1855. This comment has increased in volume, if not in insight, through the years. In 1955, the centennial of the first publication of *Leaves of Grass,* almost every professional student of Whitman had his say in numerous articles and books, including a full-scale biography. The output has not subsided, and readers of Whitman may now look forward to a completely new edition of his works, recently announced by a major university press, with some volumes already published.

There is irony in the widespread academic acceptance of Whitman as a major, probably the chief, American poet: a double irony, in fact, since Whitman looked for acceptance by common average humanity, not the intellectual classes, and during his lifetime representatives of the genteel academic world accepted him slowly and reluctantly. It seems clear now, however, that Whitman, as George Bernard Shaw observed long ago, is a classic, not a best-seller. Like other classics, *Leaves of Grass* requires, for many readers, the mediating function of criticism.

One obstacle to immediate acceptance of Whitman's poetry was its form; another, its content. Earlier commentators on Whitman's poetry were impressed, and sometimes repelled, by its "radical" form and by its revolutionary subject matter. More recent students have modified both impressions. First of all, they have found Whitman's form to be less radical than supposed and have demonstrated its kinship with other poetry and with other arts. Because of changing standards of decorum, Whitman's subject matter also is now less likely to offend. Furthermore, increasing interest in the American literary heritage has led to familiarity with Whitman's poetry, a familiarity reinforced by the example of twentieth-century poets such as Carl Sandburg and Hart Crane. Paradoxically, some critics feel that Whitman is now *threatened* by this very familiarity—by too facile an acceptance and a consequent failure to recognize his native poetic energies, his boldness, even his "wit." Hence his poetry has recently attracted the close critical attention heretofore reserved for poets more obviously "metaphysical." Hence also the increasingly frequent comparisons with T. S. Eliot. The undertone of objection has not completely subsided, of course; but objection now is based almost entirely on the question of the poet's achievement, the adequacy of his poetic vision and the skill of his craftsmanship.

The materials excerpted in this book provide for varied approaches to Whitman's poetry. Most of the issues that have animated discussion of Whitman's poetry are represented here: the nature of his literary idiom, the degree of artistic control, the influence of his theories on language, his poetic sensitivity. Whitman was a frequent, though not always consistent, spokesman concerning his aims and intentions. Part One brings together some of Whitman's prefaces, poems, and private comments on his poetry and that of others. Part Two brings together critical essays that deal with some of the specifically poetic characteristics of his writing. These are separated according to major emphasis, though it is impossible to make such separations complete. One essay may combine a discussion of language, versification, and imagery; hence, the student should not restrict his reading to a single section even when he is investigating a single problem. For term projects, all the resources of the book should be employed. These may be supplemented by reading guided by the annotated bibliography at the end of the book. The beginning student will also wish to consult the chronology of major events and publications at the beginning of the book. For classroom discussion and for shorter critical papers, a section of questions for study and topics for writing is included.

I have tried to present exact texts in all cases, except that a few obvious misspellings have been silently corrected. Omitted portions of a text are indicated by spaced ellipses (. . .); unspaced ellipses (...) are those of the original source. For the excerpts in Part Two (and some of those in Part One) I have provided a title more nearly appropriate for the excerpted portion (the original title appears in the source note). Footnotes in the original sources have been renumbered consecutively throughout the excerpts; some footnotes have been omitted. Where necessary, some footnotes have been clarified by the addition of bracketed material. By using the bibliographical source notes and observing the bracketed page divisions, a student can document his paper by reference to some of the standard authorities on Whitman, acquiring valuable bibliographical training in situations where time is short, library facilities are limited, or a "controlled" approach is desirable.

A word about some poems by Whitman which some readers may feel are unaccountably omitted: There are omissions, but they are accountable. Although every reader may have a special favorite among the poems, Whitman's masterpieces are generally reckoned to include "Song of Myself," "Crossing Brooklyn Ferry," "Out of the Cradle Endlessly Rocking," "When Lilacs Last in the Dooryard Bloom'd," and "Passage to India." Since these poems are readily accessible in anthologies and readers, Whitman is here represented by a limited number of his best and best-known poems, supplemented by poems of the next rank from all his productive periods. The student is advised to acquaint himself with all the poems named above and as many others by Whitman as time and ambition will allow.

For their willingness to listen to my questions (and even to answer some of them), I am indebted to my colleagues William O. Harris and Robert Howren; to Floyd Stovall of the University of Virginia; to Richard P. Adams of Tulane; to the general editor of this series, Maurice Beebe of Purdue; and to Mrs. Alison Thomson of the Rare Book room of Duke University, where the Josiah C. Trent Collection of Whitman materials is housed.

A WHITMAN CHRONOLOGY*

1819   Born at West Hills, Long Island, May 31, second child of Walter and Louisa Van Velsor Whitman.

1823   Family moved to Brooklyn May 27.

1825–30   Public schooling in Brooklyn.

1830–36   Held various jobs in Brooklyn and New York, mostly in printing and newspaper offices.

1836–41   Schoolteaching on Long Island, interspersed with work on Long Island newspapers, one of these his own, the Huntington *Long Islander*.

1841–47   Editor of New York and Brooklyn newspapers, contributor to various periodicals, and author of *Franklin Evans* (a temperance novel).

1848   February to May in New Orleans with his brother Jeff to work for a newspaper. Returned to Brooklyn by way of the Mississippi River and the Great Lakes.

1849–51   Editor and contributor to periodicals, including some poetic contributions.

1850–55   Apparently wrote and printed poems to be published in 1855 *Leaves of Grass*.

1852–54   Carpenter and housebuilder in Brooklyn.

1855   First edition of *Leaves of Grass* published in July, shortly before death of Whitman's father July 11. Edition contained twelve poems and a prose preface, the chief poem being "Song of Myself."

1856   Second edition of *Leaves of Grass* published about September 1; contained twenty additional poems including "Crossing Brooklyn Ferry" and "Song of the Open Road," along with Ralph Waldo Emerson's congratulatory letter and Whitman's reply.

1857–59   Brooklyn editor and frequenter of Pfaff's restaurant in New York.

---

* In preparing this chronology I have relied heavily on the one in *Walt Whitman: Representative Selections,* ed. Floyd Stovall, American Writers Series (New York: American Book Co., 1939); and on Gay Wilson Allen, *The Solitary Singer* (New York: The Macmillan Co., 1955). Significant publication dates are printed in bold face.

1860 Arrived in Boston, March 15, to arrange third edition of *Leaves of Grass,* published in early May by Thayer and Eldridge. New poems included "A Word out of the Sea" ("Out of the Cradle Endlessly Rocking") and almost all poems included in *Enfans d'Adam* and *Calamus,* two sections celebrating the love of man for woman and man for man, respectively. Famous talk with Ralph Waldo Emerson about the contents.

1860–62 Visited hospitalized stage drivers in New York and wrote antiquarian articles about Brooklyn.

1862 Left Brooklyn December 16 for army camp in Virginia to attend brother George, reportedly wounded.

1863–73 Lived mostly in Washington, D.C., with regular vacations and other visits to Brooklyn. Occupied first as volunteer hospital visitor, then as government employee in the Department of Interior and Attorney General's office. Established important friendships with the William O'Connors, John Burroughs, and others.

1865 *Drum-Taps* published in May. *Sequel to Drum-Taps* published in the fall. Mostly poems on the Civil War and on the death of Lincoln, including "When Lilacs Last in the Dooryard Bloom'd."

1867 Fourth edition of *Leaves of Grass* published in November. Contained few new poems but much revision.

1868 Selected edition of *Poems of Walt Whitman* published in England in February, with introduction by William Michael Rossetti.

1870 Publication of *Democratic Vistas,* a prose pamphlet based on three articles written for magazine publication two or three years earlier.

1871 Fifth edition of *Leaves of Grass* published, incorporating *Drum-Taps* and *Sequel,* in approximately final arrangement. *Passage to India* published—pamphlet with "Passage to India" as title poem.

1872 Pamphlet, *As a Strong Bird on Pinions Free and Other Poems,* published with significant preface.

1873 Suffered paralytic stroke on January 23, followed by death of his mother four months later in Camden, New Jersey, at the home of his brother George. Except for trips and visits, Whitman lived in Camden for the rest of his life.

1876 Sixth edition of *Leaves of Grass,* published as one of two volumes with *Two Rivulets,* a collection of poetry and prose including *Passage to India* supplement and *Democratic Vistas.* Spent summer at farm home of George Stafford.

1879 Traveled through West and Southwest for several months. Visited brother Jeff in St. Louis.

1880 Visited Dr. R. M. Bucke in Canada.

1881 Visited Boston to supervise preparation of seventh edition of *Leaves of Grass,* published by James R. Osgood, with the final arrangement of the poems (except for additional sections composed during the 1880's and added as "Annexes"). After threatened prosecution for obscenity, Osgood dissociated himself from the publication.

1882 *Specimen Days and Collect* published in fall—autobiographical sketches and miscellaneous prose.

1884 Purchased house at 328 Mickle Street in Camden, where he lived out his life.

1888 *November Boughs* published in November with preface, "A Backward Glance o'er Travel'd Roads." Poems later "annexed" as *Sands at Seventy* in 1892 edition. *Walt Whitman: Complete Poems and Prose. 1855–1888* published; large single-volume reprint of 1881, 1882, and 1888 editions of writings.

1888–92 In declining health, confined mostly to his room, ministered to by Horace Traubel, Thomas B. Harned, and other friends.

1889 Pocket-size edition of *Leaves of Grass* published for seventieth birthday.

1891–92 Final edition of *Leaves of Grass* published.

1892 Died March 26. Buried March 30.

PART ONE
Writings by Whitman

WHITMAN'S PREFACES

Preface to *Leaves of Grass*

FROM *Leaves of Grass,* 1st edition (1855). In *The Complete Writings of Walt Whitman,* Camden Edition (hereafter identified as *Complete Writings,* Camden Edition), 10 vols., edited by Richard Maurice Bucke, Thomas B. Harned, and Horace L. Traubel (New York and London: G. P. Putnam's Sons, 1902), V, 161–184.

America does not repel the past, or what the past has produced under its forms, or amid other politics, or the idea of castes, or the old religions—accepts the lesson with calmness—is not impatient because the slough still sticks to opinions and manners in literature, while the life which served its requirements has passed into the new life of the new forms—perceives that the corpse is slowly borne from the eating and sleeping rooms of the house—perceives that it waits a little while in the door—that it was fittest for its days—that its action has descended to the stalwart and well-shaped heir who approaches—and that he shall be fittest for his days.

The Americans of all nations at any time upon the earth have probably the fullest poetical nature. The United States themselves are essentially the greatest poem. In the history of the earth hitherto, the largest and most stirring appear tame and orderly to their ampler largeness and stir. Here at last is something in the doings of man that corresponds with the broadcast doings of the day and night.[161]

. . . The largeness of the nation, however, were monstrous without a corresponding largeness and generosity of the spirit of the citizen. Not swarming states, nor streets and steamships, nor prosperous business, nor farms, nor capital, nor learning, may suffice for the ideal of man—nor suffice the poet. No reminiscences may suffice either. A live nation can always cut a deep mark, and can have the best authority the cheapest—namely, from[162] its own soul. This is the sum of the profitable uses of individuals or states, and of present action and grandeur, and of the subjects of poets. (As if it were necessary to trot back generation after generation to the Eastern records! As if the beauty and sacredness of the demonstrable must fall behind that of the mythical! As if men do not make their mark out of any times! As if the opening of the Western Continent by discovery, and what has transpired in North and South America, were less than the small theatre of the antique, or the aimless sleep-walking of the Middle Ages!) The pride of the United States leaves the wealth and finesse of the cities, and all returns of commerce and agriculture, and all the magnitude of geography or shows of exterior victory, to enjoy the sight and realization of full-sized men, or one full-sized man unconquerable and simple.

The American poets are to enclose old and new, for America is the race of races. The expression of the American poet is to be transscendent and new. It is to be indirect, and not direct or descriptive or epic. Its quality goes through these to much more. Let the age and wars of other nations be chanted, and their eras and characters be illustrated, and that finish the verse. Not so the great psalm of the republic. Here the theme is creative, and has vistas.[163]

. . . The poetic quality is not marshal'd in rhyme or uniformity, or abstract addresses to things, nor in melancholy complaints or good precepts, but is the life of these and much else, and is in the soul. The profit of rhyme is that it drops seeds of a sweeter and more luxuriant rhyme, and of uniformity that it conveys itself into its own roots in the ground out of sight. The rhyme and uniformity of perfect poems show the free growth of metrical laws, and bud from them as unerringly and loosely as lilacs and roses on a bush, and take shapes as compact as the shapes of chestnuts and oranges, and melons and pears, and shed the perfume impalpable to form. The fluency and ornaments of the finest poems or music or orations or recitations are not independent but dependent. All beauty comes from beautiful blood and a beautiful brain. If the greatnesses are in conjunction in a man or woman, it is enough—the fact will prevail through the universe; but the gaggery and gilt of a million years will not prevail. Who troubles himself about his ornaments or fluency is lost. This is what you shall do: Love the earth and sun and the animals, despise riches, give alms to every one that asks, stand up for the stupid and crazy, devote[166] your income and labor to others, hate tyrants, argue not concerning God, have patience and indulgence towards the people, take off your hat to nothing known or unknown, or to any man or number of men—go freely with powerful uneducated persons, and with the young, and with the mothers of families—re-examine all you have been told in school or church or in any book, and dismiss whatever insults your own soul; and your very flesh shall be a great poem, and have the richest fluency, not only in its words, but in the silent lines of its lips and face, and between the lashes of your eyes, and in every motion and joint of your body. . . .[167]

The art of art, the glory of expression and the sunshine of the light of letters, is simplicity. Nothing is better than simplicity—nothing can make up for excess, or for the lack of definiteness. To carry on the heave of impulse and pierce intellectual depths and give all subjects their articulations, are powers neither common nor very uncommon. But to speak in literature with the perfect rectitude and insouciance of the movements of animals, and the unimpeachableness of the sentiment of trees in the woods and grass by the roadside, is the flawless triumph of art. If you have look'd on him who has achiev'd it you have look'd on one of the masters of the artists of all nations and times. You shall not contemplate the flight of the gray gull over the bay, or the mettlesome action of the blood horse, or the tall leaning of sunflowers on their stalk, or the appearance of the sun journeying through heaven, or the appearance of the moon afterward, with any more satisfaction[170] than you shall contemplate him. The great poet has less a mark'd style, and is more the channel of thoughts and things without increase or diminution, and is the free channel of himself. He swears to his art, I will not be meddlesome, I will not have in my writing any elegance, or effect, or originality, to hang in the way between me and the rest like curtains. I will have nothing hang in the way, not the richest curtains. What I tell I tell for precisely what it is. . . .[171]

There will soon be no more priests. Their work is done. A new order shall arise, and they shall be[182] the priests of man, and every man shall be his own priest. They shall find their inspiration in real objects to-day, symptoms of the past and future. They shall not deign to defend immortality or God, or the perfection of things, or liberty, or the exquisite beauty and reality of the soul. They shall arise in America, and be responded to from the remainder of the earth.

The English language befriends the grand American expression— it is brawny enough, and limber and full enough. On the tough stock of a race who through all change of circumstance was never without the idea of political liberty, which is the animus of all liberty, it has attracted the terms of daintier and gayer and subtler and more elegant tongues. It is the powerful language of resistance—it is the dialect of common sense. It is the speech of the proud and melancholy races, and of all who aspire. It is the chosen tongue to express growth, faith, self-esteem, freedom, justice, equality, friendliness, amplitude, prudence, decision and courage. It is the medium that shall wellnigh express the inexpressible.[183] . . .

Letter to Ralph Waldo Emerson

FROM "Leaves-Droppings." In *Leaves of Grass,* 2nd edition (Brooklyn, New York, 1856), pp. 343–384. "Leaves-Droppings" was a collection containing comments about the 1855 Edition; Emerson's letter to Whitman (see p. 66 below); and Whitman's reply.

Here are thirty-two Poems, which I send you, dear Friend and Master, not having found how I could satisfy myself with sending any usual acknowledgment of your letter. . . . I much enjoy making poems. Other work I have set for myself to do, to meet people and The States face to face, to confront them with an American rude tongue; but the work of my life is making poems. . . . In poems or in speeches I say the word or two that has got to be said, adhere to the body, step with the countless common footsteps, and remind every man and woman of something.[346] . . .

What else can happen The States [*sic*], even in their own despite? That huge English flow, so sweet, so undeniable, has done incalculable good here, and is to be spoken of for its own sake with generous praise and with gratitude. Yet the price The States have had to lie under for the same has not been a small price. . . . [America!] Open the doors of The West. Call for new great masters to comprehend new arts, new perfections, new wants. Submit to the most robust bard till he remedy your barrenness. Then you will not need to adopt the heirs of others; you will have true heirs, begotten of yourself, blooded with your own blood.[348]

. . . Of course all literature, in all nations and years, will share marked attributes in common, as we all, of all ages, share the common human attributes. America is to be kept coarse and broad. What is to be done is to withdraw from precedents, and be directed to men and women—also to The States in their federalness; for the union of the parts of the body is not more necessary to their life than the union of These States is to their life.[350] . . . The genius of all foreign literature is clipped and cut small, compared to our genius, and is essentially insulting to our usages, and to the organic compacts of These States. Old forms, old poems, majestic and proper in their own lands here in this land are exiles; the air here is very strong. . . . Authorities, poems, models, laws, names, imported into America, are useful to America today to destroy them, and so move disencumbered to great works, great days.[351]

. . . Always America will be agitated and turbulent. This day it is taking shape, not to be less so, but to be more so, stormily, capriciously, on native principles, with such vast proportions of parts! As for me, I love screaming, wrestling, boiling-hot days.

Of course, we shall have a national character, an identity. . . . Such character, strong, limber, just, open-mouthed, American-blooded, full of ease, of passionate friendliness, is to stand compact upon that vast basis of the supremacy of Individuality—that new moral[357] American continent without which, I see, the physical continent remained incomplete. . . .

Those shores you found. I say you have led The States there— have led Me there. I say that none has ever done, or ever can do, a greater deed for The States, than your deed. . . .[358]

Three Unpublished Prefaces

IN *Walt Whitman's Workshop. A Collection of Unpublished Manuscripts*, edited by Clifton Joseph Furness (Cambridge: Harvard Uni-

versity Press, 1928), pp. 131 ff. Reprinted by permission of the publisher. All of these prefaces seem to have been prepared during the
1860's.

INSCRIPTION TO THE READER
AT THE ENTRANCE OF LEAVES OF GRASS

Dear friend, whoe'er you are, at last arriving hither, accept from
me (as one in waiting for you at this entrance,) a word of living
hospitality and love. I almost feel the curving hold and pressure of your
hand, which I return, and thus throughout upon the journey linked
together will we go. Indeed this is no book but more a man, within
whose breast the common heart is throbbing; no leaves of paper these
must prove but lips for your sake freely speaking. . . .[131] Dear
friend![1] I put not in the following leaves melodious narratives, or
pictures for you to con at leisure, as bright creations finished all outside yourself. With such the world is well enough supplied. But of
Suggestiveness alone out of the things around us, with steady reference
to the life to come, and to the miracles of everyday this is the song—
naught made by me for you, but only hinted, to be made by you
yourself. Indeed I have not done the work, and cannot do it. But you
must do the work to really make what is within the following song—
which, if you do, I promise you return & satisfaction earned by you
yourself far more than ever book before has given you. For from this
book Yourself, before unknown, shall now rise up & be revealed.[2] This
book shall[132] hint the poem of America, and its mighty masses of men,
and a new and grand race of women.[3] [133]

INTRODUCTION TO THE LONDON EDITION

America—that new world in so many respects besides its geography—has perhaps afforded nothing even in the astonishing products
of the fields of its politics, its mechanical invention, material growth,

---

[1] Variant reading (probably first draft): *Dear friend! I put not in these Leaves,
melodious narratives or pictures for you to con at leisure for bright creations all
outside yourself. Not so—but of Suggestiveness to you alone this is*[236] *the song—
naught made & finished for you, but all invited to be made by you and from you.
Indeed I have not done the work*, etc. (The remainder shows little variation from
the reading given in text.)

[2] Cf. the thoughts Whitman recorded on "Suggestiveness" in his old age
("A Backward Glance . . ."); also this report from an interview, in the Springfield
Republican, July 23, 1875: "*My book compels,* absolutely necessitates every reader
to transpose him or herself into that central position, and become the living
fountain, actor, experiencer himself or herself, of every page, every aspiration,
every line."

[3] Alternative reading (on "trial sheet"): *America and all its mighty masses of
men and a new grand race of women will appear.* Also: *America and all its mighty
masses of men in their workshops, and the men of steamships and engines, and the
turbulent friendly, free cities, and the great masses everywhere, and a new and
grand race of women will appear.*[237]

& the like, more original, more autochthonic, than its late contribution in the field of literature, the Poem, or poetic writings, named Leaves of Grass, which in the following pages we present to the British public.

At first sight, the form of these verses, not only without rhyme, but wholly regardless of the customary verbal melody & regularity so much labored after by modern poets, will strike the reader with incredulous amazement. Then the perusal of the book will open to his view other still profounder innovations. The absolute & unqualified acceptance of Nature; the unprecedentedly candid treatment of the human body, & the exulting celebration of it in its entirety & in all its parts, without the exclusion of any; the absence, ostensibly at least, of any thing like plot, or definite point or purpose in the poems; their boundless outcroppage of arrogant animal muscle & brawn, closely tracked everywhere by an equal outcroppage of the most refined transcendentalism, & loftiest spirituality;—these, expressed through phraseology of never-surpassed earnestness and determination, make indeed a book whose presence & pages, & the action between them & their reader, resemble the struggles of the gymnastic arena, more than the usual orderly entertainment given by authors.

Taken as a unity, Leaves of Grass, true to its American origin, is a song of "the great pride of man in himself." It assumes to[150] bring the materials & outline the architecture of a more complete, more advanced, idiocratic, masterful, Western personality—the combination and model of a new Man. It does not dwell on the past, & celebrates in no way the superb old feudal world, or its gorgeous reminiscences; it is built forward in the demesne(s)[1] of the future, and it would seem as if somehow, a great coming and regnant Democracy—the dream of poets from the time of Plato, & before him, & since, too—had advanced sufficiently,[2] & here given genesis to every line.[3] —It possesses, more than any other known book, the magnetism of living flesh & blood, sitting near the reader, & looking & talking. It is marvelously cosmopolitan. Always manly friendship, the ties of nations & cities, & their common sympathies & common brotherhood—never their jealousies, vaunts[,] special glories or any thought or thing calculated to keep them apart—are encouraged & persistently upheld. The book may be further described as a genuine confession & conference of one single representative humanity, a free, yet ardently intensified *tete-a-tete*. The crowded parlor or a promiscuous audience is not its sphere. It is the most emotional & yearning of poems, & really unfolds itself only in the presence of you, the reader, with no third person near.

Like the world itself, it is not without passages that will puzzle,

---

1 In the Ms. the *s* is added as a separate letter, and written very small, as if Whitman were not sure whether it should be there.

2 *advanced sufficiently*, as well as *already*, written in above the line, are all crossed through.

3 Originally *page & line.*[243]

cause hesitation, & even shock the conventional, well-meaning student & beholder. But its fervent & powerful efflux evidently flows from a devout soul, & its writer as evidently writes from deep plan & science, & with an elaborated ethic intention, born of & designed to justify, the Democratic theory of his country & carry it out far beyond the merely political beginning already made.[151] . . .

FROM AN UNTITLED MANUSCRIPT

The theory of the poem [i.e., *Leaves of Grass*] involves both the expression of the hottest, wildest passion, bravest, sturdiest character, not however illustrated after any of the well-known types, the identities of the great bards old or modern.[1] Nor Prometheus is here, nor Agamemnon, nor Aeneas, nor Hamlet, nor Iago, nor Antony, nor any of Dante's scenes or persons,[2] nor ballad of lord or lady, nor Lucretian philosophy nor any special system of philosophy nor striking lyric achievement, nor Childe Harold, nor any epic tale with beginning, climax and termination, yet something of perhaps similar purpose, very definite, compact, (and curiously digesting & including all the list we have just named) very simple even and applying directly to the reader at first hand, is the main result (& purpose) of this book, namely to suggest the substance and form of a large, sane, perfect Human Being or character for an American man and for woman. While other things are in the book, studies, digressions of various sorts, this is undoubtedly its essential purpose and its key, so that in the poems taken as a whole unquestionably appears a great Person, entirely modern, at least as great as anything in the Homeric or Shakespearean characters, a person with the free courage of Achilles, the craft of Ulysses, the attributes even of the Greek deities. Majesty, passion, temper, amativeness, Romeo, Lear, Antony, immense self-esteem, but after democratic forms, measureless love, the old eternal elements of first-class humanity. Yet worked over, cast in a new mould, and[136] here chanted or anyhow put down & stated with invariable reference to the United States & the occasions of today & the future.[137]

Preface to *As a Strong Bird*

FROM *As a Strong Bird on Pinions Free and Other Poems* (1872). In *Complete Writings*, Camden Edition, V, 185–192.

The impetus and ideas urging me, for some years past, to an utterance, or attempt at utterance, of New World songs, and an epic

---

[1] At the top of this paragraph is written: *Some good points.*
[2] The following marginal note seems to refer to these literary figures: *They are the negative suggestions & here is the positive.*[238]

of Democracy, having already had their publish'd expression, as well as I can expect to give it, in *Leaves of Grass*, the present and any future pieces from me are really but the surplusage forming after that volume, or the wake eddying behind it. I fulfill'd in that an imperious conviction, and the commands of my nature as total and irresistible as those which make the sea flow, or the globe revolve. But of this supplementary volume, I confess I am not so certain. Having from early manhood abandon'd the business pursuits and applications usual in my time and country, and obediently yielded myself up ever since to the impetus mention'd, and to the work of expressing those ideas, it may be that mere habit has got dominion of me, when there is no real need of saying anything further. But what is life but an experiment? and mortality but an exercise? with reference to results beyond. And so shall my poems be. If incomplete here, and superfluous there, *n'importe*—the earnest trial and persistent exploration shall at least be mine, and other success failing shall be success enough. I have been more anxious, anyhow, to suggest the songs of vital endeavor and manly evolution, and furnish something for races of outdoor athletes, than to make perfect rhymes, or reign in the parlors. I[185] ventur'd from the beginning my own way, taking chances—and would keep on venturing.

I will therefore not conceal from any persons, known or unknown to me, who take an interest in the matter, that I have the ambition of devoting yet a few years to poetic composition. The mighty present age! To absorb and express in poetry, anything of it—of its world—America—cities and States—the years, the events of our Nineteenth century—the rapidity of movement—the violent contrasts, fluctuations of light and shade, of hope and fear—the entire revolution made by science in the poetic method—these great new underlying facts and new ideas rushing and spreading everywhere; truly a mighty age! . . .[186]

. . . (The moral of a late well-written book on civilization seems to be that the only real foundation-walls and bases—and also the *sine qua non* afterward—of true and full civilization, is the eligibility and certainty of boundless products for feeding, clothing, sheltering everybody—perennial fountains of physical and domestic comfort, with intercommunication, and with civil and ecclesiastical freedom—and that then the esthetic and mental business will take care of itself. Well,[188] the United States have establish'd this basis, and upon scales of extent, variety, vitality, and continuity, rivaling those of Nature; and have now to proceed to build an edifice upon it. I say this edifice is only to be fitly built by new literatures, especially the poetic. I say a modern image-making creation is indispensable to fuse and express the modern political and scientific creations—and then the trinity will be complete.)

When I commenced, years ago, elaborating the plan of my poems, and continued turning over that plan, and shifting it in my mind through many years (from the age of twenty-eight to thirty-five), experimenting much, and writing and abandoning much, one deep purpose underlay the others, and has underlain it and its execution ever since—and that has been the religious purpose. Amid many changes, and a formulation taking far different shape from what I at first supposed, this basic purpose has never been departed from in the composition of my verses. Not of course to exhibit itself in the old ways, as in writing hymns or psalms with an eye to the church-pew, or to express conventional pietism, or the sickly yearnings of devotees, but in new ways, and aiming at the widest sub-bases and inclusions of humanity, and tallying the fresh air of sea and land. I will see (said I to myself), whether there is not, for my purposes as poet, a religion, and a sound religious germenancy in the average human[189] race, at least in their modern development in the United States, and in the hardy common fiber and native yearnings and elements, deeper and larger, and affording more profitable returns, than all mere sects or churches—as boundless, joyous, and vital as Nature itself—a germenancy that has too long been unencouraged, unsung, almost unknown. With science, the old theology of the East, long in its dotage, begins evidently to die and disappear. But (to my mind) science—and maybe such will prove its principal service—as evidently prepares the way for One indescribably grander—Time's young but perfect offspring—the new theology—heir of the West—lusty and loving, and wondrous beautiful. For America, and for today, just the same as any day, the supreme and final science is the science of God—what we call science being only its minister—as Democracy is, or shall be also. And a poet of America (I said) must fill himself with such thoughts, and chant his best out of them. And as those were the convictions and aims, for good or bad, of *Leaves of Grass,* they are no less the intention of this volume. . . .[190]

   Leaves of Grass, already publish'd, is, in its intentions, the song of a great composite *democratic individual,* male or female. And following on and amplifying the same purpose, I suppose I have in my mind to run through the chants of this volume (if ever completed), the thread-voice, more or less audible, of an aggregated, inseparable, unprecedented, vast, composite, electric *democratic nationality.*

   Purposing, then, to still fill out, from time to time through years to come, the following volume (unless prevented), I conclude this preface to the first instalment of it, pencil'd in the open air, on my fifty-third birthday, by wafting to you, dear reader, whoever you are (from amid the fresh scent of the grass, the pleasant coolness of the forenoon breeze, the lights and shades of tree-boughs silently dappling and playing around me, and the notes of the cat-bird for undertone and accompaniment), my true good-will and love.   w. w.[192]

Preface to *Leaves of Grass* and *Two Rivulets*

FROM *Leaves of Grass,* 6th edition (published with *Two Rivulets*); two-volume Centennial Edition (1876). In *Complete Writings,* Camden Edition, V, 193–204.

At the eleventh hour, under grave illness, I gather up the pieces of prose and poetry left over since publishing, a while since, my first and main volume, *Leaves of Grass*—pieces, here, some new, some old—nearly all of them (sombre as many are, making this almost death's book) composed in by-gone atmospheres of perfect health—and preceded by the freshest collection, the little *Two Rivulets,* now send them out embodied in the present mélange, partly as my contribution and outpouring to celebrate, in some sort, the feature of the time, the first centennial of our New World nationality—and then as chyle and nutriment to that moral, indissoluble union, equally representing all, and the mother of many coming centennials.

And e'en for flush and proof of our America—for reminder, just as much, or more, in moods of towering pride and joy, I keep my special chants of death and immortality* to stamp the coloring-finish

---

* "PASSAGE TO INDIA."—As in some ancient legend-play, to close the plot and the hero's career, there is a farewell gathering on ship's deck and on shore, a loosing of hawsers and ties, a spreading of sails to the wind—a starting out on unknown seas, to fetch up no one knows whither—to return no more—and the curtain falls, and there is the end of it—so I have reserv'd that poem, with its cluster, to finish and explain much that, without them, would not be explain'd, and to take leave, and escape for good, from all that has preceded them. (Then probably *Passage to India,* and its cluster, are but freer vent and fuller expression to what, from the first, and so on throughout, more or less lurks in my writings, underneath every page, every line, everywhere.) . . .

It was originally my intention, after chanting in *Leaves of Grass* the songs of the body and existence, to then compose a further, equally needed volume, based on those convictions of perpetuity and conservation which, enveloping all precedents, make the unseen soul govern absolutely at last. I meant, while in a sort continuing the theme of my first chants, to shift the slides, and exhibit the problem and paradox of the same ardent and fully appointed personality entering the sphere of the resistless gravitation of spiritual law, and with cheerful face estimating death, not at all as the cessation, but as somehow what I feel it must be, the entrance upon by far the greatest part of existence, and something that life is at least as much for, as it is for itself. But the full construction of such a work is beyond my powers, and must remain for some bard in the future. The physical and the sensuous, in themselves or in their immediate continuations, retain holds upon me which I think are never entirely releas'd; and those holds I have not only not denied, but hardly wish'd to weaken.

Meanwhile, not entirely to give the go-by to my original plan, and far more to avoid a mark'd hiatus in it, than to entirely fulfill it, I end my books with thoughts,[194] or radiations from thoughts, on death, immortality, and a free entrance into the spiritual world. In those thoughts, in a sort, I make the first steps or studies toward the mighty theme, from the point of view necessitated by my foregoing poems, and by modern science. . . .

of all,[193] present and past. For terminus and temperer to all, they were originally written; and that shall be their office at the last. . . .[194]

Of the whole, poems and prose (not attending at all to chronological order, and with original dates and passing allusions in the heat and impression of the hour, left shuffled in, and undisturb'd), the chants of *Leaves of Grass,* my former volume, yet serve as the indispensable deep soil, or basis, out of which, and out of which only, could come the roots[196] and stems more definitely indicated by these later pages. (While that volume radiates physiology alone, the present one, though of the like origin in the main, more palpably doubtless shows the pathology which was pretty sure to come in time from the other.)

In that former and main volume, composed in the flush of my health and strength, from the age of 30 to 50 years, I dwelt on birth and life, clothing my ideas in pictures, days, transactions of my time, to give them positive place, identity—saturating them with that vehemence of pride and audacity of freedom necessary to loosen the mind of still-to-be-form'd America from the accumulated folds, the superstitions, and all the long tenacious and stifling anti-democratic authorities of the Asiatic and European past—my enclosing purport being to express, above all artificial regulation and aid, the eternal bodily composite, cumulative, natural character of one's self.*[197]

---

* Namely, a character, making most of common and normal elements, to the superstructure of which not only the precious accumulations of the learning and experiences of the Old World, and the settled social and municipal necessities and current requirements, so long a-building, shall still faithfully contribute, but which at its foundations and carried up thence, and receiving its impetus from the democratic spirit, and accepting its gauge in all departments from the democratic formulas, shall again directly be vitalized by the perennial influences of Nature at first hand, and the old heroic stamina of Nature, the strong air of prairie and mountain, the dash of the briny sea, the primary antiseptics—of the passions, in all their fullest heat and potency, of courage, rankness, amativeness, and of immense pride. . . .

Not but what the brawn of *Leaves of Grass* is, I hope, thoroughly spiritualized everywhere, for final estimate, but, from the very subjects, the direct effect is a[197] sense of the life, as it should be, of flesh and blood, and physical urge, and animalism. . . .

. . . I have felt temporary depression more than once, for fear that in *Leaves of Grass* the *moral* parts were not sufficiently pronounc'd. But in my clearest and calmest moods I have realized that as those *Leaves,* all and several, surely prepare the way for, and necessitate morals, and are adjusted to them, just the same as Nature does and is, they are what, consistently with my plan, they must and probably should be. . . .

Then I meant *Leaves of Grass,* as publish'd, to be the Poem of average Identity (of *yours,* whoever you are, now reading these lines). A man is not greatest as victor in war, nor inventor or explorer, nor even in science, or in his intellectual or artistic capacity, or exemplar in some vast benevolence. To the highest democratic[198] view, man is most acceptable in living well the practical life and lot which happens to him as ordinary farmer, sea-farer . . . [etc.] To sing the Song of that law of average Identity, and of Yourself, consistently with the divine law of the universal, is a main intention of those *Leaves.*

Something more may be added—for, while I am about it, I would make a full confession. I also sent out *Leaves of Grass* to arouse and set flowing in men's and women's hearts, young and old, endless streams of living, pulsating love and friendship, directly from them to myself, now and ever. . . .

Then, for enclosing clue of all, it is imperatively and ever to be borne in mind that *Leaves of Grass* entire is not to be construed as an intellectual or scholastic effort or poem mainly, but more as a radical utterance out of the Emotions and the Physique—an utterance adjusted to, perhaps born of, Democracy and the Modern— in its very nature regardless of the old conventions, and, under the great laws, following only its own impulses.[199]

Preface to *November Boughs*

FROM "A Backward Glance o'er Travel'd Roads" (1888). In *Complete Writings,* Camden Edition, III, 39–66.

. . . I consider *Leaves of Grass* and its theory experimental—as, in the deepest sense, I consider our American republic itself to be, with its theory. (I think I have at least enough philosophy not to be too absolutely certain of anything, or any results.) In the second place, the volume is a *sortie*—whether to prove triumphant, and conquer its field of aim and escape and construction, nothing less than a hundred years from now can fully answer. I consider the point that I have positively gain'd a hearing, to far more than make up for any and all other lacks and withholdings. Essentially, *that* was from the first, and has remain'd throughout, the main object. Now it seems to be achiev'd, I am certainly contented to waive any otherwise momentous drawbacks, as of little account. Candidly and dispassionately reviewing all my intentions, I feel that they were creditable—and I accept the result, whatever it may be.[43]

After continued personal ambition and effort, as a young fellow, to enter with the rest into competition for the usual rewards, business, political, literary, &c.—to take part in the great *mêlée,* both for victory's prize itself and to do some good—after years of those aims and pursuits, I found myself remaining possess'd, at the age of thirty-one to thirty-three, with a special desire and conviction. Or rather, to be quite exact, a desire that had been flitting through my previous life, or hovering on the flanks, mostly indefinite hitherto, had steadily advanced to the front, defined itself, and finally dominated everything else. This was a feeling or ambition to articulate and faithfully express in literary or poetic form, and uncompromisingly, my own physical, emotional, moral, intellectual, and aesthetic Personality, in the midst of, and tallying, the momentous spirit and facts of its immediate days, and of current America—and to exploit that Personality, identified with place and date, in a far more candid and comprehensive sense than any hitherto poem or book.

Perhaps this is in brief, or suggests, all I have sought to do. Given the nineteenth century, with the United States, and what they furnish as area and points of view, *Leaves of Grass* is, or seeks to be, simply a faithful and doubtless self-will'd record. In the midst of all, it gives one man's—the author's—identity, ardors, observations, faiths, and thoughts, color'd hardly at all with any decided coloring[44] from other faiths or other identities. Plenty of songs had been sung—beautiful, matchless songs—adjusted to other lands than these—another spirit and stage of evolution; but I would sing, and leave out or put in, quite solely with reference to America and to-day. Modern science and democracy seem'd to be throwing out their challenge to poetry to put them in statements in contradistinction to the songs and myths of the past. As I see it now (perhaps too late), I have unwittingly taken up that challenge and made an attempt at such statements—which I certainly would not assume to do now, knowing more clearly what it means.

For grounds for *Leaves of Grass,* as a poem, I abandon'd the conventional themes, which do not appear in it: none of the stock ornamentation, or choice plots of love or war, or high, exceptional personages of Old-World song; nothing, as I may say, for beauty's sake—no legend, or myth, or romance, nor euphemism, nor rhyme. But the broadest average of humanity and its identities in the now ripening nineteenth century, and especially in each of their countless examples and practical occupations in the United States to-day.[45]

. . . I know very well that my *Leaves* could not possibly have emerged or been fashion'd or completed, from any other era than the latter half of the nineteenth century, nor any other land than democratic America, and from the absolute triumph of the National Union arms.

And whether my friends claim it for me or not, I know well enough, too, that in respect to pictorial[49] talent, dramatic situations, and especially in verbal melody and all the conventional technique of poetry, not only the divine works that to-day stand ahead in the world's reading, but dozens more, transcend (some of them immeasurably transcend) all I have done, or could do. But it seem'd to me, as the objects in Nature, the themes of aestheticism, and all special exploitations of the mind and soul, involve not only their own inherent quality, but the quality just as inherent and important, of *their point of view,** the time had come to reflect all themes and things, old and new, in the lights thrown on them by the advent of America and democracy— to chant those themes through the utterance of one, not only the grateful and reverent legatee of the past, but the born child of the New World—to illustrate all through the genesis and ensemble of

---

* According to Immanuel Kant, the last essential reality, giving shape and significance to all the rest.

to-day; and that such illustration and ensemble are the chief demands of America's prospective imaginative literature. . . .[50]

But I set out with the intention also of indicating or hinting some point-characteristics which I since see (though I did not then, at least not definitely) were bases and object-urgings toward those *Leaves* from the first. The word I myself put primarily for the description of them as they stand at last, is the word Suggestiveness. I round and finish little, if anything; and could not, consistently with my scheme. The reader will always have his or her part to do, just as much as I have had mine. I seek less to state or display any theme or thought, and more to bring you, reader, into the atmosphere of the theme or thought—there to pursue your own flight. . . .[58]

Leaves of Grass indeed (I cannot too often reiterate) has mainly been the outcropping of my own emotional and other personal nature— an attempt, from first to last, to put *a Person*, a human being (myself, in the latter half of the nineteenth century, in America,) freely, fully and truly on record. I could not find any similar personal record in current literature that satisfied me. But it is not on *Leaves of Grass* distinctively as *literature*, or a specimen thereof, that I feel to dwell, or advance claims. No one will get at my verses who insists upon viewing them as a literary performance, or attempt at such performance, or as aiming mainly toward art or aestheticism.[65] . . .

There Was a Child Went Forth

FROM *Complete Writings,* Camden Edition, II, 135–138. First published in *Leaves of Grass,* 1st edition (1855). The text for this and the following poems is Whitman's final (usually revised) version.

THERE was a child went forth every day,
And the first object he look'd upon, that object he became,
And that object became part of him for the day or a certain part
    of the day,
Or for many years or stretching cycles of years.

The early lilacs became part of this child,
And grass and white and red morning-glories, and white and red
    clover, and the song of the phoebe-bird,
And the Third-month lambs and the sow's pink-faint litter, and the
    mare's foal and the cow's calf,
And the noisy brood of the barnyard or by the mire of the pond-
    side,
And the fish suspending themselves so curiously below there, and
    the beautiful curious liquid,[135]
And the water-plants with their graceful flat heads, all became
    part of him.   10
The field-sprouts of Fourth-month and Fifth-month became part of
    him,
Winter-grain sprouts and those of the light-yellow corn, and the
    esculent roots of the garden,
And the apple-trees cover'd with blossoms and the fruit afterward,
    and wood-berries, and the commonest weeds by the road,
And the old drunkard staggering home from the outhouse of the
    tavern whence he had lately risen,
And the schoolmistress that pass'd on her way to the school,
And the friendly boys that pass'd, and the quarrelsome boys,
And the tidy and fresh-cheek'd girls, and the barefoot negro boy
    and girl,
And all the changes of city and country wherever he went.

His own parents, he that had father'd him and she that had con-
    ceiv'd him in her womb and birth'd him,
They gave this child more of themselves than that,   20
They gave him afterward every day, they became part of him.

The mother at home quietly placing the dishes on the supper-table,
The mother with mild words, clean her cap and gown, a wholesome
  odor falling off her person and clothes as she walks by,[136]
The father, strong, self-sufficient, manly, mean, anger'd, unjust,
The blow, the quick loud word, the tight bargain, the crafty lure,
The family usages, the language, the company, the furniture, the
  yearning and swelling heart,
Affection that will not be gainsay'd, the sense of what is real, the
  thought if after all it should prove unreal,
The doubts of day-time and the doubts of night-time, the curious
  whether and how,
Whether that which appear so is so, or is it all flashes and specks?
Men and women crowding fast in the streets, if they are not flashes
  and specks what are they?   30
The streets themselves and the façades of houses, and goods in the
  windows,
Vehicles, teams, the heavy-plank'd wharves, the huge crossing at the
  ferries,
The village on the highland seen from afar at sunset, the river
  between,
Shadows, aureola and mist, the light falling on roofs and gables of
  white or brown two miles off,
The schooner near by sleepily dropping down the tide, the little
  boat slack-tow'd astern,
The hurrying tumbling waves, quick-broken crests, slapping, .
The strata of color'd clouds, the long bar of maroon-tint away solitary by itself, the spread of purity it lies motionless in,
The horizon's edge, the flying sea-crow, the fragrance of salt marsh
  and shore mud,[137]
These became part of that child who went forth every day, and who
  now goes, and will always go forth every day.[138]

Crossing Brooklyn Ferry

FROM *Complete Writings*, Camden Edition, I, 191–199. First published
in *Leaves of Grass*, 2nd edition (1856).

1

FLOOD-TIDE below me! I see you face to face!
Clouds of the west—sun there half an hour high—I see you also face
  to face.
Crowds of men and women attired in the usual costumes, how
  curious you are to me!
On the ferry-boats the hundreds and hundreds that cross, returning
  home, are more curious to me than you suppose,

And you that shall cross from shore to shore years hence are more
   to me, and more in my meditations, than you might suppose.

2

The impalpable sustenance of me from all things at all hours of
   the day,
The simple, compact, well-join'd scheme, myself disintegrated,
   every one disintegrated yet part of the scheme,
The similitudes of the past and those of the future,
The glories strung like beads on my smallest sights and hearings,
   on the walk in the street and the passage over the river,
The current rushing so swiftly and swimming with me far away,[191]   10
The others that are to follow me, the ties between me and them,
The certainty of others, the life, love, sight, hearing of others.

Others will enter the gates of the ferry and cross from shore to
   shore,
Others will watch the run of the flood-tide.
Others will see the shipping of Manhattan north and west, and the
   heights of Brooklyn to the south and east,
Others will see the islands large and small;
Fifty years hence, others will see them as they cross, the sun half
   an hour high,
A hundred years hence, or ever so many hundred years hence,
   others will see them,
Will enjoy the sunset, the pouring-in of the flood-tide, the falling-
   back to the sea of the ebb-tide.

3

It avails not, time nor place—distance avails not,   20
I am with you, you men and women of a generation, or ever so
   many generations hence,
Just as you feel when you look on the river and sky, so I felt,
Just as any of you is one of a living crowd, I was one of a crowd,
Just as you are refresh'd by the gladness of the river and the bright
   flow, I was refresh'd,
Just as you stand and lean on the rail, yet hurry with the swift
   current, I stood yet was hurried,
Just as you look on the numberless masts of ships and the thick-
   stemm'd pipes of steamboats, I look'd.[192]
I too many and many a time cross'd the river of old,
Watched the Twelfth-month sea-gulls, saw them high in the air
   floating with motionless wings, oscillating their bodies,
Saw how the glistening yellow lit up parts of their bodies and left
   the rest in strong shadow,
Saw the slow-wheeling circles and the gradual edging toward the
   south,   30

Saw the reflection of the summer sky in the water,
Had my eyes dazzled by the shimmering track of beams,
Look'd at the fine centrifugal spokes of light round the shape of
    my head in the sunlit water,
Look'd on the haze on the hills southward and south-westward,
Look'd on the vapor as it flew in fleeces tinged with violet,
Look'd toward the lower bay to notice the vessels arriving,
Saw their approach, saw aboard those that were near me,
Saw the white sails of schooners and sloops, saw the ships at anchor,
The sailors at work in the rigging or out astride the spars,
The round masts, the swinging motion of the hulls, the slender
    serpentine pennants,   40
The large and small steamers in motion, the pilots in their pilot-
    houses,
The white wake left by the passage, the quick tremulous whirl of
    the wheels,
The flags of all nations, the falling of them at sunset,
The scallop-edged waves in the twilight, the ladled cups, the frolic-
    some crests and glistening,
The stretch afar growing dimmer and dimmer, the gray walls of the
    granite storehouses by the docks,[193]
On the river the shadowy group, the big steam-tug closely flank'd
    on each side by the barges, the hay-boat, the belated lighter,
On the neighboring shore the fires from the foundry chimneys
    burning high and glaringly into the night,
Casting their flicker of black contrasted with wild red and yellow
    light over the tops of houses, and down into the clefts of
    streets.

4

These and all else were to me the same as they are to you,
I loved well those cities, loved well the stately and rapid river,   50
The men and women I saw were all near to me,
Others the same—others who look back on me because I look'd for-
    ward to them,
(The time will come, though I stop here to-day and to-night.)

5

What is it then between us?
What is the count of the scores or hundreds of years between us?

Whatever it is, it avails not—distance avails not, and place avails
    not,
I too lived, Brooklyn of ample hills was mine,
I too walk'd the streets of Manhattan island, and bathed in the
    waters around it,

I too felt the curious abrupt questionings stir within me.
In the day among crowds of people sometimes they came upon
    me,[194]   60
In my walks home late at night or as I lay in my bed they came
    upon me,
I too had been struck from the float forever held in solution,
I too had receiv'd identity by my body,
That I was I knew was of my body, and what I should be I knew
    I should be of my body.

6

It is not upon you alone the dark patches fall,
The dark threw its patches down upon me also,
The best I had done seem'd to me blank and suspicious,
My great thoughts as I supposed them, were they not in reality
    meagre?
Nor is it you alone who know what it is to be evil,
I am he who knew what it was to be evil,   70
I too knitted the old knot of contrariety,
Blabb'd, blush'd, resented, lied, stole, grudg'd,
Had guile, anger, lust, hot wishes I dared not speak,
Was wayward, vain, greedy, shallow, sly, cowardly, malignant,
The wolf, the snake, the hog, not wanting in me,
The cheating look, the frivolous word, the adulterous wish, not
    wanting,
Refusals, hates, postponements, meanness, laziness, none of these
    wanting,
Was one with the rest, the days and haps of the rest,
Was call'd by my nighest name by clear loud voices of young men
    as they saw me approaching or passing,
Felt their arms on my neck as I stood, or the negligent leaning of
    their flesh against me as I sat,[195]   80
Saw many I loved in the street or ferry-boat or public assembly, yet
    never told them a word,
Lived the same life with the rest, the same old laughing, gnawing,
    sleeping,
Play'd the part that still looks back on the actor or actress,
The same old role, the role that is what we make it, as great as we
    like,
Or as small as we like, or both great and small.

7

Closer yet I approach you,
What thought you have of me now, I had as much of you—I laid in
    my stores in advance,
I consider'd long and seriously of you before you were born.

Who was to know what should come home to me?
Who knows but I am enjoying this?   90
Who knows, for all the distance, but I am as good as looking at you
    now, for all you cannot see me?

                                    8

Ah, what can ever be more stately and admirable to me than mast-
    hemm'd Manhattan?
River and sunset and scallop-edg'd waves of flood-tide?
The sea-gulls oscillating their bodies, the hay-boat in the twilight,
    and the belated lighter?

What gods can exceed these that clasp me by the hand, and with
    voices I love call me promptly and loudly by my nighest name
    as I approach?[196]
What is more subtle than this which ties me to the woman or man
    that looks in my face?
Which fuses me into you now, and pours my meaning into you?

We understand then do we not?
What I promis'd without mentioning it, have you not accepted?
What the study could not teach—what the preaching could not ac-
    complish is accomplish'd, is it not?   100

                                    9

Flow on, river! flow with the flood-tide, and ebb with the ebb-tide!
Frolic on, crested and scallop-edg'd waves!
Gorgeous clouds of the sunset! drench with your splendor me,
    or the men and women generations after me!
Cross from shore to shore, countless crowds of passengers!
Stand up, tall masts of Mannahatta! stand up, beautiful hills of
    Brooklyn!
Throb, baffled and curious brain! throw out questions and answers!
Suspend here and everywhere, eternal float of solution!
Gaze, loving and thirsting eyes, in the house or street or public
    assembly!
Sound out, voices of young men! loudly and musically call me by
    my nighest name!
Live, old life! play the part that looks back on the actor or actress!   110
Play the old role, the role that is great or small according as one
    makes it![197]
Consider, you who peruse me, whether I may not in unknown ways
    be looking upon you;
Be firm, rail over the river, to support those who lean idly, yet haste
    with the hasting current;

Fly on, sea-birds! fly sideways, or wheel in large circles high in
    the air;
Receive the summer sky, you water, and faithfully hold it till all
    downcast eyes have time to take it from you!
Diverge, fine spokes of light, from the shape of my head, or any
    one's head, in the sunlit water!
Come on, ships from the lower bay! pass up or down, white-sail'd
    schooners, sloops, lighters!
Flaunt away, flags of all nations! be duly lower'd at sunset!
Burn high your fires, foundry chimneys! cast black shadows at
    nightfall! cast red and yellow light over the tops of the houses!
Appearances, now or henceforth, indicate what you are,   120
You necessary film, continue to envelop the soul,
About my body for me, and your body for you, be hung our divin-
    est aromas,
Thrive, cities—bring your freight, bring your shows, ample and
    sufficient rivers,
Expand, being than which none else is perhaps more spiritual,
Keep your places, objects than which none else is more lasting,

You have waited, you always wait, you dumb, beautiful ministers,
We receive you with free sense at last, and are insatiate hence-
    forward,[198]
Not you any more shall be able to foil us, or withhold yourselves
    from us,
We use you, and do not cast you aside—we plant you permanently
    within us,
We fathom you not—we love you—there is perfection in you also,   130
You furnish your parts toward eternity,
Great or small, you furnish your parts toward the soul.[199]

A Song of the Rolling Earth

FROM *Complete Writings*, Camden Edition, I, 268–275. First published in
Leaves of Grass, 2nd edition (1856).

1

A SONG of the rolling earth, and of words according,
Were you thinking that those were the words, those upright lines?
    those curves, angles, dots?
No, those are not the words, the substantial words are in the
    ground and sea,
They are in the air, they are in you.

Were you thinking that those were the words, those delicious
    sounds out of your friends' mouths?
No, the real words are more delicious than they.
Human bodies are words, myriads of words,
(In the best poems re-appears the body, man's or woman's well-
    shaped, natural, gay,
Every part able, active, receptive, without shame or the need of
    shame.)
Air, soil, water, fire—those are words,   10
I myself am a word with them—my qualities interpenetrate with
    theirs—my name is nothing to them,
Though it were told in the three thousand languages, what should
    air, soil, water, fire, know of my name?[268]
A healthy presence, a friendly or commanding gesture, are words,
    sayings, meanings,
The charms that go with the mere looks of some men and women,
    are sayings and meanings also.

The workmanship of souls is by those inaudible words of the earth,
The masters know the earth's words and use them more than audi-
    ble words.

Amelioration is one of the earth's words,
The earth neither lags nor hastens,
It has all attributes, growths, effects, latent in itself from the jump,
It is not half beautiful only, defects and excrescences show just as
    much as perfections show.   20

The earth does not withhold, it is generous enough,
The truths of the earth continually wait, they are not so conceal'd
    either,
They are calm, subtle, untransmissible by print,
They are imbued through all things conveying themselves willingly,
Conveying a sentiment and invitation, I utter and utter,
I speak not, yet if you hear me not of what avail am I to you?
To bear, to better, lacking these of what avail am I?

(Accouche! accouchez!
Will you rot your own fruit in yourself there?
Will you squat and stifle there?)   30

The earth does not argue,
Is not pathetic, has no arrangements,[269]
Does not scream, haste, persuade, threaten, promise,
Makes no discriminations, has no conceivable failures,
Closes nothing, refuses nothing, shuts none out,
Of all the powers, objects, states, it notifies, shuts none out.

The earth does not exhibit itself nor refuse to exhibit itself, possesses still underneath,
Underneath the ostensible sounds, the august chorus of heroes, the
   wail of slaves,
Persuasions of lovers, curses, gasps of the dying, laughter of young
   people, accents of bargainers,
Underneath these possessing words that never fail.   40

To her children the words of the eloquent dumb great mother
   never fail,
The true words do not fail, for motion does not fail and reflection
   does not fail,
Also the day and night do not fail, and the voyage we pursue does
   not fail.

Of the interminable sisters,
Of the ceaseless cotillons of sisters,
Of the centripetal and centrifugal sisters, the elder and younger
   sisters,
The beautiful sister we know dances on with the rest.

With her ample back towards every beholder,
With the fascinations of youth and the equal fascinations of age,
Sits she whom I too love like the rest, sits undisturb'd,[270]   50
Holding up in her hand what has the character of a mirror, while
   her eyes glance back from it,
Glance as she sits, inviting none, denying none,
Holding a mirror day and night tirelessly before her own face.

Seen at hand or seen at a distance,
Duly the twenty-four appear in public every day,
Duly approach and pass with their companions or a companion,
Looking from no countenances of their own, but from the counte-
   nances of those who are with them,
From the countenances of children or women or the manly counte-
   nance,
From the open countenances of animals or from inanimate things,
From the landscape or waters or from the exquisite apparition of
   the sky,   60
From our countenances, mine and yours, faithfully returning them,
Every day in public appearing without fail, but never twice with
   the same companions.

Embracing man, embracing all, proceed the three hundred and
   sixty-five resistlessly round the sun;
Embracing all, soothing, supporting, follow close three hundred
   and sixty-five offsets of the first, sure and necessary as they.

Tumbling on steadily, nothing dreading,
Sunshine, storm, cold, heat, forever withstanding, passing, carrying,
The soul's realization and determination still inheriting,[271]
The fluid vacuum around and ahead still entering and dividing,
No balk retarding, no anchor anchoring, on no rock striking,
Swift, glad, content, unbereav'd, nothing losing,   70
Of all able and ready at any time to give strict account,
The divine ship sails the divine sea.

2

Whoever you are! motion and reflection are especially for you,
The divine ship sails the divine sea for you.

Whoever you are! you are he or she for whom the earth is solid
    and liquid,
You are he or she for whom the sun and moon hang in the sky,
For none more than you are the present and the past,
For none more than you is immortality.

Each man to himself and each woman to herself, is the word of the
    past and present, and the true word of immortality;
No one can acquire for another—not one,   80
Not one can grow for another—not one.

The song is to the singer, and comes back most to him,
The teaching is to the teacher, and comes back most to him,
The murder is to the murderer, and comes back most to him,
The theft is to the thief, and comes back most to him,
The love is to the lover, and comes back most to him,
The gift is to the giver, and comes back most to him—it cannot fail,
The oration is to the orator, the acting is to the actor and actress
    not to the audience,[272]
And no man understands any greatness or goodness but his own, or
    the indication of his own.

3

I swear the earth shall surely be complete to him or her who shall
    be complete,   90
The earth remains jagged and broken only to him or her who re-
    mains jagged and broken.

I swear there is no greatness or power that does not emulate those
    of the earth,
There can be no theory of any account unless it corroborate the
    theory of the earth,
No politics, song, religion, behavior, or what not, is of account,
    unless it compare with the amplitude of the earth,

Unless it face the exactness, vitality, impartiality, rectitude of the earth.

I swear I begin to see love with sweeter spasms than that which responds love,
It is that which contains itself, which never invites and never refuses.

I swear I begin to see little or nothing in audible words,
All merges toward the presentation of the unspoken meanings of the earth,
Toward him who sings the songs of the body and of the truths of the earth,   100
Toward him who makes the dictionaries of words that print cannot touch.[273]
I swear I see what is better than to tell the best,
It is always to leave the best untold.

When I undertake to tell the best I find I cannot,
My tongue is ineffectual on its pivots,
My breath will not be obedient to its organs,
I become a dumb man.

The best of the earth cannot be told anyhow, all or any is best,
It is not what you anticipated, it is cheaper, easier, nearer,
Things are not dismiss'd from the places they held before,   110
The earth is just as positive and direct as it was before,
Facts, religions, improvements, politics, trades, are as real as before,

But the soul is also real, it too is positive and direct,
No reasoning, no proof has establish'd it,
Undeniable growth has establish'd it.

4

These to echo the tones of souls and the phrases of souls,
(If they did not echo the phrases of souls what were they then?
If they had not reference to you in especial what were they then?)

I swear I will never henceforth have to do with the faith that tells the best,
I will have to do only with that faith that leaves the best untold.   120

Say on, sayers! sing on, singers!
Delve! mould! pile the words of the earth!
Work on, age after age, nothing is to be lost,[274]
It may have to wait long, but it will certainly come in use,
When the materials are all prepared and ready, the architects shall appear.

I swear to you the architects shall appear without fail,
I swear to you they will understand you and justify you,
The greatest among them shall be he who best knows you, and
encloses all and is faithful to all,
He and the rest shall not forget you, they shall perceive that you
are not an iota less than they,
You shall be fully glorified in them.[275]   130

One Hour to Madness and Joy

FROM *Complete Writings,* Camden Edition, I, 129–130. First published in *Leaves of Grass,* 3rd edition (1860).

ONE hour to madness and joy! O furious! O confine me not!
(What is this that frees me so in storms?
What do my shouts amid lightnings and raging winds mean?)

O to drink the mystic deliria deeper than any other man!
O savage and tender achings! (I bequeath them to you, my children,
I tell them to you, for reasons, O bridegroom and bride.)[129]
O to be yielded to you whoever you are, and you to be yielded to
me in defiance of the world!
O to return to Paradise! O bashful and feminine!
O to draw you to me, to plant on you for the first time the lips of
a determin'd man.

O the puzzle, the thrice-tied knot, the deep and dark pool, all un-
tied and illumin'd!   10
O to speed where there is space enough and air enough at last!
To be absolv'd from previous ties and conventions, I from mine
and you from yours!
To find a new unthought-of nonchalance with the best of Nature!
To have the gag remov'd from one's mouth!
To have the feeling to-day or any day I am sufficient as I am.

O something unprov'd! something in a trance!
To escape utterly from others' anchors and holds!
To drive free! to love free! to dash reckless and dangerous!
To court destruction with taunts, with invitations!
To ascend, to leap to the heavens of the love indicated to me!   20
To rise thither with my inebriate soul!
To be lost if it must be so!
To feed the remainder of life with one hour of fulness and free-
dom!
With one brief hour of madness and joy.[130]

I Saw in Louisiana a Live-Oak Growing

FROM *Complete Writings,* Camden Edition, I, 152–153. First published in *Leaves of Grass,* 3rd edition (1860).

I SAW in Louisiana a live-oak growing,
All alone stood it and the moss hung down from the branches,
Without any companion it grew there uttering joyous leaves of
   dark green,
And its look, rude, unbending, lusty, made me think of myself,
But I wonder'd how it could utter joyous leaves standing alone
   there without its friend near, for I knew I could not,
And I broke off a twig with a certain number of leaves upon it, and
   twined around it a little moss,[152]
And brought it away, and I have placed it in sight in my room,
It is not needed to remind me as of my own dear friends,
(For I believe lately I think of little else than of them,)
Yet it remains to me a curious token, it makes me think of manly
   love;   10
For all that, and though the live-oak glistens there in Louisiana
   solitary in a wide flat space,
Uttering joyous leaves all its life without a friend a lover near,
I know very well I could not.[153]

Of the Terrible Doubt of Appearances

FROM *Complete Writings,* Camden Edition, I, 145–146. First published in *Leaves of Grass,* 3rd edition (1860).

Of the terrible doubt of appearances,
Of the uncertainty after all, that we may be deluded,
That may-be reliance and hope are but speculations after all,
That may-be identity beyond the grave is a beautiful fable only,
May-be the things I perceive, the animals, plants, men, hills, shin-
   ing and flowing waters,
The skies of day and night, colors, densities, forms, may-be these
   are (as doubtless they are) only apparitions, and the real some-
   thing has yet to be known,
(How often they dart out of themselves as if to confound me and
   mock me!
How often I think neither I know, nor any man knows, aught of
   them,)
May-be seeming to me what they are (as doubtless they indeed but

seem) as from my present point of view, and might prove (as of
course they would) nought of what they appear, or nought
anyhow, from entirely changed points of view;
To me these and the like of these are curiously answer'd by my
lovers, my dear friends,[145]
When he whom I love travels with me or sits a long while holding
me by the hand,
When the subtle air, the impalpable, the sense that words and
reason hold not, surround us and pervade us,
Then I am charged with untold and untellable wisdom, I am silent,
I require nothing further,
I cannot answer the question of appearances or that of identity
beyond the grave,
But I walk or sit indifferent, I am satisfied,
He ahold of my hand has completely satisfied me.[146]

Vigil Strange I Kept
on the Field One Night

FROM *Complete Writings,* Camden Edition, II, 67–69. First published
in *Drum-Taps* (1865).

VIGIL strange I kept on the field one night;
When you my son and my comrade dropt at my side that day,
One look I but gave which your dear eyes return'd with a look I
shall never forget,[67]
One touch of your hand to mine O boy, reach'd up as you lay on
the ground,
Then onward I sped in the battle, the even-contested battle,
Till late in the night reliev'd to the place at last again I made
my way,
Found you in death so cold dear comrade, found your body son of
responding kisses, (never again on earth responding,)
Bared your face in the starlight, curious the scene, cool blew the
moderate night-wind,
Long there and then in vigil I stood, dimly around me the battle-
field spreading,
Vigil wondrous and vigil sweet there in the fragrant silent night.   10
But not a tear fell, not even a long-drawn sigh, long, long I gazed,
Then on the earth partially reclining sat by your side leaning my
chin in my hands,
Passing sweet hours, immortal and mystic hours with you dearest
comrade—not a tear, not a word,
Vigil of silence, love and death, vigil for you my son and my soldier,

As onward silently stars aloft, eastward new ones upward stole,
Vigil final for you brave boy, (I could not save you, swift was your
    death,
I faithfully loved you and cared for you living, I think we shall
    surely meet again,)
Till at latest lingering of the night, indeed just as the dawn ap-
    pear'd,
My comrade I wrapt in his blanket, envelop'd well his form,[68]
Folded the blanket well, tucking it carefully over head and care-
    fully under feet,   20
And there and then and bathed by the rising sun, my son in his
    grave, in his rude-dug grave I deposited,
Ending my vigil strange with that, vigil of night and battle-field
    dim,
Vigil for boy of responding kisses, (never again on earth re-
    sponding,)
Vigil for comrade swiftly slain, vigil I never forget, how as day
    brighten'd,
I rose from the chill ground and folded my soldier well in his
    blanket,
And buried him where he fell.[69]

O Captain! My Captain!

FROM *Complete Writings,* Camden Edition, II, 105. First published in
Sequel to Drum-Taps (1865).

O CAPTAIN! my Captain! our fearful trip is done,
The ship has weather'd every rack, the prize we sought is won,
The port is near, the bells I hear, the people all exulting,
While follow eyes the steady keel, the vessel grim and daring;
    But O heart! heart! heart!
      O the bleeding drops of red,
        Where on the deck my Captain lies,
          Fallen cold and dead.

O Captain! my Captain! rise up and hear the bells;
Rise up—for you the flag is flung—for you the bugle trills,   10
For you bouquets and ribbon'd wreaths—for you the shores
    a-crowding
For you they call, the swaying mass, their eager faces turning;
    Here Captain! dear father!
      This arm beneath your head!
        It is some dream that on the deck,
          You've fallen cold and dead.

My Captain does not answer, his lips are pale and still,
My father does not feel my arm, he has no pulse nor will,
The ship is anchor'd safe and sound, its voyage closed and done,
From fearful trip the victor ship comes in with object won;   20
    Exult O shores, and ring O bells!
      But I with mournful tread,
        Walk the deck my Captain lies,
          Fallen cold and dead.[105]

Tears

FROM *Complete Writings,* Camden Edition, II, 17–18. First published
in *Leaves of Grass,* 4th edition (1867).

TEARS! tears! tears!
In the night, in solitude, tears,
On the white shore dripping, dripping, suck'd in by the sand,
Tears, not a star shining, all dark and desolate,
Moist tears from the eyes of a muffled head;
O who is that ghost? that form in the dark, with tears?
What shapeless lump is that, bent, crouch'd there on the sand?
Streaming tears, sobbing tears, throes, choked with wild cries;
O storm, embodied, rising, careering with swift steps along the
    beach!
O wild and dismal night storm, with wind—O belching and des-
    perate![17]   10
O shade so sedate and decorous by day, with calm countenance and
    regulated pace,
But away at night as you fly, none looking—O then the unloosen'd
    ocean
Of tears! tears! tears![18]

One's-Self I Sing

FROM *Complete Writings,* Camden Edition, I, 1. First published in
Leaves of Grass, 4th edition (1867).

ONE'S-SELF I sing, a simple separate person,
Yet utter the word Democratic, the word En-Masse.

Of physiology from top to toe I sing,

Not physiognomy alone nor brain alone is worthy for the Muse[, I]
    say the Form complete is worthier far,
The Female equally with the Male I sing.

Of Life immense in passion, pulse, and power,
Cheerful, for freest action form'd under the laws divine,
The Modern Man I sing.

Passage to India

FROM *Complete Writings*, Camden Edition, II, 186–197. First published
as title poem of pamphlet *Passage to India* (1871).

1

SINGING my days,
Singing the great achievements of the present,
Singing the strong light works of engineers,
Our modern wonders, (the antique ponderous Seven outvied,)
In the Old World the east the Suez canal,
The New by its mighty railroad spann'd,
The seas inlaid with eloquent gentle wires;
Yet first to sound, and ever sound, the cry with thee O soul,
The Past! the Past! the Past!

The Past—the dark unfathom'd retrospect!   10
The teeming gulf—the sleepers and the shadows!
The past—the infinite greatness of the past!
For what is the present after all but a growth out of the past?
(As a projectile form'd, impell'd, passing a certain line, still
    keeps on,
So the present, utterly form'd, impell'd by the past.)

2

Passage O soul to India!
Eclaircise the myths Asiatic, the primitive fables.[186]
Not you alone proud truths of the world,
Nor you alone ye facts of modern science,
But myths and fables of eld, Asia's, Africa's fables,   20
The far-darting beams of the spirit, the unloos'd dreams,
The deep diving bibles and legends,
The daring plots of the poets, the elder religions;
O you temples fairer than lilies pour'd over by the rising sun!
O you fables spurning the known, eluding the hold of the known,
    mounting to heaven!

You lofty and dazzling towers, pinnacled, red as roses, burnished
    with gold!
Towers of fables immortal fashion'd from mortal dreams!
You too I welcome and fully the same as the rest!
You too with joy I sing.

Passage to India!   30
Lo, soul, seest thou not God's purpose from the first?
The earth to be spann'd, connected by network,
The races, neighbors, to marry and be given in marriage,
The oceans to be cross'd, the distance brought near,
The lands to be welded together.

A worship new I sing,
You captains, voyagers, explorers, yours,
You engineers, you architects, machinists, yours,
You, not for trade or transportation only,
But in God's name, and for thy sake O soul.   40

3

Passage to India!
Lo soul for thee of tableaus twain,[187]
I see in one the Suez canal initiated, open'd,
I see the procession of steamships, the Empress Eugenie's leading
    the van,
I mark from on deck the strange landscape, the pure sky, the level
    sand in the distance,
I pass swiftly the picturesque groups, the workmen gather'd,
The gigantic dredging machines.

In one again, different, (yet thine, all thine O soul, the same,)
I see over my own continent the Pacific railroad surmounting every
    barrier,
I see continual trains of cars winding along the Platte carrying
    freight and passengers,   50
I hear the locomotives rushing and roaring, and the shrill steam-
    whistle,
I hear the echoes reverberate through the grandest scenery in the
    world,
I cross the Laramie plains, I note the rocks in grotesque shapes,
    the buttes,
I see the plentiful larkspur and wild onions, the barren, colorless,
    sage-deserts,
I see in glimpses afar or towering immediately above me the great
    mountains, I see the Wind river and the Wahsatch mountains,
I see the Monument mountain and the Eagle's Nest, I pass the
    Promontory, I ascend the Nevadas,

I scan the noble Elk mountain and wind around its base,
I see the Humboldt range, I thread the valley and cross the river,
I see the clear waters of lake Tahoe, I see forests of majestic
    pines,[188]
Or crossing the great desert, the alkaline plains, I behold enchant-
    ing mirages of waters and meadows,   60
Marking through these and after all, in duplicate slender lines,
Bridging the three or four thousand miles of land travel,
Tying the Eastern to the Western sea,
The road between Europe and Asia.

(Ah Genoese thy dream! thy dream!
Centuries after thou art laid in thy grave,
The shore thou foundest verifies thy dream.)

4

Passage to India!
Struggles of many a captain, tales of many a sailor dead,
Over my mood stealing and spreading they come,   70
Like clouds and cloudlets in the unreach'd sky.

Along all history, down the slopes,
As a rivulet running, sinking now, and now again to the surface
    rising,
A ceaseless thought, a varied train—lo, soul, to thee, thy sight,
    they rise,
The plans, the voyages again, the expeditions;
Again Vasco de Gama sails forth,
Again the knowledge gain'd, the mariner's compass,
Lands found and nations born, thou born America,
For purpose vast, man's long probation fill'd,
Thou rondure of the world at last accomplish'd.   80

5

O vast Rondure, swimming in space,
Cover'd all over with visible power and beauty,[189]
Alternate light and day and the teeming spiritual darkness,
Unspeakable high processions of sun and moon and countless stars
    above,
Below, the manifold grass and waters, animals, mountains, trees,
With inscrutable purpose, some hidden prophetic intention,
Now first it seems my thought begins to span thee.

Down from the gardens of Asia descending radiating,
Adam and Eve appear, then their myriad progeny after them,
Wandering, yearning, curious, with restless explorations,   90
With questionings, baffled, formless, feverish, with never-happy
    hearts,

With that sad incessant refrain, *Wherefore unsatisfied soul?* **and**
  Whither O mocking life?

Ah who shall soothe these feverish children?
Who justify these restless explorations?
Who speak the secret of impassive earth?
Who bind it to us? what is this separate Nature so unnatural?
What is this earth to our affections? (unloving earth, without a
  throb to answer ours,
Cold earth, the place of graves.)
Yet soul be sure the first intent remains, and shall be carried out,
Perhaps even now the time has arrived.   100
After the seas are all cross'd, (as they seem already cross'd,)
After the great captains and engineers have accomplish'd their
  work,
After the noble inventors, after the scientists, the chemist, the
  geologist, ethnologist,[190]
Finally shall come the poet worthy that name,
The true son of God shall come singing his songs.

Then not your deeds only O voyagers, O scientists and inventors,
  shall be justified,
All these hearts as of fretted children shall be sooth'd,
All affection shall be fully responded to, the secret shall be told,
All these separations and gaps shall be taken up and hook'd and
  link'd together,
The whole earth, this cold, impassive, voiceless earth, shall be com-
  pletely justified,   110
Trinitas divine shall be gloriously accomplish'd and compacted by
  the true son of God, the poet,
(He shall indeed pass the straits and conquer the mountains,
He shall double the cape of Good Hope to some purpose,)
Nature and Man shall be disjoin'd and diffused no more,
The true son of God shall absolutely fuse them.

6

Year at whose wide-flung door I sing!
Year of the purpose accomplish'd!
Year of the marriage of continents, climates and oceans!
(No mere doge of Venice now wedding the Adriatic,)
I see O year in you the vast terraqueous globe given and giving
  all,   120
Europe to Asia, Africa join'd, and they to the New World,
The lands, geographies, dancing before you, holding a festival
  garland,
As brides and bridegrooms hand in hand.[191]

Passage to India!
Cooling airs from Caucasus far, soothing cradle of man,
The river Euphrates flowing, the past lit up again.

Lo soul, the retrospect brought forward,
The old, most populous, wealthiest of earth's lands,
The streams of the Indus and the Ganges and their many affluents,
(I my shores of America walking to-day behold, resuming all,)   130
The tale of Alexander on his warlike marches suddenly dying,
On one side China and on the other side Persia and Arabia,
To the south the great seas and the bay of Bengal,
The flowing literatures, tremendous epics, religions, castes,
Old occult Brahma interminably far back, the tender and junior
        Buddha,
Central and southern empires and all their belongings, possessors,
The wars of Tamerlane, the reign of Aurungzebe,
The traders, rulers, explorers, Moslems, Venetians, Byzantium, the
        Arabs, Portuguese,
The first travelers famous yet, Marco Polo, Batouta the Moor,
Doubts to be solv'd, the map incognita, blanks to be fill'd,   140
The foot of man unstay'd, the hands never at rest,
Thyself O soul that will not brook a challenge.

The mediaeval navigators rise before me,
The world of 1492, with its awaken'd enterprise,
Something swelling in humanity now like the sap of the earth in
        spring,
The sunset splendor of chivalry declining.[192]

And who art thou sad shade?
Gigantic, visionary, thyself a visionary,
With majestic limbs and pious beaming eyes,
Spreading around with every look of thine a golden world,   150
Enhuing it with gorgeous hues.

As the chief histrion,
Down to the footlights walks in some great scena,
Dominating the rest I see the Admiral himself,
(History's type of courage, action, faith,)
Behold him sail from Palos leading his little fleet,
His voyage behold, his return, his great fame,
His misfortunes, calumniators, behold him a prisoner, chain'd,
Behold his dejection, poverty, death.

(Curious in time I stand, noting the efforts of heroes,   160
Is the deferment long? bitter the slander, poverty, death?
Lies the seed unreck'd for centuries in the ground? lo, to God's due
        occasion,

Uprising in the night, it sprouts, blooms,
And fills the earth with use and beauty.)

7

Passage indeed O soul to primal thought,
Not lands and seas alone, thy own clear freshness,
The young maturity of brood and bloom,
To realms of budding bibles.

O soul, repressless, I with thee and thou with me,
Thy circumnavigation of the world begin,   170
Of man, the voyage of his mind's return,[193]
To reason's early paradise,
Back, back to wisdom's birth, to innocent intuitions,
Again with fair creation.

8

O we can wait no longer,
We too take ship O soul,
Joyous we too launch out on trackless seas,
Fearless for unknown shores on waves of ecstasy to sail,
Amid the wafting winds, (thou pressing me to thee, I thee to me,
    O soul,)
Caroling free, singing our song of God,   180
Chanting our chant of pleasant exploration.

With laugh and many a kiss,
(Let others deprecate, let others weep for sin, remorse, humilia-
    tion,)
O soul thou pleasest me, I thee.

Ah more than any priest O soul we too believe in God,
But with the mystery of God we dare not dally.

O soul thou pleasest me, I thee,
Sailing these seas or on the hills, or waking in the night,
Thoughts, silent thoughts, of Time and Space and Death, like
    waters flowing,
Bear me indeed as through the regions infinite,   190
Whose air I breathe, whose ripples hear, lave me all over,
Bathe me O God in thee, mounting to thee,
I and my soul to range in range of thee.[194]

O Thou transcendent,
Nameless, the fibre and the breath,
Light of the light, shedding forth universes, thou centre of them,
Thou mightier centre of the true, the good, the loving,
Thou moral, spiritual fountain—affection's source—thou reservoir,

(O pensive soul of me—O thirst unsatisfied—waitest not there,
Waitest not haply for us somewhere there the Comrade perfect?)   200
Thou pulse—thou motive of the stars, suns, systems,
That, circling, move in order, safe, harmonious,
Athwart the shapeless vastnesses of space,
How should I think, how breathe a single breath, how speak, if,
        out of myself,
I could not launch, to those, superior universes?

Swiftly I shrivel at the thought of God,
At Nature and its wonders, Time and Space and Death,
But that I, turning, call to thee O soul, thou actual Me,
And lo, thou gently masterest the orbs,
Thou matest Time, smilest content at Death,   210
And fillest, swellest full the vastnesses of Space.

Greater than stars or suns,
Bounding O soul thou journeyest forth;
What love than thine and ours could wider amplify?
What aspirations, wishes, outvie thine and ours O soul?
What dreams of the Ideal? what plans of purity, perfection,
        strength,
What cheerful willingness for others' sake to give up all?
For others' sake to suffer all?[195]

Reckoning ahead O soul, when thou, the time achiev'd,
The seas all cross'd, weather'd the capes, the voyage done,   220
Surrounded, copest, frontest God, yieldest, the aim attain'd,
As fill'd with friendship, love complete, the Elder Brother found,
The Younger melts in fondness in his arms.

                              9

Passage to more than India!
Are thy wings plumed indeed for such far flights?
O soul, voyagest thou indeed on voyages like those?
Disportest thou on waters such as those?
Soundest below the Sanscrit and the Vedas?
Then have thy bent unleash'd.

Passage to you, your shores, ye aged fierce enigmas!   230
Passage to you, to mastership of you, ye strangling problems!
You, strew'd with the wrecks of skeletons, that, living, never reach'd
        you.

Passage to more than India!
O secret of the earth and sky!
Of you O waters of the sea! O winding creeks and rivers!
Of you O woods and fields! of you strong mountains of my land!

Of you O prairies! of you gray rocks!
O morning red! O clouds! O rain and snows!
O day and night, passage to you!

O sun and moon and all you stars! Sirius and Jupiter!   240
Passage to you!

Passage, immediate passage! the blood burns in my veins!
Away O soul! hoist instantly the anchor![196]
Cut the hawsers—haul out—shake out every sail!
Have we not stood here like trees in the ground long enough?
Have we not grovel'd here long enough, eating and drinking like
    mere brutes?
Have we not darken'd and dazed ourselves with books long enough?

Sail forth—steer for the deep waters only,
Reckless O soul, exploring, I with thee, and thou with me,
For we are bound where mariner has not yet dared to go,   250
And we will risk the ship, ourselves and all.

O my brave soul!
O farther farther sail!
O daring joy, but safe! are they not all the seas of God?
O farther, farther, farther sail![197]

On the Beach at Night

FROM *Complete Writings,* Camden Edition, II, 19–20. First published in
Leaves of Grass, 5th edition (1871).

ON the beach at night,
Stands a child with her father,
Watching the east, the autumn sky.

Up through the darkness,
While ravening clouds, the burial clouds, in black masses spread-
    ing,
Lower sullen and fast athwart and down the sky,
Amid a transparent clear belt of ether yet left in the east,
Ascends large and calm the lord-star Jupiter,[19]
And nigh at hand, only a very little above,
Swim the delicate sisters the Pleiades.   10

From the beach the child holding the hand of her father,
Those burial clouds that lower victorious soon to devour all,
Watching, silently weeps.

Weep not, child,
Weep not, my darling,
With these kisses let me remove your tears,
The ravening clouds shall not long be victorious,
They shall not long possess the sky, they devour the stars only in
    apparition,
Jupiter shall emerge, be patient, watch again another night, the
    Pleiades shall emerge,
They are immortal, all those stars both silvery and golden shall
    shine out again,   20
The great stars and the little ones shall shine out again, they
    endure,
The vast immortal suns and the long-enduring pensive moons shall
    again shine.
Then dearest child mournest thou only for Jupiter?
Considerest thou alone the burial of the stars?

Something there is,
(With my lips soothing thee, adding I whisper,
I give thee the first suggestion, the problem and indirection,)
Something there is more immortal even than the stars,
(Many the burials, many the days and nights, passing away,)
Something that shall endure longer even than lustrous Jupiter,   30
Longer than sun or any revolving satellite,
Or the radiant sisters the Pleiades.[20]

Prayer of Columbus

FROM *Complete Writings*, Camden Edition, II, 198–200. First published
in *Harper's Monthly*, March 1874. Reprinted in *Two Rivulets* (1876).

A BATTER'D, wreck'd old man,
Thrown on this savage shore, far, far from home,
Pent by the sea and dark rebellious brows, twelve dreary months.
Sore, stiff with many toils, sicken'd and nigh to death,
I take my way along the island's edge,
Venting a heavy heart.

I am too full of woe!
Haply I may not live another day;
I cannot rest O God, I cannot eat or drink or sleep,
Till I put forth myself, my prayer, once more to Thee,   10
Breathe, bathe myself once more in Thee, commune with Thee,
Report myself once more to Thee.

Thou knowest my years entire, my life,
My long and crowded life of active work, not adoration merely;
Thou knowest the prayers and vigils of my youth,
Thou knowest my manhood's solemn and visionary meditations,
Thou knowest how before I commenced I devoted all to come to
    Thee,
Thou knowest I have in age ratified all those vows and strictly
    kept them,
Thou knowest I have not once lost nor faith nor ecstasy in
    Thee,[198]
In shackles, prison'd, in disgrace, repining not,   20
Accepting all from Thee, as duly come from Thee.

All my emprises have been fill'd with Thee,
My speculations, plans, begun and carried on in thoughts of Thee,
Sailing the deep or journeying the land for Thee;
Intentions, purports, aspirations mine, leaving results to Thee.

O I am sure they really came from Thee,
The urge, the ardor, the unconquerable will,
The potent, felt, interior command, stronger than words,
A message from the Heavens whispering to me even in sleep,
These sped me on.   30

By me and these the work so far accomplish'd,
By me earth's elder cloy'd and stifled lands uncloy'd, unloos'd,
By me the hemispheres rounded and tied, the unknown to the
    known.

The end I know not, it is all in Thee,
Or small or great I know not—haply what broad field, what lands,
Haply the brutish measureless human undergrowth I know,
Transplanted there may rise to stature, knowledge worthy Thee,
Haply the swords I know may there indeed be turn'd to reaping-
    tools,
Haply the lifeless cross I know, Europe's dead cross, may bud and
    blossom there.

One effort more, my altar this bleak sand;   40
That thou O God my life has lighted,[199]
With ray of light, steady, ineffable, vouchsafed of Thee,
Light rare untellable, lighting the very light,
Beyond all signs, descriptions, languages;
For that O God, be it my latest word, here on my knees,
Old, poor, and paralyzed, I thank Thee.

My terminus near,
The clouds already closing in upon me,

The voyage balk'd, the course disputed, lost,
I yield my ships to Thee.   50

My hands, my limbs grow nerveless,
My brain feels rack'd, bewilder'd,
Let the old timbers part, I will not part,
I will cling fast to Thee, O God, though the waves buffet me,
Thee, Thee at least I know.

Is it the prophet's thought I speak, or am I raving?
What do I know of life? what of myself?
I know not even my own work past or present,
Dim ever-shifting guesses of it spread before me,
Of newer better worlds, their mighty parturition,   60
Mocking, perplexing me.

And these things I see suddenly, what mean they?
As if some miracle, some hand divine unseal'd my eyes,
Shadowy vast shapes smile through the air and sky,
And on the distant waves sail countless ships,
And anthems in new tongues I hear saluting me. [200]

Spirit That Form'd This Scene

FROM *Complete Writings,* Camden Edition, II, 268. First published in
Leaves of Grass, 7th edition (1881). According to the subtitle, the poem
was "Written in Platte Cañon, Colorado."

SPIRIT that form'd this scene,
These tumbled rock-piles grim and red,
These reckless heaven-ambitious peaks,
These gorges, turbulent-clear streams, this naked freshness,
These formless wild arrays, for reasons of their own,
I know thee, savage spirit—we have communed together,
Mine too such wild arrays, for reasons of their own;
Was't charged against my chants they had forgotten art?
To fuse within themselves its rules precise and delicatesse?
The lyrist's measur'd beat, the wrought-out temple's grace—column
    and polish'd arch forgot?   10
But thou that revelest here—spirit that form'd this scene,
They have remember'd thee.

REVISIONS OF "BARDIC SYMBOLS"

First Version

"Bardic Symbols," *Atlantic Monthly,* V (April 1860), 445–447.

Bardic Symbols

I

ELEMENTAL drifts!
Oh, I wish I could impress others as you and the waves have just
    been impressing me!

II

As I ebbed with an ebb of the ocean of life,
As I wended the shores I know,
As I walked where the sea-ripples wash you, Paumanok,
Where they rustle up, hoarse and sibilant,
Where the fierce old mother endlessly cries for her castaways,
I, musing, late in the autumn day, gazing off southward,
Alone, held by the eternal self of me that threatens to get the better
    of me and stifle me,
Was seized by the spirit that trails in the lines underfoot,   10
In the ruin, the sediment, that stands for all the water and all the
    land of the globe.

III

Fascinated, my eyes, reverting from the south, dropped, to follow
    those slender windrows,
Chaff, straw, splinters of wood, weeds, and the sea-gluten,
Scum, scales from shining rocks, leaves of salt-lettuce, left by the
    tide.

IV

Miles walking, the sound of breaking waves the other side of me,
Paumanok, there and then as I thought the old thought of like-
    nesses,
These you presented to me, you fish-shaped island,
As I wended the shores I know,
As I walked with that eternal self of me, seeking types.

V

As I wend the shores I know not,   20
As I listen to the dirge, the voices of men and women wrecked,

As I inhale the impalpable breezes that set in upon me,
As the ocean so mysterious rolls toward me closer and closer,
At once I find, the least thing that belongs to me, or that I see or
   touch, I know not;
I, too, but signify a little washed-up drift,—a few sands and dead
   leaves to gather,
Gather, and merge myself as part of the leaves and drift.

VI

Oh, baffled, lost,
Bent to the very earth, here preceding what follows
Terrified with myself that I have dared to open my mouth,
Aware now, that, amid all the blab whose echoes recoil upon me,
   I have not once had the least idea who or what I am,[445]   30
But that before all my insolent poems the real me still stands un-
   touched, untold, altogether unreached,
Withdrawn far, mocking me with mock-congratulatory signs and
   bows,
With peals of distant ironical laughter at every word I have written
   or shall write,
Striking me with insults, till I fall helpless upon the sand!

VII

O, I think I have not understood anything,—not a single object,—
   and that no man ever can!

VIII

I think Nature here, in sight of the sea, is taking advantage of me
   to oppress me,
Because I was assuming so much,
And because I have dared to open my mouth to sing at all.

IX

You oceans both! You tangible land! Nature!
Be not too stern with me,—I submit,—I close with you—   40
These little shreds shall, indeed, stand for all.

X

You friable shore, with trails of debris!
You fish-shaped island! I take what is underfoot:
What is yours is mine, my father!

XI

I, too, Paumanok,
I, too, have bubbled up, floated the measureless float, and been
   washed on your shores.

XII

I, too, am but a trail of drift and debris,—
I, too, leave little wrecks upon you, you fish-shaped island!

XIII

I throw myself upon your breast, my father!
I cling to you so that you cannot unloose me,—   50
I hold you so firm, till you answer me something.

XIV

Kiss me, my father!
Touch me with your lips, as I touch those I love!
Breathe to me, while I hold you close, the secret of the wondrous
    murmuring I envy!
For I fear I shall become crazed, if I cannot emulate it, and utter
    myself as well as it.

XV

Sea-raff! Torn leaves!
O, I sing, some day, what you have certainly said to me![446]

XVI

Ebb, ocean of life! (the flow will return,)—
Cease not your moaning, you fierce old mother!
Endlessly cry for your castaways! Yet fear not, deny not me,—   60
Rustle not up so hoarse and angry against my feet, as I touch you,
    or gather from you.

XVII

I mean tenderly by you,—
I gather for myself, and for this phantom, looking down where we
    lead, and following me and mine.

XVIII

Me and mine!
We, loose windrows, little corpses,
Froth, snowy white, and bubbles,
Tufts of straw, sands, fragments,
Buoyed hither from many moods, one contradicting another,
From the storm, the long calm, the darkness, the swell,
Musing, pondering, a breath, a briny tear, a dab of liquid or soil,   70
Up just as much out of fathomless workings fermented and thrown,
A limp blossom or two, torn, just as much over waves floating,
    drifted at random,

Just as much for us that sobbing dirge of Nature,
Just as much, whence we come, that blare of the cloud-trumpets,—
We, capricious, brought hither, we know not whence, spread out
    before you,—you, up there, walking or sitting,
Whoever you are,—we, too, lie in drifts at your feet.[447]

Three Revised Versions

The lists below tabulate changes made in three intermediate versions of the poem, leading to the final 1881 version, entitled "As I Ebb'd with the Ocean of Life," which follows the lists of revisions. All changes are keyed to the line numbers of "Bardic Symbols." Changes, once made, continue through subsequent editions. Bracketed page references are included for all the later editions.

1. [Walt Whitman,] *Leaves of Grass.* Boston: Thayer and Eldridge, 1860–61, pp. 196–199.
    [Title: "Leaves of Grass" 1. Arabic section numbers in left margin at first line of section: i.e., by lines 1, 3, 12, 20, 27, 35, 36, 39, 42, 45, 49, 52, 56, 58, 62, 64.]

REVISIONS

l. 2	. . . me.
l. 11	In the rim . . .
l. 12	. . . winrows.
l. 25	[separated into two lines after "drift,"]
l. 27	O baffled, balked,
l. 29	Oppressed with myself . . . my mouth,[196]
l. 31	. . . the real ME . . .
l. 35	O I perceive . . .
l. 36	I perceive Nature here . . . advantage of me, to dart upon me, and sting me,
l. 40	. . . too rough with me . . .
l. 43	. . . underfoot;
l. 46	. . . shores;[197]
l. 47	. . . debris,
l. 48	. . . island.
l. 53	. . . love,
l. 54	. . . envy,
l. 56	Sea-raff! Crook-tongued waves
l. 57	O, I will yet sing, some day, what you have said to me.
l. 58	. . . life, . . . return,)
l. 59	. . . mother,
l. 60	. . . castaways—but fear not, deny not me,
l. 62	. . . you,
l. 65	. . . winrows . . .

l. 66   . . . bubbles,[198]
added   (See from my dead lips the ooze exuding at last!
         See—the prismatic colors, glistening and rolling!)
l. 74   . . . cloud-trumpets;
l. 75   . . . before You, up there, . . .

2. [Walt Whitman,] *Leaves of Grass.* New York, 1867, pp. 331–334.
     [Title: "Elemental Drifts." Marginal section numbers retained, but supplemented by four centered Arabic division numbers before lines 1, 20, 39, 58.]

REVISIONS

l. 3   As I ebb'd with an ebb . . .
l. 5   As I walk'd . . .
l. 9   Alone, held by this eternal self of me, out of the pride of which I have utter'd my poems,
l. 10   Was seiz'd . . .
l. 12   . . . drop't . . .
l. 16   [end of page 331]
l. 19   As I walk'd . . .
l. 20   As I wend to the shores . . .
l. 21   As I list to the dirge, . . . wreck't,
l. 24   [deleted]
l. 25   . . . wash'd-up drift,
l. 27 f   O baffled, balk'd, bent to the very earth
         Opprest with myself . . .
l. 31   . . . untouch'd . . . unreach'd,
l. 33   . . . at every word I have written,
l. 34   Pointing in silence to all these songs, and then to the sand beneath.
l. 35   Now I perceive . . . can.[332]
l. 36   I perceive Nature, here in sight . . .
l. 37   [deleted]
l. 38   Because I have . . .
l. 39   You oceans both! I close with you;
l. 40   [deleted]
l. 46   . . . wash'd . . .
l. 55   [deleted]
l. 56   [deleted]
l. 57   [deleted]
l. 61   [end of page 333]
l. 70   . . . soil;
l. 71   . . . thrown;
l. 72   . . . random;
l. 73   . . . Nature;
l. 75 ff   We, capricious, brought hither, we know not whence, spread out before you,
         You, up there, walking or sitting
         Whoever you are . . . feet.[334]

3. [Walt Whitman,] *Passage to India*. Washington, D.C., 1872, pp. 78–82.
    [Title: "Elemental Drifts," in a group called "Sea-Shore Memories."
Marginal numbers and division numbers as before.]

REVISIONS

l. 2	How I wish . . .
l. 4	[end of page 78]
l. 5	As I walk'd where the ripples continually wash . . .
l. 9	. . . eternal Self . . . of which I utter . . .
l. 12	. . . dropt . . .
l. 14	. . . tide:
l. 19	. . . eternal Self . . .
l. 21	. . . wreck'd,
l. 26	[end of page 79]
l. 29	Oppress'd with myself . . .
l. 34	. . . silence to these songs . . .
l. 39 ff	. . . you;
added	We murmur alike reproachfully, rolling our sands and drift, knowing not why,
	Those little shreds indeed, standing for you and me and all.
l. 48	[end of page 80]
l. 62	I mean tenderly by you and all,

Final Version

"As I Ebb'd with the Ocean of Life," in *Leaves of Grass*, third edition
[*sic*]. Boston: James R. Osgood and Company, 1881–82, pp. 202–204.
Poem included in a group called "Sea-Drift."

As I Ebb'd with the Ocean of Life

1

As I ebb'd with the ocean of life,
As I wended the shores I know,
As I walk'd where the ripples continually wash you Paumanok
Where they rustle up hoarse and sibilant,
Where the fierce old mother endlessly cries for her castaways,
I musing late in the autumn day, gazing off southward,
Held by this electric self out of the pride of which I utter poems,
Was seiz'd by the spirit that trails in the lines underfoot,
The rim the sediment that stands for all the water and all the land
    of the globe.

Fascinated, my eyes reverting from the south, dropt, to follow those
    slender winrows,   10
Chaff, straw, splinters of wood, weeds, and the sea-gluten,

Scum, scales from shining rocks, leaves of salt-lettuce, left by the
    tide,
Miles walking, the sound of breaking waves the other side of me,
Paumanok there and then as I thought the old thought of like-
    nesses,
These you presented to me you fish-shaped island,
As I wended the shores I know,
As I walk'd with that electric self seeking types.

2

As I wend to the shores I know not,
As I list to the dirge, the voices of men and women wreck'd,
As I inhale the impalpable breezes that set in upon me,   20
As the ocean so mysterious rolls toward me closer and closer,
I too but signify at the utmost a little wash'd-up drift,
A few sands and dead leaves to gather,
Gather, and merge myself as part of the sands and drift.

O baffled, balk'd, bent to the very earth,
Oppress'd with myself that I have dared to open my mouth,
Aware now that amid all the blab whose echoes recoil upon me I
    have not once had the least idea who or what I am,
But that before all my arrogant poems the real ME still stands un-
    touch'd, untold, altogether unreach'd,
Withdrawn far, mocking me with mock-congratulatory signs and
    bows,
With peals of distant ironical laughter at every word I have written, 30
Pointing in silence to these songs, and then to the sand beneath.[202]
I perceive I have not understood any thing, not a single object,
    and that no man ever can.
Nature here in sight of the sea taking advantage of me to dart upon
    me and sting me,
Because I have dared to open my mouth to sing at all.

3

You oceans both, I close with you,
We murmur alike reproachfully rolling sands and drift, knowing
    not why,
These little shreds indeed standing for you and me and all.

You friable shore with trails of debris,
You fish-shaped island, I take what is underfoot,
What is yours is mine my father.   40

I too Paumanok,
I too have bubbled up, floated the measureless float, and been
    wash'd on your shores,
I too am but a trail of drift and debris,

I too leave little wrecks upon you, you fish-shaped island.
I throw myself upon your breast my father,
I cling to you so that you cannot unloose me,
I hold you so firm till you answer me something.

Kiss me my father,
Touch me with your lips as I touch those I love,
Breathe to me while I hold you close the secret of the murmuring
    I envy.   50

4

Ebb, ocean of life, (the flow will return,)
Cease not your moaning you fierce old mother,
Endlessly cry for your castaways, but fear not, deny not me,
Rustle not up so hoarse and angry against my feet as I touch you or
    gather from you.
I mean tenderly by you and all,
I gather for myself and for this phantom looking down where we
    lead, and following me and mine.
Me and mine, loose winrows, little corpses,
Froth, snowy white, and bubbles,
(See, from my dead lips the ooze exuding at last,[203]
See, the prismatic colors glistening and rolling,)   60
Tufts of straw, sands, fragments,
Buoy'd hither from many moods, one contradicting another,
From the storm, the long calm, the darkness, the swell,
Musing, pondering, a breath, a briny tear, a dab of liquid or soil,
Up just as much out of fathomless workings fermented and thrown.

A limp blossom or two, torn, just as much over waves floating,
    drifted at random,
Just as much for us that sobbing dirge of Nature,
Just as much whence we come that blare of cloud-trumpets,
We, capricious, brought hither we know not whence, spread out
    before you,
You up there walking or sitting,   70
Whoever you are, we too lie in drifts at your feet.[204]

OBITER DICTA ON
POETRY AND LANGUAGE

Poets Here and Abroad

FROM Whitman's miscellaneous criticisms of books and authors, written mainly for newspapers. In *The Uncollected Poetry and Prose of Walt Whitman*, 2 vols. edited by Emory Holloway (Garden City: Doubleday Page & Co., 1921). Reprinted with permission of Emory Holloway and Doubleday & Company, Inc.

AMERICAN GENIUS AND FOREIGN TRASH

He who desires to see this noble Republic independent, not only in name but in fact, of all unwholesome foreign sway must ever bear in mind the influence of European literature over us—its tolerable amount of good, and its, we hope, "not to be endured" much longer, immense amount of evil. That there is often some clap-trap in denunciations of English books, we have no disposition to deny,—but the evil generally leans on the other side: we receive with a blind homage whatever comes to us stamped with the approbation of foreign critics—merely because it *is* so stamped. We have not enough confidence in our own judgment; we forget that God has given the American mind powers of analysis and acuteness superior to those possessed by any other nation on earth.[I,121]

But where is the remedy? says the inquisitive reader. *In ourselves* we must look for it. Let those who read (and in this country who does not read?) no more condescend to patronize an inferior foreign author, when they have so many respectable writers at home. Shall Hawthorne get a paltry *seventy-five dollars* for a two-volume work—shall real American genius shiver with neglect—while the public run after this foreign trash?[I,123]

[Brooklyn *Daily Eagle*, July 11, 1846]

THOMAS CARLYLE

Under his rapt, weird (grotesque?) style the writer of this work has placed—we may almost say *hidden*—many noble thoughts. That his eyes are clear to the numerous ills which afflict humanity, and that he is a Democrat in that enlarged sense [in] which we would fain see more men Democrats;—that he is quick to champion the down-trodden, and earnest in his wrath at tyranny—is evident enough in almost any one page of Mr. Carlyle's writings. . . . We must confess, however, that we would have preferred to get the thoughts of this truly good thinker, in a plainer and more customary garb. No great writer achieves anything worthy of him, by merely inventing a new *style*. Style in writing, is much as dress in society; sensible people will conform to the prevalent mode, and it is not of infinite importance anyhow, and can always be so varied as to fit one's peculiar way, convenience, or circumstance.[I,129]

[Brooklyn *Daily Eagle*, October 17, 1846]

One likes Mr. Carlyle, the more he communes with him; there is a sort of fascination about the man. His weird wild way—his phrases, welded together as it were, with strange twistings of the terminatives of words—his startling suggestions—his taking up, fish-hook like, certain matters of abuse—make an *original* kind of composition, that gets, after a little usage, to be strangely agreeable! This "Past and Present, and Chartism," now—who would ever puzzle out the drift of the book from the chapter-heads? from such phrases as "Plugson on undershot," or "the One institution," or "Gospel of Dilletantism"? And yet there lies rich ore under that vague surface.[I,130]

[Brooklyn *Daily Eagle*, April 14, 1847]

JOHN MILTON

As a writer Milton is stern, lofty, and grand; his themes are heavenly high, and profoundly deep. A man must have something of the poet's own vast abruptness (if we [may] use such a term), in order to appreciate this writer, who, apparently conscious of his own gigantic proportions, disdains the usual graces and tricks of poets who are read more widely, and understood more easily, because they have *not* his qualities. The towering pile of cliffs, with yawning caverns in the side, the mysterious summits piercing the clouds, while the lightning plays on their naked breasts, is not, to the usual world, half so favorite an object as the landscape of cultivated meadows fringed with a little wood, and watered by a placid stream.[I,134]

[Brooklyn *Daily Eagle,* January 10, 1848]

GOETHE'S AUTOBIOGRAPHY

What a prodigious gain would accrue to the world, if men who write well would as much think of writing life, as they (most of them) think it necessary to write one of the million things evolved from life—Learning! What a gain it would be, if we could forego some of the heavy tomes, the fruit of an age of toil and scientific study, for the simple easy truthful narrative of the existence and experience of a man of genius,—how his mind unfolded in his earliest years—the impressions things made upon him—how and where and when the religious sentiment dawned in him—what he thought of God before he was inoculated with books' ideas—the development of his soul—when he first loved—the way circumstance imbued his nature, and did him good, or worked him ill—with all the long train of occurrences, adventures, mental processes, exercises within, and trials without, which go to make up the man—for *character* is the man, after all. Such a work, fully and faithfully performed, would be a rare treasure! . . . This Life of Goethe—this famous *Wahrheit und Dichtung*—seems shaped with the intention of rendering a history of soul and body's growth, such as alluded to. It is not full enough, perhaps; but it is a real history, and no man but will learn much in the reading of it. It (like Shakespere's writing) does not bear every now and then the inscription, "See the moral of this!" or "Behold how vice is punished!" It goes right on, stating what it has to say, exuberant in its seeds of reflection and inference—though it doesn't reflect or draw the inference. [I,140]

[Brooklyn *Daily Eagle,* November 19, 1846]

EMERSON AND LITERARY GENIUS

I call it one of the chief acts of art, and the greatest trick of literary genius (which is a higher sanity of insanity), to hold the reins firmly, and to preserve the mastery in its wildest escapades. Not to deny the most ecstatic and even irregular moods, so called—rather indeed to favor them—at the same time never to be entirely carried away with them, and always feeling, by a fine caution, when and wherein to limit or prune them, and at such times relentlessly applying restraint and negation. Few even of the accepted great artists or writers hit the happy balance of this principle—this paradox. . . .

Coming, for further illustration, to R. W. Emerson, is not his fault, finally, too great prudence, too rigid a caution? I am not certain it is so. Indeed I have generally felt that Emerson was altogether adjusted to himself, in every attribute, as he should be (as a pine tree is a pine tree, not a quince or a rose bush). But upon the whole, and notwithstanding the many unsurpassed beauties of his poetry first, and prose only second to[II,53] it, I am disposed to think (picking out spots against the sun) that his constitutional distrust and doubt—almost finical in their nicety—have been too much for him—have not perhaps stopped him short of first-class genius, but have veiled it—have certainly clipped and pruned that free luxuriance of it which only satisfies the soul at last.[II,54]

[*Christmas Graphic,* 1874, p. 5]

THE POET'S LANGUAGE

Every soul has its own individual language, often unspoken, or feebly lamely spoken; but a true fit for that man and perfectly adapted for haltingly his use.—The truths I tell to you or to any other may not be plain to you, because I do not translate them fully from my idiom into yours. —If I could do so, and do it well, they would be as apparent to you as they are to me; for they are truths—No two have exactly the same language, and the great translator and joiner of the whole is the poet.

He has the divine grammar of all tongues, and says indifferently and alike, How are you friend? to the President in the midst of his cabinet, and Good day my brother, to Sambo, among the hoes of the sugar field, and both understand him and know that his speech is right.[II,65]

[Manuscript Notebook, 1847]

Memoranda to Himself

FROM "Notes on the Meaning and Intention of 'Leaves of Grass.'" In *Complete Writings,* Camden Edition, IX, 3–44. Whitman's literary executors inherited a mass of manuscript material, including clippings, scrapbooks, and miscellaneous jottings. Dr. Richard M. Bucke put together a great many of these fragmentary jottings. Those numbered 16 and 58 he dated very early, 1856 or earlier.

1

My poems when complete should be a *unity,* in the same sense that the earth is, or that the human body, (senses, soul, head, trunk, feet, blood, viscera, man-root, eyes, hair,) or that a perfect musical composition is.

Great constituent elements of my poetry—Two, viz.: Materialism—Spirituality—The Intellect, the Esthetic is what is to be the medium of these and to beautify and make serviceable there.[3]. . .

7

Make no quotations and no reference to any other writers.[4]

Lumber the writing with nothing—let it go as lightly as a bird flies in the air—or a fish swims in the sea.

Be careful not to temper down too much. . . .[5]

16

Make *the Works*—Do not go into criticisms or arguments at all. Make full-blooded, rich, flush, natural *works.* Insert natural things, indestructibles, idioms, characteristics, rivers, states, persons, &c. Be full of strong sensual germs.[7]. . .

21

Poet! beware lest your poems are made in the spirit that comes from the study of pictures of things—and not from the spirit that comes from the contact with real things themselves.[10] . . .

24

The greatest poems may not be immediately, fully understood by outsiders any more than astronomy or engineering may. The work of the poet is as deep[10] as the astronomer's or engineer's, and his art is also as far-fetched. Science proves itself.—Let poets . . .[11]

58

Rules for Composition—A perfectly transparent, plate-glassy style, artless, with no ornaments, or attempts[34] at ornaments, for their own sake—they only looking well when like the beauties of the person or character by nature and intuition, and never lugged in to show off, which nullifies the best of them, no matter when and where.

Take no illustrations whatever from the ancients or classics, nor from the mythology, nor Egypt, Greece or Rome—nor from the royal and aristocratic institutions and forms of Europe. Make no mention or allusion to them whatever except as they relate to the new, present things—to our country—to American character or interests. Of specific mention of them, even for these purposes, as little as possible.

Too much attempt at ornament is the blur upon nearly all literary styles.

Clearness, simplicity, no twistified or foggy sentences, at all—the most translucid clearness without variation.

Common idioms and phrases—Yankeeisms and vulgarisms—cant expressions, when very pat only.[35]

The Poetry of the Future

FROM "Poetry To-Day in America." In *Complete Writings,* Camden Edition, V, 207–229. Originally included in *Specimen Days and Collect* (1882).

Leaving unnoticed at present the great masterpieces of the antique, or anything from the middle ages, the prevailing flow of poetry for the last fifty or eighty years, and now at its height, has been and is (like the music) an expression of mere surface[215] melody, within narrow limits, and yet, to give it its due, perfectly satisfying to the demands of the ear, of wondrous charm, of smooth and easy delivery, and the triumph of technical art. Above all things it is fractional and select. It shrinks with aversion from the sturdy, the universal, and the democratic.

The poetry of the future (a phrase open to sharp criticism, and not satisfactory to me, but significant, and I will use it)—the poetry of the future aims at the free expression of emotion, (which means far, far more than appears at first,) and to arouse and initiate, more than to define or finish. Like all modern tendencies, it has direct or indirect reference continually to the reader, to you or me, to the central identity of everything, the mighty Ego. . . . It is more akin, likewise, to outside life and landscape, (returning mainly to the antique feeling,) real sun and gale, and woods and shores—to the elements themselves—not sitting at ease in parlor or library listening to a good tale of them, told in good rhyme. Character, a feature far above style or polish—a feature not absent at any time, but now first brought to the fore—gives predominant stamp to advancing poetry. Its born sister, music, already responds to[216] the same influences. "The music of the present, Wagner's, Gounod's, even the later Verdi's, all tends toward this free expression of poetic emotion, and demands a vocalism totally unlike that required for Rossini's splendid roulades, or Bellini's suave melodies."

Is there not even now, indeed, an evolution, a departure from the masters?[217] . . .

On Poetic Power

FROM "Notes Left Over." In *Complete Writings,* Camden Edition, V, 262–301. Originally included in *Specimen Days and Collect* (1882).

RALPH WALDO EMERSON

At times it has been doubtful to me if Emerson really knows or feels what Poetry is at its highest, as in the Bible, for instance, or Homer or Shakspere. I see he covertly or plainly likes best superb verbal polish, or something old or odd—Waller's *Go, lovely rose,* or Lovelace's lines *To Lucasta*—the quaint conceits of the old French bards, and the like. Of *power* he seems to have a gentleman's admiration—but in his inmost heart the grandest attribute of God and Poets is always subordinate to the octaves, conceits, polite kinks, and verbs.[269]

PROSE AND POETRY

In my opinion the time has arrived to essentially break down the barriers between prose and poetry.[271] I say the latter is henceforth to win and maintain its character regardless of rhyme, and the measurement-rules of iambic, spondee, dactyl, &c., and that even if rhyme and those measurements continue to furnish the medium for inferior writers and themes, (especially for persiflage and the comic, as there seems henceforward, to the perfect taste, something inevitably comic in rhyme, merely in itself, and anyhow,) the truest and greatest Poetry, (while subtly and necessarily always rhythmic, and distinguishable easily enough,) can never again, in the English language, be express'd in arbitrary and rhyming metre, any more than the greatest eloquence, or the truest power and passion. . . .[272]

Of poems of the third or fourth class, (perhaps even some of the second,) it makes little or no difference who writes them—they are good enough for what they are; nor is it necessary that they should be actual emanations from the personality and life of the writers. The very reverse sometimes gives piquancy. But poems of the first class, (poems of the depth, as distinguished from those of the surface,) are to be sternly tallied with the poets themselves, and tried by them and their lives. Who wants a glorification of courage and manly defiance from a coward[273] or a sneak? . . .[274]

Conversations with Traubel

FROM Horace Traubel, *With Walt Whitman in Camden*, 4 vols. Vols. 1 and 2—New York: D. Appleton and Company, 1908 (Vol. 1 first published Boston, 1906). Vol. 3—New York: Mitchell Kennerly, 1914. Vol. 4—Philadelphia: University of Pennsylvania Press, 1953 (ed. Sculley Bradley). Reprinted by permission of Gertrude Traubel.

Tuesday, May 15, 1888

. . . [Whitman:] Referring to Passage to India: "There's more of me, the essential ultimate me, in that than in any of the poems. There is no philosophy, consistent or inconsistent, in that poem—there [Daniel G.] Brinton would be right—[I,156]but the burden of it is evolution—the one thing escaping the other—the unfolding of cosmic purposes."[I,157]

Wednesday, May 16, 1888

. . . [Whitman:] "But let me tell you a little more about [Ernest] Rhys. He is very interesting to me. We talked of the poetic lilt. Rhys insists on it; insists on it, come good or bad. Well—the lilt is all right: yes, right enough: but there's something anterior—more imperative. The first thing necessary is the thought—the rest may follow if it chooses—may play its part—but must not be too much sought after. The two things being equal I should prefer to have the lilt present with the idea, but if I got down my thought and the rhythm was not there I should not work to secure it. I am very deliberate—I take a good deal of trouble with words: yes, a good deal: but what I am after is the content not the music of words. Perhaps the music happens—it does no harm; I do not go in search of it. Two centuries back or so much of the poetry passed from lip to lip—was oral: was literally made to be sung: then the lilt, the formal rhythm, may have been necessary. The case is now somewhat changed: now, when the poetic work in literature is more than nineteen-twentieths of it by print, the simply tonal aids are

not so necessary, or if necessary, have considerably shifted their character."[I,163]

Thursday, May 17, 1888

. . . [Whitman] naturally diverted to [Sidney] Lanier. "The recent published adverse reference to me from Lanier as reported in the
Memorial volume was objected to by his wife, I am told, on the ground
of its unfairness, not only to me but to Lanier, since other things said
by Lanier about me, reflecting a more favorable mood, should also have
been given. I know nothing about that myself and care less. I had
several letters from Lanier—very warm letters. One of them is still
about here somewhere: I want you to have it some day: the severely
critical paragraphs in the book were therefore rather a surprise to me.
I suppose we will all survive the anomaly. Lanier was tragic in life
and death. He had the soul of the musician—was a flute player: indeed,
in the accounts, was phenomenally fine. This extreme sense of the
melodic, a virtue in itself, when carried into [I,170] the art of the writer
becomes a fault. Why? Why, because it tends to place the first emphasis
on tone, sound—on the lilt as Rhys so often puts it. Study Lanier's
choice of words—they are too often fit rather for sound than for sense.
His ear was over-sensitive. He had a genius—a delicate, clairvoyant
genius: but this over-tuning of the ear, this extreme deference paid to
oral nicety, reduced the majesty, the solid worth, of his rhythms."[I,171]

Wednesday, June 6, 1888

. . . [Whitman was led] to some reflections upon the character
of these latest poems. "I often ask myself, is this expression of the life
of an old man consonant with the fresher, earlier, delvings, faiths,
hopes, stated in the original Leaves? I have my doubts—minor doubts—
but somehow I decide the case finally on my own side. It belongs to the
scheme of the book. As long as I live the Leaves must go on. Am I, as
some think, losing grip?—taking in my horns? No—no—no: I am sure
that could not be. I still wish to be, am, the radical of my stronger
days—to be the same uncompromising oracle of democracy—to maintain undimmed the light of my deepest faith. I am sure I have not gone
back on that—sure, sure. The Sands [Sands at Seventy, an "annex" of
the 1880's] have to be taken as the utterances of an old man—a very
old man. I desire that they may be interpreted as confirmations, not
denials, of the work that has preceded. [William Dean] Howells,
[Henry] James and some others appear to think I rest my philosophy,
my democracy, upon braggadocio, noise, rough assertion, such integers.
While I would not be afraid to assent to this as a part of the truth
I still insist that I am on the whole to be thought of in other terms.
I recognize, have always recognized, the importance of the lusty, strong-
limbed, big-bodied American[I,271] of the Leaves: I do not abate one
atom of that belief now, today. But I hold to something more than

that, too, and claim a full, not a partial, judgment upon my work—I am not to be known as a piece of something but as a totality."[I,272]

Thursday, June 7, 1888

. . . Was he on the whole satisfied with the Hotten book [London edition of *Leaves of Grass* published by John Camden Hotten]? "On the whole—yes. Yet any volume of extracts must misrepresent the Leaves—any volume—the best. The whole theory of the book is against gems, abstracts, extracts: the book needs each of its parts to keep its perfect unity. Above everything else it stands for unity. Take it to pieces—even with a gentle hand—and it is no longer the same product."[I,282]

Tuesday, June 26, 1888

[Whitman] asked me if I "could make anything out of the Conway document"* I had "taken away yesterday?" Said further of it himself: "I do not remember the incident with which it seems to belong. For one thing, it gives my idea of my own book: a man's idea of his own book—his serious idea—is not to be despised. I do not lack in egotism, as you know—the sort of egotism that is willing to know itself as honestly as it is willing to know third or fourth parties. Why shouldn't a man be allowed to weigh himself? He can't do worse than go wrong: going wrong is no hurt." I might as well copy "the Conway document" right here.

"2. Critically, a significant, if not the most significant, fact about Leaves of Grass is, that the genesis and fashioning of them have evidently not had in view literary purposes merely or even mainly, and the poet has not, either in mass or in detail, tried his work as it progressed by the *sine qua non* of current literary or esthetic standards. The Book is a product, not of literature merely, but of the largest universal law and play of things, and of Kosmical beauty, of which literature, however important, is but a fraction. This is the clue to, the explanation of, the puzzle of the widest vexatious literary and esthetic questions involved in Leaves of Grass.

"3. The summed-up idea however which, in this man's contribution, compared even with the vast Biblical and Homeric poetry, looms and towers as athwart the giants of the Himalayas, the dim head of the more gigantic Kunchainjunga, rises over the rest: idea of Totality, of the All-perfect, All-successful final certainties of each individual[I,383] Man, as well as of the world he inhabits. Joyousness, and certain ultimate triumph, only of new and unthought of descriptions, ringing through every verse. He alone holds the solution, the spell, giving full satisfaction; and his talisman is *Ensemble*. This is the word that belongs to the book, turned with the word Modernness."[I,384]

---

* A letter from William O'Connor to Moncure Conway, Nov. 10, 1867, originally composed by Whitman himself. The letter was possibly written to provide William Rossetti with information and judgments about Whitman for his forthcoming edition of the poet's work (appeared 1868). [Ed.]

Monday, July 2, 1888

. . . I will copy here the sheet of pencilled paper. It had had a headline—"The question of form"—which was marked out. [The sheet was apparently composed by Whitman in the early 1870's.]

"The want for something finished, completed, and technically beautiful will certainly not be supplied by this writer, as it is by existing esthetic works. For the best poems both the old ones and later ones now accepted as first class are polished, rhymed regular, with all the elegance of fine conceits, carefully elaborated, showing under all the restraints of art, language and phrase chosen after very much has been rejected, and only the best admitted, and then all joined and cemented together, and finally presenting the beauty of some architectural temple—some palace, proudly rising in proportions of marble, entered from superb porticos and adorned with statuary satisfying the art sense and that of form, fulfilling beauty and inviting criticism. Not so his poetry. Its likeness is not the solid stately palace, nor the sculpture that adorns it, nor the paintings on its walls. Its analogy is *the Ocean*. Its verses are the liquid, billowy waves, ever rising and falling, perhaps sunny and smooth, perhaps wild with storm, always moving, always alike[I,414] in their nature as rolling waves, but hardly any two exactly alike in size or measure (meter), never having the sense of something finished and fixed, always suggesting something beyond."[I,415]

Thursday, August 2, 1888

. . . Returned him [W. E.] Henley's poems. Told him I had read the book through. He exclaimed: "All through? Why, I had no idea anybody was capable of that. I read only the fore part of it—the hospital pieces—was peculiarly, intensely, interested in that—but as for the rest—" After a pause: "It struck me as extremely deliberate verse—verse written of malice prepense—all laid out, designed, on mathematical principles. Did you get that impression of it? Or did it carry you right along as if you could not help it?"[II,77]

Friday, August 24, 1888

I found a poem by [Algernon Charles] Swinburne—A Double Ballad of August. [Whitman] said: "Oh yes, I did see that. And if Swinburne had a few grains of thought with all his music wouldn't he be the greatest charmer of all? I never liked him from the first—Swinburne—from the very first: could not take him in, adapt myself to him. I know of nothing I think of so little account as pretty words, pretty thoughts, pretty china, pretty arrangements."[II,188]

Monday, September 24th, 1888

. . . [Whitman:] "If there is anything whatever in Leaves of Grass—anything that sets it apart as a fact of any importance—that thing must be its totality—its massings. I respond to no other explanation: no other explanation comes up to my purpose—tallies the long steady pull of my many years of adhesion to a first purpose. I chose the fundamentals for Leaves of Grass—heart, spirit: the initiating passions of character: chose that it should stand for, be, a human being, with all the impulses, desires, aspirations, gropings, triumphs, that go with human life: comprehended at no time by its parts, at all times by its unity." He was very earnest. Then he went on: "Leaves of Grass is not intellectual alone (I do not despise the intellectual— far from it: it is not to be despised—has its uses) nor sympathetic alone (though sympathetic enough, too) nor yet vaguely emotional—least of all this. I have always stood in Leaves of Grass for something higher than qualities, particulars. It is atmosphere, unity: it is never to be set down in traits but as a symphony: is no more to be stated by super- ficial criticism than life itself is to be so stated: is not to be caught by a smart definition or all given up to any one extreme state- ment." [II,373]

Monday, October 22, 1888

[During a discussion of Edmund Gosse, the British critic:] Gosse had remarked Poe's great influence upon English writers. [Whitman] said: "He means in technique—of all things, metrical niceties! Gosse's applause of Poe is like admiration for a shop window crowded with delicacies: is like a polite Episcopal preacher's estimate, analysis, of a Catholic priest." [II,518]

Wednesday, October 31, 1888

. . . [Whitman:] "The best gift to our age so far is what we have come to know as the scientific spirit . . . It is the crowning glory of our time that this new evangel has appeared. There is no salvation if not in that: it is an appeal to nature, an appeal to final meanings—to facts, to the sun itself: it is an absolute surrender to the truth: it never asks us: Do you want this thing to be true? or, Is it ugly, hateful? but, Is it true, and if it is true that settles it. That's all there is to it—that's all there needs to be to it; that's enough. Here science and literature are one, as they everywhere and always should be one in fact, and it is here, in such a noble equipment, that [Heinrich] Heine lustrously shines. Brilliants, gems, crystallizations, in the requisites of a writer— bright epigrams, splendid learning, eloquent roundings-off of phrase— all these, I can see, have an importance, too, though second-rate, third- rate, at the best. But in all imaginative work, all pure poetic work, there must especially come in a primal quality, not to be mentioned, named, described, but always felt when present: the direct off-throwing of nature, parting the ways between formal, conventional, borrowed expression and the fervor of genuine spirit. Heine had it—so do all the big fellows have it. More than any other agent, science has been further- ing it." Was it not also in Leaves of Grass? [Whitman] exclaimed fervidly: "Oh! I hope so, I believe so: it has been in the air: I have sucked it in as the breath of life: unconsciously, not by determination, but with full recognition now of its great value, of its wonderful significance. Yes, Leaves of Grass would lose much if it lost that.[II,562] that [sic] is the ground underlying all: the fact, the fact: that alone: the fact devotedly espoused, sacred, uplifting! The whole mass of people are being leavened by this spirit of scientific worship—this noblest of religions coming after all the religions that came before. . . . That's where science becomes religion—where the new spirit utters the highest truth—makes the last demonstration of faith: looks the universe full in the face—its bad in the face, its good—and says yes to it."[II,563]

Tuesday, November 6, 1888

Reference having been made to Shakespeare, [Whitman] said: "Shakespeare shows undoubted defects: he often uses a hundred words where a dozen would do: it is true that there[III,35] are many pithy terse sentences everywhere: but there are countless prolixities: though as for the overabundances of words more might be said: as, for instance, that he was not ignorantly prolific; that he was like nature itself: nature, with her trees, the oceans: nature, saying 'there's lots of this, infinitudes of it—therefore, why spare it? If you ask for ten I give you a hundred, for a hundred I give you a thousand, for a thousand I give you ten thousand.' It may be that we should look at it in that way: not complain of it: rather understanding its amazing intimations."[III,36]

Monday, November 26, 1888

. . . [Whitman:] "I could never go Milton: he is turgid, heavy, overstately." I said: "Take Paradise Lost: don't its vogue come mainly from a sort of Christian theological self-interest rather than from pure delight in its beauty?" He responded at once: "Oh! an immense lot! Besides, it seems to me that Milton is a copy, not only [of] Homer but the Aeneid: a sort of modern repetition of the same old story: legions of angels, devils; war is declared, waged: moreover, even as a story it enlists little of my attention: he seems to me like a bird—soaring yet overweighted: dragged down, as if burdened—too greatly burdened: a lamb in its beak: its flight not graceful, powerful, beautiful, satisfying, like the gulls we see over the Delaware in mid-winter—their simple motion a delight—attracting you when they first break upon your sight: soaring, soaring, irrespective of cold or storm. It is true, Milton soars, but with dull, unwieldy motion."[III,185]

Monday, December 17, 1888

. . . [Concerning Emerson's advice that some of the poems on sex be omitted from the 1860 edition of Leaves of Grass:] "Emerson—well, Emerson had his rights, too, but in his argument failed to realize the orbic character of the Leaves, supposing that an important piece could be taken out without injury to the whole. . . ."[III,321]

Sunday, February 10, 1889

. . . He [Whitman] continued: "The trouble is that writers are too literary—too damned literary. There has grown up—Swinburne I think an apostle of it—the doctrine (you have heard of it? it is dinned everywhere), art for art's sake: think of it—art for art's sake. Let a man really accept that—let that be his ruling thought—and he is lost." I suggested: "If we say politics for politics' sake they get mad." [Whitman:] "So they do: that is very good: it's true: politics for politics' sake, church for church's sake, talk for talk's sake, government for government's sake: state it any way you choose it becomes offensive: it's all out of the same pit. Instead of regarding literature as only a weapon, an instrument, in the service of something larger than itself, it looks upon itself as an end—as a fact to be finally worshipped, adored. To me that's all a horrible blasphemy—a bad-smelling apostasy." [IV,121]

Monday, March 11, 1889

[Whitman:] ". . . it is that catalogue business* that wrecks them all—that hauls them up short, that determines their opposition: they shudder at it." He smiled: "They call the catalogue names: but suppose they do? it *is* names: but what could be more poetic than names?" [Dr. Richard Maurice] Bucke said: "Yes: look at those lines of Indian names!" adding: "It is one of the choice bits in Leaves of Grass." [Whitman] said: "I almost think so myself: at least I like it: I have often resolved within myself that I would write a book on names—simply names: it has been one of my pet ambitions never realized." [IV,324]

Thursday, March 28, 1889

Reference to Song of the Open Road. [J. V.] Blake told [Whitman] how he used it in his New Year's service. It had been suggested by [Sidney B.] Morse's reading some extracts to [Blake] one day. [Whitman] said: "I have wondered if in my work there is not too much of that." I asked: "Of what?" He answered: "Of indirection." Blake demurred. [Whitman] said: "It has often occurred to me that perhaps all through the poems I assume too largely the responding, sympathetic gifts of the reader." Blake again expressed his dissent. [IV,439]

A Self-Review

FROM "Walt Whitman and His Poems." In *In Re Walt Whitman,* edited by Horace L. Traubel, Richard Maurice Bucke, and Thomas B. Harned

---

* A reference to Whitman's technique of including seemingly random lists of persons, occupations, or scenes in his poetry. [Ed.]

(Philadelphia: David McKay, 1893), pp. 13–21. First published as unsigned review in *United States Review*, XXXVI (September 1855), 205–
212.

Self-reliant, with haughty eyes, assuming to himself all the
attributes of his country, steps Walt Whitman into literature, talking
like a man unaware that there was ever hitherto such a production as
a book, or such a being as a writer. . . . With light and rapid touch
he first indicates in prose the principles of the foundation of a race
of poets so deeply to spring from the American people, and become
ingrained through them, that their Presidents shall not be the common
referees so much as that great race of poets shall. He proceeds himself
to exemplify this new school, and set models for their expression and
range of subjects. . . . His work is to be achieved by unusual methods.
Neither classic nor romantic is he, nor a materialist any more than a
spiritualist. Not a whisper comes out of him of the old stock talk and
rhyme of poetry—not the first recognition of gods or goddesses, or[14]
Greece or Rome. No breath of Europe, or her monarchies or priestly
conventions, or her notions of gentlemen and ladies, founded on the
idea of caste, seems ever to have fanned his face or been inhaled into
his lungs.

The movement of his verses is the sweeping movement of great
currents of living people . . . Undecked also is this poet with senti-
mentalism, or jingle, or nice conceits, or flowery similes . . .[15] The
style of the bard that is waited for, is to be transcendent and new. It is
to be indirect, and not direct or descriptive or epic. . . .

The style of these poems, therefore, is simply their own style, just
born and red. Nature may have given the hint to the author of the
"Leaves of Grass," but there exists no book or fragment of a book
which can have given the hint to them. All beauty, he says, comes from
beautiful blood and a beautiful brain. His rhythm and uniformity he
will conceal in the roots of his verses, not to be seen of themselves, but
to break forth loosely as lilacs on a bush, and take shapes compact, as
the shapes of melons, or chestnuts, or pears.[16]

PART TWO
WRITINGS ABOUT WHITMAN

5

CONTEMPORARY CRITICAL ESTIMATES
1855–1892

The Beginning of a Great Career

Ralph Waldo Emerson

FROM "Leaves-Droppings." In *Leaves of Grass,* 2nd edition (Brooklyn, N.Y., 1856). Emerson's letter was written July 21, 1855.

Dear Sir—I am not blind to the worth of the wonderful gift of "LEAVES OF GRASS." I find it the most extraordinary piece of wit and wisdom that America has yet contributed. I am very happy in reading it, as great power makes us happy. It meets the demand I am always making of what seemed the sterile and stingy nature, as if too much handiwork, or too much lymph in the temperament, were making our western wits fat and mean.

I give you joy of your free and brave thought. I have great joy in it. I find incomparable things said incomparably well, as they must be. I find the courage of treatment which so delights us, and which large perception only can inspire.

I greet you at the beginning of a great career, which yet must have had a long foreground somewhere, for such a start. I rubbed my eyes a little, to see if this sunbeam were no illusion; but the solid sense of the book is a sober certainty. It has the best merits, namely, of fortifying and encouraging.

I did not know until I last night saw the book advertised in a newspaper that I could trust the name as real[345] and available for a post-office. I wish to see my benefactor, and have felt much like striking my tasks and visiting New York to pay you my respects.[346]

Yankee Transcendentalism
and New York Rowdyism

Charles Eliot Norton

FROM "Whitman's Leaves of Grass." Unsigned review in *Putnam's Monthly,* VI (September 1855), 321–323. The reviewer was later identified as Charles Eliot Norton. See *A Leaf of Grass From Shady Hill . . .* (Cambridge, 1928).

Our account of the last month's literature would be incomplete without some notice of a curious and lawless collection of poems, called *Leaves of Grass,* and issued in a thin quarto without the name of publisher or author. The poems, twelve in number, are neither in rhyme nor blank verse, but in a sort of excited prose broken into lines without any attempt at measure or regularity, and, as many readers will perhaps think, without any idea of sense or reason. The writer's scorn for the wonted usages of good writing, extends to the vocabulary he adopts; words usually banished from polite society are here employed without reserve and with perfect indifference to their effect on the reader's mind; and not only is the book one not to be read aloud to a mixed audience, but the introduction of terms, never before heard or seen, and of slang expressions, often renders an otherwise striking passage altogether laughable. . . . The application of these principles [of the Preface], and of many others equally peculiar, which are expounded in a style equally oracular throughout the long preface,—is made *passim,* and often with comical success, in the poems themselves, which may briefly be described as a compound of the New England transcendentalist and New York rowdy. A fireman or omnibus driver, who had intelligence enough to absorb the speculations of that school of thought which culminated at Boston some fifteen or eighteen years ago, and resources of expression to put them forth again in a form of his own, with sufficient self-conceit and contempt for public taste to affront all usual propriety of diction, might have written this gross yet elevated, this superficial yet profound, this preposterous, yet somehow fascinating book. As we say, it is a mixture of Yankee transcendentalism and New York rowdyism, and, what must be surprising to both these elements, they here seem to fuse and combine with the most perfect harmony.[321] . . .

A Keen Memory and a Vivid Imagination

Edward Everett Hale

FROM *"Leaves of Grass," North American Review,* LXXXII (January 1856), 275–277.

Everything about the external arrangement of this book was odd and out of the way. The author printed it himself, and it seems to have been left to the winds of heaven to publish it. So it happened that we had not discovered it before our last number, although we believe the sheets had then passed the press. It bears no publisher's name, and, if the reader goes to a bookstore for it, he may expect to be told at first, as we were, that there is no such book, and has not been. Nevertheless, there is such a book, and it is well worth going twice to the bookstore to buy it. Walter Whitman, an American,—one of the roughs,—no sentimentalist,—no stander above men and women, or apart from them,—no more modest than immodest,—has tried to write down here, in a sort of prose poetry, a good deal of what he has seen, felt, and guessed at in a pilgrimage of some thirty-five years. He has a horror of conventional language of any kind. His theory of expression is, that, "to speak in literature with the perfect rectitude and *insouciance* of the movements of animals, is the flawless triumph of art." Now a great many men have said this before. But generally it is the introduction to something more artistic than ever,—more conventional and strained. Antony began by saying he was no orator, but none the less did an oration follow. In this book, however, the prophecy is fairly fulfilled in the accomplishment. "What I experience or portray shall go from my composition without a shred of my composition. You shall stand by my side and look in the mirror with me."

So truly accomplished is this promise,—which anywhere else would be a flourish of trumpets,—that this thin quarto deserves its name. That is to say, one reads and enjoys the freshness, simplicity, and reality of what he reads, just as the tired man, lying on the hill-side in summer, enjoys the leaves of grass around him,—enjoys the shadow,— enjoys the flecks of sunshine,—not for what they "suggest to him," but for what they are.[275] . . .

The book is divided into a dozen or more sections, and in each one of these some thread of connection may be traced, now with ease, now with difficulty,—each being a string of verses, which claim to be written without effort and with entire *abandon*. So the book is a collection of observations, speculations, memories, and prophecies, clad in the simplest, truest, and often the most nervous English,—in the midst of which the reader comes upon something as much out of place as a piece of rotten wood would be among leaves of grass in the meadow, if the meadow had no object but to furnish a child's couch. . . .[276]

. . . It is very clear, that with him, as with most other effective writers, a keen, absolute memory, which takes in and holds every detail of the past,—as they say the exaggerated power of the memory does when a man is drowning,—is a gift of his organization as remarkable as his vivid imagination. What he has seen once, he has seen forever. . . .

For the purpose of showing that he is above every conventionalism, Mr. Whitman puts into the book one or two lines which he would not address to a woman, nor to a company of men. There is not anything, perhaps, which modern usage would stamp as more indelicate than are some passages in Homer. There is not a word in it meant to attract readers by its grossness, as there is in half the literature of the last century, which holds its place unchallenged on the tables of our drawing-rooms. For all that, it is a pity that a book where everything else is natural should go out of the way to avoid the suspicion of being prudish.[277]

Pantheism, Libidinousness, and Ridiculous Self-Applause

The Christian Examiner

FROM Anonymous Review of 1855 and 1856 Editions, *The Christian Examiner,* LXI (November 1856), 471–473.

. . . The book might pass for merely hectoring and ludicrous, if it were not something a great deal more offensive. We are bound in conscience to call it impious and obscene. . . . We know only, that, in point of style, the book is an impertinence towards the English language, and in point of sentiment, an affront upon the recognized morality of respectable people. Both its language and thought seem to have just broken out of Bedlam. It sets off upon a sort of distracted philosophy, and openly deifies the bodily organs, senses, and appetites, in terms that admit of no double sense. To its pantheism and libidinousness it adds the most ridiculous swell of self-applause; for the author is "one of the roughs, a Kosmos, disorderly, fleshy, sensual, divine inside and out. This head more than churches or bibles or creeds. . . ." These quotations are made with cautious delicacy. We pick our way as cleanly as we can between other passages which are more detestable.

A friend whispers as we write, that there is nevertheless a vein of benevolence running through all this vagabondism and riot. Yes; there is plenty of that philanthropy, which cares as little for social rights as for the laws of God. . . .[472] Indeed, we should even now hardly be tempted to make the slightest allusion to this crazy outbreak of conceit and vulgarity, if a sister Review had not praised it, and even undertaken to set up a plea in apology for its indecencies. We must be allowed to say, that it is not good to confound the blots upon great compositions with the compositions that are nothing but a blot. . . .

There is one feature connected with the second edition of this foul work . . . [which] involves the grossest violation of literary comity and courtesy that ever passed under our notice. Mr. Emerson had written a letter of greeting to the author on the perusal of the first edition, the warmth and eulogium of which amaze us. But "Walt Whitman" has taken the most emphatic sentence of praise from this letter, and had it stamped in gold, signed "R. W. Emerson," upon the back of his *second* edition. . . . Thus the honored name of Emerson . . . is made to indorse a work that teems with abominations.[473]

Mr. Whitman's Declamations

Henry James

FROM "Mr. Walt Whitman," *The Nation,* I (November 16, 1865), 625–626. A review of *Drum-Taps.*

. . . if Mr. Whitman does not write verse, he does not write ordinary prose. The reader has seen that liberty is "libertad." In like manner comrade is "camerado;" Americans are "Americanos;" a pavement is a "trottoir," and Mr. Whitman himself is a "chansonnier." If there is one thing that Mr. Whitman is not, it is this, for Béranger was a *chansonnier.* To appreciate the force of our conjunction, the reader should compare his military lyrics with Mr. Whitman's declamations. Our author's novelty, however, is not in his words, but in the form of his writing. As we have said, it begins for all the world like verse and turns out to be arrant prose. It is more like Mr. Tupper's proverbs than anything we have met. But what if, in form, it *is* prose? it may be asked. Very good poetry has come out of prose before this. To this we would reply that it must first have gone into it. Prose, in order to be good poetry, must first be good prose. As a general principle, we know of no circumstance more likely to impugn a writer's earnestness than the adoption of an anomalous style. He must have something very original to say if none of the old vehicles will carry his thoughts. Of course he *may* be surprisingly original. Still, presumption is against him. If on examination the matter of his discourse proves very valuable, it justifies, or at any rate excuses, his literary innovations.

But if, on the other hand, it is of a common quality, with nothing new about it but its manners, the public will judge the writer harshly. The most that can be said of Mr. Whitman's vaticinations is, that, cast in a fluent and familiar manner, the average substance of them might escape unchallenged. But we have seen that Mr. Whitman prides himself especially on the substance—the life—of his poetry. It may be rough, it may be grim, it may be clumsy—such we take to be the author's argument—but it is sincere, it is sublime, it appeals to the soul of man, it is the voice of a people. He tells us, in the lines quoted [from "Shut Not Your Doors"], that the words of his book are nothing. To our perception they are everything, and very little at that. A great deal of verse that is nothing but words has, during the war, been sympathetically sighed over and cut out of newspaper corners, because it possessed a certain simple melody. But Mr. Whitman's verse, we are confident, would have failed even of this triumph, for the simple reason that no triumph, however small, is won but through the exercise of art, and that this volume is an offense against art. It is not enough to be grim and rough and careless; common sense is also necessary, for it is by common sense that we are judged. There exists in even the commonest minds, in literary matters, a certain precise instinct of conservatism, which is very shrewd in detecting wanton eccentricities. To this instinct Mr. Whitman's attitude seems monstrous. It is monstrous because it pretends to persuade the soul while it slights the intellect; because it pretends to gratify the feelings while it outrages the taste. The point is that it does this *on theory*, willfully, consciously, arrogantly. It is the little nursery game of "open your mouth and shut your eyes." Our hearts are often touched through a compromise with the artistic sense, but never in direct violation of it. Mr. Whitman sits down at the outset and counts out the intelligence. This were indeed a wise precaution on his part if the intelligence were only submissive! But when she is deliberately insulted, she takes her revenge by simply standing erect and open-eyed. This is assuredly the best she can do. And if she could find a voice she would probably address Mr. Whitman as follows: ". . . We look in vain, however, through your book for a single idea. We find nothing but flashy imitations of ideas. We find a medley of extravagances and commonplaces. We find art, measure, grace, sense sneered at on every page, and nothing positive given us in their stead. To be positive one must have something to say; to be positive requires reason, labor, and art; and art requires, above all things, a suppression of one's self, a subordination of one's self to an idea. . . ."[626]

Whitman's Misconceptions

Sidney Lanier

FROM *The English Novel: A Study in the Development of Personality,* revised edition (New York: Charles Scribner's Sons, 1897). Lectures delivered in 1880–1881.

Returning to our outline of the last lecture: After we had discussed this matter [the misconception that science will destroy literature], we advanced to the second of the great misconceptions of the function of form in art—that which holds that the imaginative effort of the future will be better than that of the present, and that this improvement will come through a progress towards formlessness. After quoting several sentences from Whitman which seemed to contain the substantial argument—to-wit, that the poetry of the future is to be signalized by independence of form, and is, by virtue of this independence, to gain strength, and become a democratic poetry, as contrasted with the supposed weak and aristocratic poetry of the present—I called your attention to a notable circumstance which seems to throw a curious light along this inquiry: that circumstance being that the two English poets who have most exclusively laid claim to represent the people in poetry, to express nothing but the people's heart in the people's words, namely, Wordsworth and Whitman, are precisely the two whose audience has been most exclusively confined to the other[50] extreme of culture. Wordsworth, instead of appealing to Hodge, Nokes, and Stiles, instead of being found in penny editions on the collier's shelves, is most cherished by Mr. Matthew Arnold, the high-priest of culture. And so with Whitman. We may say with safety that no preacher was ever so decisively rejected by his own: continually crying democracy in the market-place, and crying it in forms or no-forms professing to be nothing but products of the democratic spirit; nevertheless the democracy everywhere have turned a deaf ear, and it is only with a few of the most sober and retired thinkers of our time that Whitman has found even a partial acceptance.

And finally by way of showing a reason for this state of things in Whitman's case, the last lecture closed with the assertion that Whitman's poetry, in spite of his belief (which I feel sure is most earnest) that it is democratic, is really aristocratic to the last degree; and instead of belonging, as he claims, to an early and fresh-thoughted stage of a republic, is really poetry which would be impossible except in a highly civilized state of society.[51]

And lastly, the Poetry of the Future holds that all modern poetry, Tennyson particularly, is dainty and over-perfumed, and Whitman speaks of it with that contempt which he everywhere affects for the dandy. But surely—I do not mean this disrespectfully—what age of time ever yielded such a dandy as the founder of this school, Whitman himself? The simpering beau who is the product of the tailor's art is certainly absurd enough; but what difference is there between that and the other dandy-upside-down who from equal motives of affectation throws away coat and vest, dons a slouch hat, opens his shirt so as to expose his breast, and industriously circulates his portrait, thus taken, in his own books. And this dandyism—the dandyism of the roustabout—I find in Whitman's poetry from beginning to end. Everywhere it is conscious of itself, everywhere it is analyzing itself, everywhere it is posing to see if it cannot assume a naïve and striking attitude, every-where it is screwing up its eyes, not into an eyeglass like the conventional dandy, but into an expression supposed to be fearsomely rough and barbaric and frightful to the terror-stricken reader, and it is almost safe to say that one half of Whitman's poetic work has consisted of a detailed description of the song he is going to sing. It is the extreme of sophistication in writing.

But if we must have dandyism in our art, surely the softer sort, which at least leans toward decorum and gentility, is preferable; for that at worst becomes only laughable, while the rude dandyism, when it does acquire[63] a factitious interest by being a blasphemy against real manhood, is simply tiresome.

I have thus dwelt upon these claims of the Whitman school, not so much because of any intrinsic weight they possess, as because they are advanced in such taking and sacred names,—of democracy, of manhood, of freedom, of progress. Upon the most earnest examination, I can find it nothing but wholly undemocratic; not manful, but dandy; not free, because the slave of nature; not progressive, because its whole momentum is derived from the physical-large which ceased to astonish the world ages ago, in comparison with spiritual greatness.

Indeed, this matter has been pushed so far, with the apparent, but wholly unreal sanction of so many influential names, that in speaking to those who may be poets of the future, I cannot close these hasty words upon the Whitman school without a fervent protest, in the name of all art and all artists, against a poetry which has painted a great scrawling picture of the human body and has written under it, *"This is the soul;"* which shouts a profession of religion in every line, but of a religion that, when examined, reveals no tenet, no rubric, save that a man must be natural, must abandon himself to every passion; and which constantly roars its belief in God, but with a camerado air as if it were patting the Deity on the back and bidding Him *Cheer up* and hope for further encouragement.

It seems like a curious sarcasm of time that even the form of Whitman's poetry is not poetry of the future but tends constantly into the rhythm of

"Brimmanna boda abeod eft ongean,"

which is the earliest rhythm of our poetry. The only difference which Whitman makes is in rejecting the alliteration,[64] in changing the line-division, so as to admit longer lines, and the allowance of much liberty in interrupting this general rhythm for a moment. It is remarkable indeed that this old rhythm is still distinctly the prevalent rhythm of English prose. Some years ago Walter Savage Landor remarked that the dactyl was "the bindweed of English prose," and by the dactyl he means simply a word of three syllables with the accent on the first, like Brimmanna. For example:

"I loaf and invite my soul;
I lean and loaf at my ease, observing a spear of summer grass.
I exist as I am—that is enough;
If no other in the world be aware, I sit content;
And if each and all be aware I sit content.
Washes and razors for foofoos, and for me freckles and a bristling beard."

"Walt Whitman am I, a cosmos of mighty Manhattan the sun [*sic*]."[65]

Whitmaniacs and Byronites

Algernon Charles Swinburne

FROM "Whitmania," *Fortnightly Review*, XLVIII (August 1887), 170–176.

. . .

The highest literary quality discoverable in either book [*Childe Harold* or *Drum-Taps*] is rhetoric: and very excellent rhetoric in either case it sometimes is; what it is at other times I see no present necessity to say. But Whitmaniacs and Byronites have yet to learn that if rhetoric were poetry John Bright would be a poet at least equal to John Milton, Demosthenes to Sophocles, and Cicero to Catullus. Poetry may be something more—I certainly am not concerned to deny it—than an art or a science; but not because it is not, strictly speaking, a science or an art. There is a science of verse as surely as there is a science of mathematics: there is an art of expression by metre as certainly as there is an art of representation by painting. To some poets the understanding of this science, the mastery of this art, would seem to come by a natural instinct which needs nothing but practice for its development, its application, and its perfection: others by patient and conscientious study of their own abilities attain a no less unmistakable and a scarcely less admirable success. But the man of genius and the dullard who cannot write good verse are equally out of the running. "Did you ask dulcet rhymes from me?" inquires Mr. Whitman of some extraordinary if not imaginary interlocutor; and proceeds, with some not ineffective energy of expression, to explain that "I lull nobody—and you will never understand me." No, my dear good sir . . . not in the wildest visions of a distempered slumber could I ever have dreamed of doing anything of the kind. Nor do we ask them even from such other and inferior scribes or bards as the humble Homer, the modest Milton, or the obsolete and narrow-minded Shakespeare—poets of sickly feudality, of hidebound classicism, of effete and barbarous incompetence. But metre, rhythm, cadence not merely appreciable but definable and reducible to rule and measurement, though we do not expect from you, we demand from all who claim, we discern in the works of all who have achieved, any place among poets of any class whatsoever. The question whether your work is in any sense poetry has no more to do with dulcet rhymes than with the differential calculus. The question is whether you have any more right to call yourself a poet, or to be called a poet by any man who knows verse from prose, or black from white, or speech from silence, or his right hand from his left, than to call yourself or to be called, on the strength of your published writings, a mathematician, a logician, a painter, a political economist, a sculptor, a dynamiter, an old parliamentary hand, a civil engineer, a dealer in marine stores, an amphimacer, a triptych, a rhomboid, or a rectangular parallelogram.[172] . . .

Bard, Prophet, Seer, Apostle

John Burroughs

FROM "Walt Whitman and His Recent Critics." In *In Re Walt Whitman,* edited by Horace L. Traubel, Richard Maurice Bucke, and Thomas B. Harned (Philadelphia: David McKay, 1893), pp. 93–108.

. . .
Some of the newspapers have seriously discussed the question whether or not he was a poet at all. I quite agree with a writer in the *Nineteenth Century* a few years ago, that we need not be at all zealous to claim this title for him, and with "Uncle Remus" that it is no distinction to call his writings poems. But if we give up the word poet, it must be for a designation that means more, instead of less, as bard, prophet, seer, apostle. "Leaves of Grass" is primarily a gospel and is only secondarily a poem. Its appeal is to the whole man and not merely to one set of faculties, as the aesthetic. It cannot be too often said that the book is not merely a collection of pretty poems, themes elaborated and followed out at long removes from the personality of the poet, but a series of *sorties* into the world of materials, the American world, piercing through the ostensible shows of things to the interior meanings, and illustrating in a free and large way the genesis and growth of a man, his free use of the world about[102] him, appropriating it to himself, seeking his spiritual identity through its various objects and experiences, and giving in many direct and indirect ways the meaning and satisfaction of life. There is much in it that is not poetical in the popular sense, much that is neutral and negative and yet is an integral part of the whole, as in the world we inhabit. If it offends, it is in a wholesome way, like objects in the open air.

Whitman was *un*artistic rather than *in*artistic. His orb of song was modelled after a certain other orb with which we all have at least a limited acquaintance. His long lists and enumerations, page after page of scenes, actions, trades, tools, occupations, have their purpose; they give weight and momentum; they supply negative elements and backgrounds which are just as important in his poetic scheme as the positive and select elements. . . .[103]

The whole drift of his work is to get rid for once of the artificial, and to bring to bear upon the reader's mind real nature, often rude abysmal nature. He cuts under the artificial and conventional in everything, in manners, in morals, in religion, in verse. To have used the highly wrought and elaborate poetic forms would have been at war with his purpose in this respect. He strips the soul bare, the mind bare, the conscience bare, the body bare. He strips from the muse all her customary trappings and finery.[104] . . .

Did Whitman Write Poetry?

John Addington Symonds

FROM *Walt Whitman: A Study* (London: John C. Nimmo, 1893).

Here it serves nothing to inquire whether he [Whitman] was justified in supposing that he had written poetry. It is clear that in a certain and technical sense he did not write poetry, because he did not use metre and rhyme. It is also clear that, except in his Prefaces, Democratic Vistas, Specimen Days, and so forth, he did not attempt to write prose. When he did write prose in "Leaves of Grass" and "Drum Taps," he did so involuntarily, and just as Dante in the "Paradiso," and Milton in the "Paradise Lost," and Lucretius in "De Rerum[147] Natura," unwillingly wrote prose at intervals. Therefore, it may be inferred—and one flings the suggestion with equanimity to cavillers—that what he did write in his masterpiece of literature was neither flesh nor fowl nor good red herring. It is not verse, it is not (except involuntarily) prose.

But is there no poetry outside the region of rhyme and verse? Was Sir Philip Sidney, the first accomplished critic in our language, so far wrong in his contention that "apparelled verse is but an ornament, and no cause to poetry; since there have been many most excellent poets that have never versified, and now swarm many versifiers who need never answer to the name of poets?" Are we all wrong in thinking that, when we read Job, the Psalms, the Prophets, the Song of Solomon, in our English version, we are reading the sublimest, the sweetest, the strongest, the most sensuous poetry that was ever written?

To my mind Whitman did indubitably produce poetry, and poetry of a very high order. According to the theory he had formed before he began to "strike up the songs of the New[148] World," he deliberately rejected rhyme, metre, the set stanza, all the "Ars Poetica" of his predecessors. In art it is exceedingly difficult to break with tradition, to innovate with success. And doctrine, the obedience to a settled theory, is inimical to pure spontaneous singing. From the outset Whitman was hampered by his[149] system, and he was not quite strong enough to create by a single fiat the new perfect form he aimed at. He resolved to rely on rhythm, and on the coinage of phrases which should exactly suit the matter or the emotion to be expressed.

The countless clear and perfect phrases he invented, to match most delicate and evanescent moods of sensibility, to picture exquisite and broad effects of natural beauty, to call up poignant or elusive feelings, attest to his artistic faculty of using language as a vehicle for thought. They are hung, like golden medals of consummate workmanship and incised form, in rich clusters over every poem he produced. And, what he aimed at above all, these phrases are redolent of the very spirit of the emotions they suggest, communicate the breadth and largeness of the natural things they indicate, embody the essence of realities in living words which palpitate and burn for ever.

I do not think it needful to quote examples. Those who demur and doubt may address themselves to an impartial study of his writings. It is enough for me, trained in Greek and Latin[150] classics, in the literatures of Italy and France and Germany and England, who have spent my life in continuous addiction to literature, and who am the devotee of what is powerful and beautiful in style—it is enough for me to pledge my reputation as a critic upon what I have asserted.

I have already admitted that his self-assertion and tumidity are drawbacks to his art. Furthermore it must be confessed that the lists of things, of peoples, of places, he is wont to make, exhaust our powers of attention. We tire of uncouth paragraphs, each clause of which begins with "Oh," or "See," "I see," "I hear," "I swear," or "Shapes arise." We long for humour, which is almost totally absent in his work, to relieve its seriousness and self-complacency. We are jarred by his ungrammatical constructions and crude agglutinations of jaw-breaking substantives. His ill-assimilated French or Spanish phrases—imported in obedience to the system, because America includes so many nations— hurt our ear. We could gladly dispense with *etui, trottoir, habitans, eleve, allons, accouche, mon enfant,* and so forth, in compositions which[151] after all are written in the English mother-tongue. Let us, however, be thankful that he did not think fit to borrow also from the German dictionary! Finally, we could desire more of dramatic power and a juster sense of composition in creating balanced wholes.

But when all this has been conceded, we return to the position, and declare it to be impregnable and unchallenged, that Whitman, working under the conditions of his chosen style, has produced long series of rhythmic utterances, strung together and governed by an inner law of melody, capable of transposition, augmentation, and diminution at the author's will, which have the magnetic charm of nature, the attraction of his own "fluid and attaching" personality.

In his happiest moments these periods are perfect poems, to alter which would be to ruin them. Not a word is then superfluous; not an epithet, but adds to the rhetorical effect; and when the climax is attained, our sense of music, and far more of vitalising imaginative potency, is fully satisfied.

Let those who doubt these words, or do not know Walt Whitman's writings, devote themselves[152] to the careful study of "When Lilacs last in the Door-Yard Bloomed," "Vigil Strange I kept on the Field One Night," "The Singer in the Prison," "Sleep-Chasings," "A Leaf of Faces," "A Word Out of the Sea," and those passages from the poem called "Walt Whitman" [i.e., "Song of Myself"], which begin with the lines "I am he that walks with the tender and growing night," and "You sea! I resign myself to you also."[153]

Extrinsic and Intrinsic Art

John Burroughs

FROM *Whitman: A Study* (Boston and New York: Houghton Mifflin and Co., 1896).

The truth is, Whitman's art, in its lack of extrinsic form and finish, is Oriental rather than Occidental, and is an offense to a taste founded upon the precision and finish of a mechanical age. His verse[114] is like the irregular, slightly rude coin of the Greeks compared with the exact, machine-cut dies of our own day, or like the unfinished look of Japanese pottery beside the less beautiful but more perfect specimens of modern ceramic art.

For present purposes, we may say there are two phases of art,—formal art and creative art. By formal art I mean that which makes a direct appeal to our sense of form,—our sense of the finely carved, the highly wrought, the deftly planned; and by creative art I mean that quickening, fructifying power of the masters, that heat and passion that make the world plastic and submissive to their hands, teeming with new meanings and thrilling with new life.

Formal art is always in the ascendant. Formal anything—formal dress, formal manners, formal religion, formal this and that—always counts for more than the informal, the spontaneous, the original. It is easier, it can be put off and on.

Formal art is nearly always the gift of the minor poet, and often of the major poet also. In such a poet as Swinburne, formal art leads by a great way. The content of his verse,—what is it? In Tennyson as well I should say formal art is in the ascendant. Creative art is his also; Tennyson reaches and moves the spirit, yet his skill is more noteworthy than his power. In Wordsworth, on the other hand, I should say creative art led: the content of his verse is more than its form; his spiritual and religious values are greater than his literary[115] and artistic. The same is true of our own Emerson. Poe, again, is much more as an artist than as a man or a personality.

I hardly need say that in Whitman formal art, the ostensibly artistic, counts for but very little. The intentional artist, the professional poet, is kept entirely in abeyance, or is completely merged and hidden in the man, more so undoubtedly than in any poet this side the old Oriental bards. We call him formless, chaotic, amorphous, etc., because he makes no appeal to our modern highly stimulated sense of art or artificial form. We must discriminate this from our sense of power, our sense of life, our sense of beauty, of the sublime, of the all, which clearly Whitman would reach and move. Whitman certainly has a form of his own; what would a poet, or any writer or worker in the ideal, do without some kind of form? some consistent and adequate vehicle of expression? But Whitman's form is not what is called artistic, because it is not brought within the rules of the prosodical system, and does not appeal to our sense of the consciously shaped and cultivated. It is essentially the prose form heightened and intensified by a deep, strong, lyric and prophetic note.

The bonds and shackles of regular verse-form Whitman threw off. This course seemed to be demanded by the spirit to which he had dedicated himself,—the spirit of absolute unconstraint. The restrictions and hamperings of the scholastic forms did not seem to be consistent with this spirit, which[116] he identified with democracy and the New World. A poet who sets out to let down the bars everywhere, to remove veils and obstructions, to emulate the freedom of the elemental forces, to effuse always the atmosphere of open-air growths and objects, to be as "regardless of observation" as the processes of nature, etc., will not be apt to take kindly to any arbitrary and artificial form of expression. The essentially prose form which Whitman chose is far more in keeping with the spirit and aim of his work than any conventional metrical system could have been. Had he wrought solely as a conscious artist, aiming at the effect of finely chiseled forms, he would doubtless have chosen a different medium. . . .[117]

Whitman was compelled to this negation of extrinsic art by the problem he had set before himself,—first, to arouse, to suggest, rather than to finish or elaborate, less to display any theme or thought than "to bring the reader into the atmosphere of the theme or thought;" secondly, to make his own personality the chief factor in the volume, or present it so that the dominant impression should always[118] be that of the living, breathing man as we meet him and see him and feel him in life, and never as we see him and feel him in books or art,—the man in the form and garb of actual, concrete life, not as poet or artist, but simply as man. This is doubtless the meaning of the vestless and coatless portrait of himself prefixed to the first issue of the "Leaves," . . . This portrait is symbolical of the whole attitude of the poet toward his task. It was a hint that we must take this poet with very little literary tailoring; it was a hint that he belonged to the open air, and came of the people and spoke in their spirit. . . .[119]

Whitman was not a builder. If he had the architectural power which the great poets have shown, he gave little proof of it. It was not required by the task he set before himself. His book is not a temple: it is a wood, a field, a highway; vista, vista, everywhere,—vanishing lights and shades, truths half disclosed, successions of objects, hints, suggestions, brief pictures, groups, voices, contrasts, blendings, and, above all, the tonic quality of the open air. The shorter poems are like bunches of herbs or leaves, or a handful of sprays gathered in a walk; never a thought carefully carved, and appealing to our sense of artistic form.[120]

The main poem of the book, "The Song of Myself," is a series of utterances, ejaculations, apostrophes, enumerations, associations, pictures, parables, incidents, suggestions, with little or no structural or logical connection, but all emanating from a personality whose presence dominates the page, and whose eye is ever upon us. Without this vivid and intimate sense of the man back of all, or a sane and powerful spirit sustaining ours, the piece would be wild and inchoate. . . .[121]

This simple aggregating or cataloguing style as it has been called, and which often occurs in the "Leaves," has been much criticised, but it seems to me in perfect keeping in a work that does not aim at total artistic effects, at finished structural perfection like architecture, but to picture the elements of a man's life and character in outward scenes and objects and to show how all nature tends inward to him and he outward to it. Whitman showers the elements of American life upon his reader until, so to speak, his mind is drenched with them, but never groups them into patterns to tickle his sense of form. It is charged that his method is inartistic, and it is so in a sense, but it is the Whitman art and has its own value in his work. Only the artist instinct could prompt to this succession of one line genre word painting.[126]

But this is not the way of the great artists. No, but it is Whitman's way, and these things have a certain artistic value in his work, a work that professedly aims to typify his country and times,—the value of multitude, processions, mass-movements, and the gathering together of elements and forces from wide areas. . . .[127]

Whitman is poetic in the same way in which he is democratic, in the same way in which he is religious, or American, or modern,—not by word, merely, but by deed; not by the extrinsic, but by the intrinsic; not by art, but by life.

I am never tired of saying that to put great personal qualities in a poem, or other literary work, not formulated or didactically stated, but in tone, manner, attitude, breadth of view, love, charity, good fellowship, etc., is the great triumph for our day. So put, they are a possession to the race forever; they grow and bear fruit perennially, like the grass and the trees. And shall it be said that the poet who does this has no worthy art?

Nearly all modern artificial products, when compared with the ancient, are characterised by greater mechanical finish and precision. Can we say, therefore, they are more artistic? Is a gold coin of the time of Pericles, so rude and simple, less artistic than the elaborate coins of our own day? Is Japanese pottery, the glazing often ragged and uneven, less artistic than the highly finished work of the moderns?

Are we quite sure, after all, that what we call "artistic form" is in any high or fundamental sense artistic? Are the precise, the regular, the measured,[129] the finished, the symmetrical, indispensable to our conception of art? If regular extrinsic form and measure and proportion are necessary elements of the artistic, then geometrical flower-beds, and trees set in rows or trained to some fancy pattern, ought to please the artist. But do they? If we look for the artistic in these things, then Addison is a greater artist than Shakespeare. Dr. Johnson says, "Addison speaks the language of poets, and Shakespeare of men." Which is really the most artistic? The one is the coin from the die, the other the coin from the hand.[130]

6

WHITMAN'S FORM AND TECHNIQUE

Whitman's Antecedents

Bliss Perry

FROM *Walt Whitman: His Life and Work* (Boston and New York: Houghton Mifflin and Co., 1906). Reprinted by permission of and arrangement with Houghton Mifflin Company, the authorized publishers.

. . . The wide pages of the 1855 quarto gave Whitman's long lines a dignity unapproached in any subsequent edition. Yet many of these lines were obviously sentences of prose, which, like the three opening lines [of "Song of Myself"], contained no hint of poetry. There was no use of rhyme or stanza. There was no uniformly recognizable type of metre, although many passages fell into regular metrical beats. Rhythm could indeed be felt, as in all emotional writing whether in prose or verse; but the rhythms of *Leaves of Grass* had been more cunningly modulated and disguised than any one then suspected. To most readers, no doubt, the poetical intention of the work was more apparent than the poetical pattern. The raw material of poetry was flung in with a liberal hand,—emotion, imagination, and many a singing word or phrase. Cadences rich and melancholy, periods full and orotund, made themselves instantly recognized by the attentive reader.[81] But the tunes were chiefly those of passionate speech rather than of verse. Sometimes there were memories and fragments of well-known metrical forms.

"Downhearted doubters, dull and excluded"

is a line of pure Anglo-Saxon four-stressed alliterative verse. Many passages are composed in a sort of ruined blank verse, like that employed by late Elizabethan and Jacobean dramatists; a measure so broken by pauses, by fragmentary lines, by warfare between metrical and logical accent, by sheer willfulness, as to seem of the iambic five-stressed type only through echo and reminiscence. Again, there are single lines of dactylic hexameter:—

"The married and unmarried children ride home to their Thanksgiving dinner."
"I rise ecstatic through all and sweep with the true gravitation."

Sometimes this dactylic beat continues through more than the normal six intervals, as in the second of the following lines:—

> "I laughed content when I heard the voice of my little captain,
> We have not struck, he composedly cried, we have just begun our
>   part of the fighting."

Frequently the ear catches the measure of the six-foot anapest which
Tennyson used so often[82] in his later poetry,—either in its normal
form, as when Whitman writes:—

> "And I know that the hand of God is the elder hand of my own;"
> "And reached till you felt my beard and reached till you held my feet;"

or disguised by substitution, as

> "Dark to come from under the faint red roofs of mouths."

It was evident that, however freely Whitman made use of lines or
paragraphs of sheer prose, the closing cadences of most of the poems
had been constructed with the utmost care. Very characteristic are
these final lines:—

> "Smile, for your lover comes!"
> "It is nearer and further than they."
> "And that was a jet black sunrise."

Yet the rhythmical structure of *Leaves of Grass* is scarcely to be
apprehended through the metrical analysis of single lines. Whitman
composed—and in this respect, at least, he resembled the great masters
of blank verse—with reference to the group, or paragraph of lines, and
not merely to the single unit. If read aloud, page after page, the general
rhythmic type makes itself felt. It is highly individual, and yet it is
clearly related to other well-recognized modes of impassioned literary
expression.[83]

On one side it touches the "prose poetry" of Carlyle and Emerson,
De Quincey and Poe,—writers with whom Whitman was familiar, and
some of whom he had imitated in his earlier productions. Passages from
Sartor Resartus and from Emerson's *Essays* have frequently been re-
arranged typographically, without any verbal alteration whatever, so
as to look and sound like passages from *Leaves of Grass*. It is well
known that Ruskin, for example, brought this rhythm of "prose poetry"
so near to actual metre, that the transposition of a few words, and
the addition or subtraction of a syllable here and there would turn his
prose into verse. . . .[84] . . .

Again, the heightened passages of oratory tend, in proportion to
their impassioned quality, to fall into regular stress. The natural
orators to whom Whitman loved to listen were fond of the heavily
accented periods, which, like the cadences of prose poetry, approximate, without quite reaching,[85] metrical regularity. . . .

Whitman utilized freely the characteristic effects of both "prose
poetry" and oratory, but he varied these effects not only with prose

rhythms, but with the tunes of lyric poetry. He admitted, furthermore, his indebtedness to music as suggesting rhythmical variations. He told Mrs. Fanny Raymond Ritter that more of his poems were actually inspired by music than he himself could remember. He frequently compared his interweaving of lyric with descriptive passages to the alternating aria and recitative of an oratorio. . . .[86]

"*Make this more rhythmical*" is one of the admonitions written in Whitman's notebook during the *Leaves of Grass* period. That sentence is typical of the unending labor with which he wrought at the cadences of his long irregular lines, until they suited his ear. He was making careful notes upon English prosody at the same time, and knew something of what he was rejecting, in his striving after a greater freedom and "naturalness." Whitman's impatience with the real or supposed restraints of formal art coincided, in fact, with the instinct for the "return to nature" which had already been potent for more than a generation. William Blake, for example, in the preface to one of those *Prophetic Books* which he composed in a language that was neither verse nor prose, declared: ". . .[88] I therefore have produced a variety in every line, both of cadences & number of syllables. Every word and every letter is studied and put into its fit place: the terrific numbers are reserved for the terrific parts, the mild & gentle for the mild & gentle parts, and the prosaic for inferior parts: all are necessary to each other. Poetry Fetter'd Fetters the Human Race!"

This was doctrine after Whitman's own heart, and it was more widely accepted in the middle of the nineteenth century, both in England and America, than most present-day readers suspect. Among the New England Transcendentalists strict poetic form was often looked upon as a barrier, rather than an aid to expression. The private journals of Thoreau and Emerson are full of rhapsodic passages, the first drafts for poems, which illustrate a metrical and rhythmical lawlessness that was in the very air, although the classical training of Thoreau and Emerson doubtless made them hesitate to print these fresh, formless transcripts of emotional experience.[89] There were at least two books, widely read during the fifties and on the shelves of many a family that did not own a Shakespeare, which seemed to prove that conventional poetic form was a negligible element in securing an emotional effect. One was Macpherson's *Poems of Ossian,* which Whitman had declaimed by the seashore in his youth, and which he read throughout his life. . . .

A more cogent example of the popular success then attained by a composition lacking rhyme, metre, and indeed rhythm—except such as inheres in its Biblical phraseology—was presented[90] to Whitman in Tupper's *Proverbial Philosophy.* Tiresome as they seem to-day, those jejune pages certainly satisfied the aesthetic requirements of countless readers who felt that they were reading "poetry." Take, for instance, this passage, which illustrates the enumerative method which Whitman loved.

"Where are the nobles of Nineveh, and mitred rulers of Babylon?
Where are the lords of Edom, and the royal pontiffs of Thebais?
The golden Satrap, and the Tetrarch,—the Hun, and the Druid, and the Celt" . . .[91]

A far more striking model of rhythmical prose masking as poetry was also at hand. Samuel Warren, the author of the Blackwood novel *Ten Thousand a Year*, which was immensely popular on both sides of the Atlantic, published in 1851 a "Lyrical Soliloquy" in commemoration of the Crystal Palace exhibition. Its title was *The Lily and the Bee*. It describes a day, a night, and an early morning passed in the Crystal Palace, but its real subject, the author declares, is "Man—a unity." Into its rhythmic structure, which is prevalently iambic, are woven passages from the Bible, Milton, Shakespeare, and Wordsworth. It uses almost every stylistic device now identified with Walt Whitman,—catalogue, ejaculation, apostrophe, epithet, and high astounding term. . . .[92]

His [Whitman's] own essential model, after all is said, was the rhythmical patterns of the English Bible. Here was precisely the natural stylistic variation between the "terrific," the "gentle," and the "inferior" parts, so desired by William Blake. Here were lyric fragments, of consummate beauty, imbedded in narrative or argumentative passages. The parallelism which constituted the peculiar structural device of Hebrew poetry gave the English of the King James version a heightened rhythm without destroying the flexibility and freedom natural to prose. In this strong, rolling music, this intense feeling, these concrete words expressing primal emotions in daring terms of bodily sensation, Whitman found the charter for the book he wished to write.

As a whole, therefore, *Leaves of Grass* belonged to no one accepted type of poetry. It was a hybrid, with something of the hybrid's exotic and disturbing charm. Whitman spoke of it afterwards as "a new and national declamatory expression," and of his three adjectives the last is the most weighty. *Leaves of Grass*—whatever else it may have been—was superb[96] declamation. It was so full of poetry that to deny it the name of "poem" is pedantic; yet "rhapsody" is a more closely descriptive word. To interpret as formal song what was intended for rhapsodical speech is to misread Walt Whitman. Here was no born maker of poetry, like Shelley, transforming his thought and emotions into a new medium and scarcely conscious of the miracle he is achieving; but rather a man burdened with sensations, wrestling with language, and forcing it into accents that are like the beating of his own tumultuous heart. Both Shelley and Whitman "communicate" passion; but in one case we are listening to a pure aria that might conceivably issue from a violin or a skylark, while in the other we are

listening to a declaimer with "tears in his eyes, distraction in 's aspect."
Not to apprehend *Leaves of Grass* as a *man speaking* is to miss its
purport.[97]

Whitman the Romantic

George L. Raymond

FROM *Art in Theory,* second edition revised (New York and London:
G. P. Putnam's Sons, 1909).

The classic tendency being that which prompts the artist to
imitate forms and subjects of the past, the romantic has come to mean
just the opposite,—namely, that which allows the form to be determined solely by the exigencies of expression and the expression solely
by the exigencies of the period. In fact, it is hardly right to say that
this latter tendency has *come* to mean this,—it has always meant this.
The mediaeval pictures were poorly drawn. Their forms, as forms, were
exceedingly defective. Yet they were fully successful in expressing exactly the religious ideas of the time. Similar conditions underlay also,
as first developed, mediaeval music, poetry, and sculpture.

This being so, it is evident that romanticism, if manifested to the
total exclusion of classicism cannot lead to the best results. The same
fact is still more evident when we consider that the forms and themes
of all art of the highest character, whenever and wherever it appears,
are developed upon lines of previously developed excellence; and that
to model after others, even in a slight degree, is to manifest something
of the classic tendency.[25]

Our American representative of the exclusively romantic tendency is Whitman. Most of his productions are entirely devoid of
either metre, tune, or verse, nor do they treat of subjects in themselves
aesthetic, or present them in picturesque phraseology. They are written
at times in rhythm, but so is most prose; and the prose of some, both
in spirit and form, is more poetic than that which his admirers call
his poetry. That he has been a force in literature, no one can deny.
The virility and suggestiveness both of his matter and manner cannot
but affect for good, thoughtful minds able to appreciate their scope
and meaning. But how many distinctive characteristics of poetic form
do his works embody? And if works like these are to become the models
of poetic form,[28] what, in the future, will separate poetry from poetic
prose? If poetry, *per se,* be not destined, one of these days, to become a
lost art, it is because the classic tendency, no trace of which Whitman
manifests, will never be completely overcome.[29]

Whitman's Use of Repetition

Autrey Nell Wiley

FROM "Reiterative Devices in *Leaves of Grass*," *American Literature*, I (May 1929), 161–170. Reprinted by permission of the publisher and the author.

. . .

Epanaphora, or initial repetition, appears in some form in 262 of the 403 poems that make up the latest edition of *Leaves of Grass*. It gives pattern, by my count, to no fewer than four thousand of the upward of 10,500 lines, and I believe it plays a very considerable part in the rhythmical effects of Whitman's poems. A familiar example may be cited from the opening lines of "Out of the Cradle Endlessly Rocking":

> *Out of the* cradle endlessly rocking
> *Out of the* mocking-bird's throat, the musical shuttle,
> *Out of the* Ninth-month midnight.[161] . . .

Noteworthy likewise is the number of words involved in the initial reiterative patterns; for Whitman, though repeating extensively the unit of one word or two or three words, employs also units consisting of four, five, and even eight words. The familiar style of the poets who, like Greene, are charged with having "bodged up" their blank verse with *and's* and *if's* does not appear preeminently in *Leaves of Grass*. On the contrary, Whitman employs most[162] extensively the pronoun *I*, which he repeats at the beginning of thirty-four successive lines in "Salut au Monde!"; the verb *Let*, which introduces thirty-three successive lines in "Respondez!" and the pronoun *You*, which is repeated at the beginning of twenty-seven successive lines in "Salut au Monde!" . . .[163]

But scarcely less striking—and hardly less significant for his art— is Whitman's employment of epanalepsis, or repetition within the line, as in "Out of the Cradle Endlessly Rocking":

> *Loud! loud! loud!*
> *Loud I* call to *you, my love!*
> High and clear *I* shoot my voice over the waves
> Surely *you must know who is here, is here,*
> *You must know who I* am, *my love.*[164]

. . . But epanalepsis with Whitman is not limited to the single line. Still holding to the form of successive repetition in numerous instances, it flows into a second verse, taking, for example, the following pattern:

"Blow! blow! blow!
Blow up sea-winds along Paumanok's shore."
   —"Out of the Cradle Endlessly Rocking"

As a matter of fact, this return in a second line to the final word of an immediately preceding line is an important poetic device in[166] *Leaves of Grass.* It serves frequently and fittingly as a transitional link. Such, for instance, is the use that Whitman makes of this special type of epanalepsis in several parts of "When Lilacs Last in the Dooryard Bloom'd":

I

. . . .
I mourn'd, and yet shall mourn with *ever-returning spring.*
Ever-returning spring, trinity sure to me you bring,
. . . .

IV

. . . .
Sings by himself a *song.*
Song of the bleeding throat,
. . . .

V

. . . .
Night and day journeys a *coffin.*

VI

Coffin that passes through lanes and streets.

Epanalepsis enters, not infrequently, into the texture of an entire poem, having much to do with unity, symmetry, and variety. Sometimes fifty per cent of the words in a passage—lyric passages, especially—are given over to this device. In the following stanzas of forty-nine words, for instance, twenty-seven words are parts of the reiterative pattern:

Shine! shine! shine!
Pour down your warmth, great sun!
While we bask, *we two together,*
Two together!
Winds blow south, *or winds blow* north
Day *come* white, *or* night *come* black,
Home, or rivers and mountains from *home,*
Singing all *time,* minding no *time,*
While we two keep *together.*

An especially striking use of epanalepsis occurs in "When Lilacs Last in the Dooryard Bloom'd." Sustaining a *leitmotif* of sorrow,[167] Whitman repeats at irregular intervals certain thematic words and phrases: *heart-shaped leaves of rich green, death, star, lilacs,* and *him I love. . . .*[168]

Of signal importance to rhetorical emphasis and prosodic form, epanaphora and epanalepsis are primarily the devices of a lyrist. No small part of the lyric quality of the songs and chants that make up *Leaves of Grass* derives from the extensive use of these various reiterative devices. Giving new and remarkable turns to the long-favored repetend-patterns and doubtless evolving some patterns of his own, Whitman discovered an effective sort of lyric emphasis in a lyricism of exceedingly broad circles.[170]

Three Analogies for a Poem

F. O. Matthiessen

FROM *American Renaissance: Art and Expression in the Age of Emerson and Whitman* (New York: Oxford University Press, 1941). Reprinted by permission of the publisher.

Beyond the experiments that Whitman made with words, and the attitude to which these gave utterance, lies the central question of why he devised his peculiar form. The result has been evaluated in innumerable ways: it has been commended for its freedom and blamed for its monotony; it has been viewed as an extension of the possibilities of poetry, and also as no poetry at all, as a muddy encroachment on the domains of prose. It seems most fruitful, therefore, to begin with an account of what Whitman himself believed he was doing, to try to grasp his evolving sense of what he meant by a poem, complicated though that meaning is by his three chief recurrent analogies for his 'songs': with oratory, with Italian music, and with the sea. Any one of these analogies may seem[549] confused enough; together they would appear inevitably and absurdly incompatible. Nevertheless, Whitman persisted in feeling connections between them.[550] . . .

. . . it might seem that any connections between Whitman's poetry and its forensic base constituted its heaviest liability. Yet it remains equally true that his richest feelings were aroused by the sound and action of the voice, in a way that he tried often to describe, especially in his *Primer*. He believed that you could realize the full beauty of a word only on those rare occasions when you heard it pronounced with modulation and timbre, and that such power of speech was the subtlest property of organic well-being, dependent alike on the flexible structure of the throat and chest, and on 'a developed harmonious soul.' The lurking, yet compelling charm of the voice was the ultimate token of personality. It was not something that could be taught, but was bound up inextricably with the growth of experience, and its final ripening could come only after 'the chaste drench of love.' It is no wonder, therefore, that he[554] reached the conclusion that the best poetry 'perhaps waits to be rous'd out yet, or suggested, by the perfect physiological human voice.'

In such a way he arrived again at the bodily and spiritual oneness which he wanted his poems to convey, and which made him declare of his book, 'who touches this touches a man.' He implied a great deal in his repeated use of the word 'vocalism,' in his desire that it should be 'limpid' and 'inspired' in both his speeches and poems. What he meant is developed in a poem with the word itself for title, though it was at one time called 'To Oratists.' Here he declares that 'the divine power to speak words' comes only as a product of the most vigorous assimilation of life, and rounds again to the point:

> All waits for the right voices;
> Where is the practis'd and perfect organ? where is the develop'd soul?
> For I see every word utter'd thence has deeper, sweeter, new sounds, impossible on less terms.

The formulation gropes after the main forces that moved him in his *Leaves*. He wrote in the manuscript draft of the very first lines of 'Song of Myself':

> I am your voice—It was tied in you—In me it begins to talk.
> I celebrate myself to celebrate every man and woman alive;
> I loosen the tongue that was tied in them,
> It begins to talk out of my mouth.

In these lines he experienced his birth as a poet, for the vibration of emotion *in* the voice was his first step towards poetic rhythm. His demand for the direct presence of speaking tones in poetry would put him in accord with the revolt of modern poets against the artificial muffling of such tones by Tennyson and Swinburne. . . .[555]

For his belief that poetry was not something written but uttered, he may well have been indebted to the vogue of Ossian and to the romanticization of the heroic bard as the equivalent of the Biblical prophet. But he observed that the 'Address to the Sun' was misty and windy, 'how full of diffused, only half-meaning words,' and warned himself not to 'fall into the Ossianic, *by any chance*.' The mode to which he conceived his own poems to belong is made unmistakable by the fact that he did not use the word 'write' in connection with them, but described his activity variously as 'singing,' 'warbling,' 'carolling,' 'trilling,' and 'chanting.' Moreover, he told Trowbridge, in the same conversation in 1860 in which he phrased his debt to Emerson: 'But for the opera I could never have[559] written *Leaves of Grass*.' He was fully aware that his rapt identification with this music had been the root cause of his emancipation from what he called the 'ballad-style' of poetry, which seems to have meant to him all poetry encumbered by rhyme and metre. . . .[560]

He was undoubtedly talking big in claiming any strictness for his compositions. Yet in referring to their alternating *recitative* and *aria*, he meant the kind of contrast that is used most effectively in 'Out of the cradle endlessly rocking,' between the narrative sections and the rising song of the bird. It is possible also to see likenesses to music in the varied repetitions of some of his catalogues, or to go farther and note that his method in a poem is to present a main motive, which is repeated, amplified, and recapitulated. Or you can make rough analogies of his climactic effects with operatic 'crescendo,' 'fortissimo,' and 'diminuendo.' Indeed, the quietness of the closing lines of his vision may well be judged an instance of his approximation to the last device. But in general it does not seem profitable to push such analogies any farther than he did when, in blithe ignorance of exact musical technique, he spoke of his

> Easily written loose-finger'd chords—I feel the thrum of your climax
> and close.

He often longed to rival Bettini and to fold

> or seek to fold, within my chants transmuting,
> Freedom's and Love's and Faith's unloos'd cantabile.

He seems to have believed that he could summon directly the music of the storm or that of 'the mystic trumpeter,' but his rejection of all the resources of verbal melody, of the intricacies of rhyme and assonance that enabled Dryden or Tennyson to carry off *tours de force* of musical analogy, often left his lines as flat as

> Tutti! for earth and heaven . . .[561]

Coleridge's principle that the reconciliation of opposites is essential for the creation of any great art lies behind . . . Whitman's desire that the sea should endow him with its 'cosmic elemental passion' just as much as with its delicacy and whispering 'soothe.' Whitman made his special application of this principle fairly explicit in the course of developing, on another occasion, what he meant by . . . the indirect *influence,* the invisible flowing-in of the waves upon his composition: 'Its analogy is *the Ocean*. Its verses are the liquid, billowy waves, ever rising and falling, perhaps sunny and smooth, perhaps wild with storm, always moving, always alike in their nature as rolling waves, but hardly any two exactly alike in size or measure (metre), never having[566] the sense of something finished and fixed, always suggesting something beyond.' He touches there on the widely contrasting aspects of the sea, the calm and the tempest that both correspond to his desire, but he also reveals a marked difference from Coleridge in his conception of how these might be transferred to his verse. For Coleridge, tracing the origin of metre 'to the balance in the mind effected by that spontaneous effort which strives to hold in check the workings of passion,' recognized verse as a product both of emotion *and* its control, a harmony that sprang from the resolution of the antagonism between them. Whitman seemed to sense this tension at the base of art when he spoke of the pressure of 'the whole bubble of the sea-ooze against that unspeakable something in my own soul which makes me know without being able to tell how it is that I know.' But he did not try to make his verse reflect the overcoming of that tension. He evaded the problem by throwing over the discipline of metre altogether in his eagerness 'to let nature speak, without check, with original energy.' The sea did not remain a challenge to him to master his own rhythm. He wanted to absorb its elemental power by identifying himself with it.[567]

Whitman's Tidal Rhythms

Hugh I'Anson Fausset

FROM *Walt Whitman: Poet of Democracy* (New Haven: Yale University Press, 1942). Reprinted by permission of Jonathan Cape Limited.

The pattern, however, of Whitman's verse was generally too large and loose to form a unity. Its intermingled rhythms were those of the Bible, of the natural orator whose speech falls into accentuated periods, of the prose-poetry of such writers as Emerson, Carlyle and Poe, and of the traditional metrical verse which he had unconsciously absorbed. But these rhythmic elements were seldom fused in a music that was at once his own and more than his own. They came nearest to being so in such a passage as that . . . beginning 'I am he that walks with the tender and growing night', in which we feel a tide of feeling flowing out of depths and in its movement finding its inevitable form.

But this deeper tidal rhythm was not easy to sustain. What held his verse together, however loosely, and enabled it to carry, on an unbroken current, cargoes of facts and prose-statements, was a force of measured declamation. His verse had at its most compelling the unity of passionate speech by which a reciter commands the attention of his audience, but not the deeper unity of a poetry in which diverse threads of thought and feeling are harmonized in an intimate marriage of spiritual intuitions and sensuous things. Consequently the elemental emotion it evoked, though exhilarating and continually associated with actual objects and challenging statements, tended in time to dull the reader's response, as the winds and waves of nature do to one standing on a stormy shore. There was no inward complexity to feed the more sensitive human faculties and no centre of rest at the heart of the verse's endless movement.[132]

There was, in fact, no reason why it should stop at any particular point nor would the addition or subtraction of lines have affected any but a few paragraphs. Such, in terms of verse form, was the result of the freedom which Whitman proclaimed in 'Song of the Open Road':

> From this hour I ordain myself loos'd of limits and imaginary lines,
> Going where I list, my own master total and absolute.

His desire to 'divest myself of the holds that would hold me' was well enough, so far as those 'holds' were conventional. But there was a deeper order in the universe and in the constitution of man, which those who abandoned artificial props had the greater need to realize. This order was the true quest of the poet, and pursuing it he was bound to find that art was not just a fluid Nature or a mere succession of objects and sensations.

Because civilized art had tended to lose touch with its roots in Nature, Whitman dismissed all art as artificiality and was thus relieved of much arduous effort both in self-concentration and formal discipline. 'I do not feel it to be necessary to fight for my words', he was to say in later years. 'I use them and let them go and that's an end on't.' Or again, of cultivated writers: 'I have felt they have not let go—have not been willing to let their demon work out its fate . . . have not believed enough in themselves . . . Almost any writer who is willing to be himself will amount to something, to about the same thing, at the roots.'

There was truth in this appeal to writers to 'be natural' and to be themselves. But there was a sense also in which they could only become truly themselves by ceasing to be natural. Whitman's failure to recognize this was reflected in the formless vigour of his own verse, so rich in surface aspects, so empty of inner relations.

'I know perfectly well my own egotism,' he wrote in 'Song of Myself':

> Know my omnivorous lines and must not write any less,
> And would fetch you whoever you are flush with myself.

And untroubled by the exacting need of organizing his material from within and of intricately combining immediate experience and reflection upon it in an expressive act, he was free to be an astonishingly receptive channel to the immense landscape and seething life of a new continent. His mind hardly interposed to select, still less deeply ponder, the host of details, sharply but transitorily perceived, which poured through it.[133]

His vision of the material texture of common life was in consequence often wonderfully graphic, as was his feeling for the elementary forces and fervours which animated it and which he could express, at his best, with a tidal grandeur. For one whose aim it was to impel his readers continually forward into an unlimited vista, the want of formal framework was, indeed, an advantage, while he owed, perhaps, to his very artlessness a power of strong and simple utterance of the basic human emotions which few have equalled.

And if his ego, however cosmic in the largeness of its embrace, lacked much intimate insight, it proclaimed a self-abandonment without stint or limit. The psychologist may, indeed, see, in the very extravagance of such utterance as the following, symptoms of one thwarted in the self-giving he craved. Yet a humanity magnificent in its impulse, however tainted with arrogance, spoke in such lines as:

> O despairer, here is my neck,
> By God, you shall not go down! hang your whole weight upon me.
> I dilate you with tremendous breath, I buoy you up.

And no one, perhaps, has expressed more remarkably the dissolution of the human in the elemental and elementary than Whitman did at the end of 'Song of Myself':

> I depart as air, I shake my white locks at the runaway sun,
> I effuse my flesh in eddies, and drift it in lacy jags.
> I bequeath myself to the dirt to grow from the grass I love,
> If you want me again look for me under your boot-soles.[134]

Whitman's Innovations

David Daiches

FROM "Walt Whitman as Innovator." In *The Young Rebel in American Literature: Seven Lectures,* edited by Carl Bode (London: Heinemann, 1959), pp. 25–48. Reprinted by permission of Frederick A. Praeger Inc. and William Heinemann Ltd.

. . . I think the best approach to this question is in terms of what Mr. [T. S.] Eliot has called "tradition and the individual talent." I think perhaps it can be said that Whitman's primary contribution as an innovator in literature was to offer new solutions to the problems posed by the relation between tradition and the individual talent. It has always been a problem; perhaps—as anyone who has wrestled with trying to write creatively must know—perhaps the greatest of all artistic problems; how the individual can come to terms with the general postulates about art which his culture provides him with; and also in a larger sense how individual experience can come to terms with contemporary religious or philosophical or social tradition. There is inevitably a dichotomy, a gap, between your own aesthetic experience and the lessons you learn from it and what you learn from the pulpit and the platform.

The more traditional English or European way of handling this problem has been a deliberate counterpointing of experience and tradition in all sorts of interesting and very often fruitful ways. If you are brought up in an age which has a strong communal belief, whether[27] religious or philosophical or any other, you breathe it in, as it were, without perhaps examining it too closely. In any case you accept it as representing the truth about experience.[28] . . . That is how Dante operated, and Milton, and the great Greek dramatists— they pitted a personal vision against the traditional mythology of their people. And, as I say, across the gap you get the spark of literature.

Now, when public belief becomes less insistent in its demands, when it becomes less stable and certain (as it did in the nineteenth century), the poet has no longer the two clear poles of traditional formulation and personal experience between which his sensibility must move and which he has to come to terms with simultaneously. He turns instead to the one pole, the self, the introspective self. When Keats reflects, as Milton had reflected, that he could die before writing his best poetry, he does not end by coming to terms with religion. He does not say, God knows what He is doing, "Tomorrow to fresh Woods and Pastures new." He turns instead to sheer elegiac introspection.[29]

. . . In spite of the driving egotism, the self [of Whitman, on the other hand] is somehow transmuted from the beginning, as it is in the first word of the opening inscription, 'One's-self I sing.' Whitman is concerned to build up in his own special way a picture of the relationship of his self, first to other selves, secondly to the external world of nature, and thirdly to other moments in time than the moment which he is experiencing now. There is both a spatial and a temporal relationship developed here. The relationship of the poet to external nature is not one simply of a poet who gets from nature certain scenic assistance, as though nature is the great backdrop for human emotion. . . .[32]

'Song of Myself' is like so many of Whitman's poems, full of those enormous catalogues of Americana, sweeping over the country, describing its cities, sounds, scenes, in various geographical regions and professions and walks of life. These catalogues have a purpose. They are not simply there in order to build up a picture of the size or complexity or diversity of the country. They are not simply saying, as Sidney Lanier said Whitman was simply saying, that because the Mississippi is long America is great. It is not simply what most of us on this side of the Atlantic recognize as the American preoccupation with size as a good thing. It is something much more complex and interesting than that. It is an endeavour to cultivate a kind of awareness of other people so complexly developed that your own stream of consciousness while you are in the act of contemplation takes you outside of[34] yourself and achieves a new kind of relationship between your ineradicable self (which remains the core and centre of all Whitman's poems) and the external world.

It might almost be said that Whitman is the father of that stream-of-consciousness technique which has been so popular in twentieth-century fiction. By cultivating the special kind of sensibility you can learn to depend on that sensibility. But you cannot depend on raw sensibility—or you can only if you are writing another kind of poem; it is another way of doing it. You prepare your sensibility in rather special ways. You strike certain poses, and the pose with Whitman is extremely important. It is not, as Esther Shephard tried to show in her book on Whitman's pose, something purely histrionic, although there are histrionic elements in Whitman's behaviour sometimes. This pose represents a way of chemically treating your consciousness, as it were, so that you can depend on it to register in a more than egotistical way. How can you make your stream of consciousness tell something real about the external world rather than operate only solipsistically referring back always only to yourself? That is the problem Whitman is dealing with. His aim was to make his consciousness into that sort of servant by posing it in a certain way as one poses a camera at a certain angle.[35]

What he is saying there [in the prefaces] is that he is hewing out his own kind of craftsmanship in order to contain his own particular kind of personal feeling. This is a moment of time; this individual confronts this time and it is possible, if he cultivates the proper kind of awareness, if he trains his sensibility, if he poses it in the proper way, to achieve a cosmic vision which relates all time and all space to the individual. Only by being true to one's own self can one ever come to terms with outside reality.[41]

In what respects, then, was Whitman a rebel, what did he rebel against, and how fruitful was his rebellion? It seems to me that his main objective was to come to terms with the nature of identity, the nature of personality; to explore new ways of relating a full relish of personal identity with a full savouring of life existing in the teeming[46] world around him, whether of other people or of nature. What he rebelled against was the implication of the Victorian assumption that the poet must surrender either to elegy or to didacticism, the assumption that these are incompatible alternatives and, further, that directing of sensibility into pre-determined channels was the only way of writing a poem. What he won for the future in this rebellion was a new way of relating loneliness to love, the great perennial problem of modern literature. It was a way that involved a consciousness of the *otherness* of other people, a new kind of dependence on the consciousness closely akin to the stream-of-consciousness method in modern fiction, and a mode of poetical utterance which depended for its structure on a mosaic of ideas and impressions rather than on set forms.

And where does that take us? Precisely to the heart of the one great modern poet who has ignored and undervalued Whitman—Mr. Eliot himself. Whitman's Brooklyn is not unlike Eliot's London. Both poets were similarly aware of the rhythms of modern life. Both used the mosaic of ideas, the special kind of poetic dialectic achieved by patterning fragments of the civilisation you are presenting into a kind of eloquent and symbolic jigsaw. Whitman did that in his own way before Eliot did and it seems to me that no American poet, whether he accepts or rejects Whitman, can fail to have profited. It sometimes seems to me that the tragedy of Whitman is exactly the same as the tragedy of my native Scottish poet, Robert Burns. Both were admired for the wrong reasons and the people who imitated them[47] most directly were the worst poets. The so-called Whitmanians of the twentieth century were those who cultivated a shrill patriotic rhetoric, but that is not the true Whitman idiom. I myself believe that the mosaic of ideas in Eliot, the stream of consciousness in the modern novel, and all those extraordinarily subtle devices through which the modern novelist and poet have tried to explore ways in which an individual sensibility can be modulated into an inclusive consciousness, are in the tradition of Whitman. How to escape the prison of the self and cultivate simultaneously self-consciousness and sympathy, using a sense of self-identity as a means of projecting oneself into the identity of others—that, I think, is Whitman's most valuable legacy to modern literature.[48]

7

WHITMAN'S PROSODY

Whitman's Use of Prose Rhythms

Fred Newton Scott

FROM "A Note on Walt Whitman's Prosody," *Journal of English and Germanic Philology,* VII:2 (1907–8), 134–153. Reprinted by permission of the publisher.

. . .

The rhythm of prose is not as yet very well understood, but it seems, in English at any rate, to be a different thing from metre. Instead of the short, pulsating rhythm characteristic of verse, we find in prose a long, sweeping, swaying, cumulative movement like that of ocean waves. A prose sentence seems to be made up of rushes of sound, rising and falling, hastening and delaying, swelling and dying away, in a complex and evasive sequence.

If the basic element of modern English verse is stress, that of modern English prose is probably pitch. That is to say, prose is in the main a succession of pitch-glides. The unit, or foot, is composed of a rising followed by a falling glide. These units are susceptible of considerable variation, and when artfully combined give the impression of a distinct tune or pattern.

In order to distinguish these types of rhythm I have applied to the rhythm of verse the term *nutation,* to the rhythm of prose the term *motation.*

Employing these convenient terms, we may say that Whitman, in his prosody, turned from the nutative to the motative principle, from the rhythm of beats to the rhythm of pitch-glides. Why he did so I have already indicated in part. It was because the rhythm of prose, being larger and freer than the rhythm of verse, seemed nearer to the uncramped spirit of nature from which he drew his inspiration. But another reason may be found in a peculiarity of Whitman's genius to which, I believe, sufficient attention has not hitherto been given. I mean his quick and delicate susceptibility to certain modes of motion and sequences[144] of sound. One cannot read far in Whitman, either in his poetry or his prose, without being struck by this characteristic.[145] . . .

Whitman's reasons for rejecting the stress-and-quantity principle, which has generally satisfied the ears of other English poets, should now be clear. His delight in large free movements and rushes of sound made him impatient of the short units, the quickly recurring beats, of the nutative rhythm. He wished to embody in his verse the largo of nature, especially the flux and reflux of the waves, the rise and fall of the murmur of the pines, the circling dip of bird-flight, the crescendo and dying fall of the locust-song.

Other poets had done this, to be sure, but mainly by way of making the sound an imitation of the sense. But mere imitation was not enough for Whitman. He did not wish to make a "dead set at poetizing" these sounds and movements; he sought to make them the very foundation of his prosody, the regulative principle of his rhythm.

Moved by this desire he turned from verse to prose. In the pitch-glides and speech-tunes which are the basis of the prosaic pattern, in the swift upward rush and retarded cadence of the prose sentence, he found the principle he sought. He adopted it. But, having adopted it, he found it in its ordinary form inapt to his purpose. Prose, as prose, is the instrument of communication. It suggests and implies the communicative attitude, whereas Whitman's genius, like that of every great poet, was mainly expressive. In the tide of poetic creation, therefore, he instinctively and perforce returned to nutative pattern. But he brought back with him from his incursion into prose new materials for the weaving. With these materials he created for himself a new and peculiar kind of verse, in which the dips and glides and evolutions of the prose rhythm were woven into a pattern of nutation. In this seemingly hybrid form he found a medium adequate to the expression of his peculiar genius.[149]

In general, it may be said that the Whitmanian line, scanned in routine fashion, consists, like the prose sentence, of an advancing and retreating wave. This simple movement is varied almost infinitely (1) by varying the length of the successive waves proportionally, (2) by allowing the speech-rhythm now to coincide with the routine scansion, now to conflict with it, (3) by introducing minor waves or impulses in varying numbers and proportionate lengths, (4) by the artful use of alliteration and refrain.[152] . . .

Verse Without Line-Ends

John Erskine

FROM "A Note on Whitman's Prosody," *Studies in Philology,* XX (July 1923), 336–344. Reprinted by permission of the publisher.

It has long been a conventional thing to say of Whitman's verse that it is metrically unintelligible, a barbaric yawp, as he called it himself. But this phrase of his was not so modest as it sounds, and he knew that his metre contained no novelties; we need but read his lines for their sense, he told us, and the metrical pattern will be disclosed along with the meaning. Advice not unlike this Tennyson gave to his son, commenting on "Paradise Lost"; the opening line of it, he said, with its bold rhythm, would be quite spoiled unless the reader under-stood that the story dealt with man's first disobedience, as distinguished from his later sins,—

Of Man's *first* disobedience, and the fruit, etc.

There is good reason to think that Whitman was as surprised as Milton could have been, when the readers, who had only to follow the sense in order to find the rhythm, reported no difficulty in the sense, yet confessed to have missed the rhythm altogether. We are beginning to see now that he was quite reasonable and his readers were be-fuddled; his rhythms are clear enough, and they are none of them new,—they could all be found in Milton, who was much more of an innovator. We might also see that the reader who cannot make out Whitman's rhythms, from line to line, is very unlikely to follow Milton's. For after all allowances for Whitman's individual genius and for the cadences peculiar to him and to his time, it remains true that his originality is more for the eye than for the ear—his poems seem difficult metrically only because he printed them without the tradi-tional line-end. He thought he was helping us, and at the same time rendering the art of verse more simple and sincere, by printing his verse as he knew we would read it if it were printed the traditional way. He knew we had ceased to observe the line-ends in oral reading, perhaps because we no longer understood them; he therefore made bold to mark no line-ends in the printing, but only phrases, clauses and sentences. But, as it turned out, though we do not observe line-ends in reading, we are lost if they are not there on the page for us to disregard. Whitman has therefore been a difficult metrist for the average reader.[336]

The problem that he tried to solve for us still remains to bother the inexperienced—just how to come at the rhythmic pattern the poet may have wished us to hear, and yet be true to the pre-conceived pat-tern we should like to impose on his verse. The romantic school in England as elsewhere had a tendency to break down the art of versifi-cation, to confuse the reader's ear by forcing the accent, to dull it by weak stretches in the monotony of conversation, with no accent at all. . . . But the breaking down of our skill to follow rhythm was not accompanied, unfortunately, by the abandonment of ancient methods of "scansion," so called; however ignorant of Latin or Greek the aver-age reader is today, and however incompetent to read verse rhythmi-cally, he is liable still to believe that all famous poetry (except Whit-man's) was composed by manipulating the unwilling language into a pattern that does not fit it; if you ask him to scan a line, he will try to force it back once more into the awkward mold; if, however, you ask him to read the line, he will deliver it as free from all pattern, as much like prose as possible. If you ask him, that is, to scan the opening line of *Paradise Lost,* he will announce it as

Of Mán's first dísobédience, ánd the frúit
Of thát forbídden trée . . .

for he will remember that "Paradise Lost" is in blank verse, and he has been told that a blank-verse line has ten syllables, with accents on the five even syllables. . . . But if you ask the same modern reader to *read* the line, as distinguished from scanning it, he will begin "Paradise Lost" somewhat in this fashion—[337]

Of man's first disobedience,
And the fruit of that forbidden tree,
Whose mortal taste brought death into the world and all our woe,
With loss of Eden,
Till one greater Man restore us and regain the blissful seat,
Sing, Heavenly Muse.

That is somewhat the way that Whitman would have printed the lines; but so printed, the average reader would find them metrically incomprehensible.

The difference between our conventional printing and our conventional reading of verse, is that on the page we mark a regular line-end, but with the voice we never or rarely mark it. Yet the art of verse is for the ear, not for the eye, and so long as we had an ear for such things, we followed the design of the rhythm by the pauses, slight or considerable, at the end of each line. To the ear, it is the pause at the end, not the capital at the beginning, which gives form to verse. In English poetry especially, the line-end is essential to any real distinction between the rhythms of prose and of verse, for only the line-end is invariable, or even approximately so . . . The effect of this pause [at the end of the line] in our classical poets, is to set up a normal time-beat, against which the wide variety in the lines can be measured and appreciated; it is the one fixed mark in what otherwise would be a riot of variation, and to forget or misunderstand its use is to miss entirely the secret of English verse.

We began to miss this secret at the end of the eighteenth century, in the reaction against the rimed couplet. The new poets of the day had had enough of strongly marked line-ends, and they turned most often, by way of protest, to the writing of blank verse. But having a protest in mind, and wishing to avoid as far as possible the effect of regularity which had become wooden to their ears, they cultivated a blank verse not at all like that of Shakespeare or Milton, not a sounding line, but rather a conversational stretch that ran over easily and imperceptibly from verse to verse. . . .[338]

It is important to realize how ignorant we are of English verse-music, and to prove to ourselves by experiment what havoc even educated people make of poetry, when they read it aloud, if we are to give

Whitman credit for his shrewd innovation in prosody. Since we no longer understood the line-end and almost always omitted it, he wrote verse without line-ends. With respect to line-ends, his verse was to be fool-proof. To give up the subtle art of the end-pause was to give up a characteristic charm of English verse, and many poets have hesitated to imitate Whitman's method, but it is only fair to remember that not he, but the general public, gave up the line-ends first; he merely composed as people in this country read. And if you take from Shakespeare or Milton the essential pauses at the close of the lines, their verse is pale beside the best of Whitman's, which has its rhythm only from the accent of the words.[343] . . .

Units of Sense and End-Stopped Lines

E. C. Ross

"Whitman's Verse." Reprinted from *Modern Language Notes,* XLV (June 1930), 363–364, by permission of The Johns Hopkins Press, Baltimore, Maryland.

Whitman's verse—with the exception that it is not metered—is farther removed from prose than is traditional verse itself, for the reason that traditional verse is, like prose, composed in sentences, whereas Whitman's verse is composed in lines. Structurally, traditional verse is but metered prose. It is written in sentences,[363] abounds in run-on lines, and, except metrically, the line itself is not a unit. This is just as true of the practice of Pope and his school as it is of any other English verse. The first sixteen-line stanza of *An Essay on Man* is a series of sentences which runs on from line to line and couplet to couplet. Between all traditional verse and prose there is no structural distinction except that of meter.

But Whitman's verse differs from both prose and traditional verse, and in the same way: it is composed in lines. not in sentences.

> Something startles me where I thought I was safest,
> I withdraw from the still woods I loved,
> I will not go now on the pastures to walk,
> I will not strip the clothes from my body to meet my lover the sea,
> I will not touch my flesh to the earth as to other flesh to renew me.

A run-on line is rare in Whitman—so rare that it may be considered a "slip." The law of his structure is that *the unit of sense is the measure of the line.* The lines, in sense, are end-stopped. Whitman employed everywhere a system of punctuation to indicate his structure. Look down any page of *Leaves of Grass,* and you will find almost every line ending in a comma; you will find a period at the end of a group of lines or a whole poem. Syntactically, there may be many sentences in the group or the whole poem; there may be two or three sentences in one line. But Whitman was composing by lines, not by sentences, and he punctuated accordingly.

Nor is *Leaves of Grass* "prose poetry," which, as in the case of Ruskin, for example, is, like ordinary prose, written in sentences, not in lines.

Musically, the accumulative effect of a number of Whitman lines is that of the chant. Whitman often refers to *Leaves of Grass* as "these chants." And one might go on to cite his comparison of his rhythm with the rolling of the sea ("Had I the Choice"), or with the undulation of the mountain range ("Spirit that Form'd This Scene"). One might guess that *Leaves of Grass,* in its structure, was an answer to Whitman's desire for a loose form befitting what he felt to be the experimental spirit of the New World. But what has already been pointed out is the thing of importance.[364]

Organic Rhythms and Hovering Accents

Sculley Bradley

FROM "The Fundamental Metrical Principle in Whitman's Poetry," *American Literature,* X (January 1939), 437–459. Reprinted by permission of the publisher and the author.

. . .

That the organic theory of composition had influenced Whitman[1] profoundly is shown by a study of the rhythm of his individual lines. Perhaps even more strikingly it is demonstrated by an analysis of the longer sections of composition which he substituted for more conventional and traditional stanzas. Although he nowhere speaks of his artistic devices as being "organic," he continuously refers to them as being based upon nature itself. It seems clear that the critical principle, originating in the rise of romanticism in Germany, had somehow reached Whitman. It is unlikely that he had derived it directly from such German critics as Herder, Schelling, or Goethe, although his notes refer to the reading of the works of Goethe and Friedrich Schlegel. However, the organic theory had such a wide currency in romanticism that the quest for an immediate source is not perhaps necessary. To seek no further, Whitman must have become

---

[1] Since this article was written, Mr. Fred W. Lorch has published an article, "Thoreau and the Organic Principle in Poetry," *PMLA,* LIII, 286–302 (March, 1938), in which is given an interesting account of the manner in which identical influences operated in the case of Thoreau.

well aware of this critical attitude in the work of Emerson, Carlyle, and Coleridge, with which he was familiar.

To achieve this impalpable subtlety of form, this rhythmic shape of nature, required endless rewriting and revision, both in manuscript and between successive editions. Every close student of Whitman's manuscripts and of the variorum readings has perceived the poet's increasing sensitiveness to a rhythmical principle. That this principle was rooted in the very nature of English speech, and had been employed in English poetry, especially in popular poetry, continuously since the Old English period, is the fact that seems to have escaped critical attention.

It has been pointed out that so much emphasis has been laid upon the classical ancestry of our English prosody that criticism has frequently lost sight of the earlier and very strong Germanic and Old English ancestry. The classical system employed a rhythm based on the inherent quality, long or short, contained in the syllables of words. But the English language largely lacked from the beginning, and subsequently lost entirely, the fixed quantities which rendered the classical system rational. Old English poetry did not, and could not, regulate itself by counting syllables. Quantity was [441] felt as the duration of time elapsing between stresses, and this elapsed time was a relatively fixed interval throughout the entire extent of any composition. Between stresses the number of unstressed syllables was variable. Such a verse as the following, in which the number of syllables between principal stresses varies from one to four, is not unusual:

Ic þǽt hogode þa ic on hólm gèstáh[2]

What is not generally recognized is that the prosodic principles represented by that line have survived throughout the history of our poetry. The amount of freedom in respect to syllabic regularity in the poetry of various periods of English poetry bears direct relationship to the strength or weakness of classicism at the time. From the beginning of the romantic movement onward, freedom in respect to syllabic regularity has increased, partly as a result of the influence of the popular ballad, in which the Old English tendency persisted strongly.[3] Walt Whitman's verse merely marked an extreme instance of the general evolution. Unfortunately for the reception of *Leaves of Grass,* most critics and prosodists have been of the classical school. Even so clear an exposition as that of T. S. Omond[4] of the freedom in English meter resulting from the compromise between the Old English and the classical prosody, has been lost sight of by recent writers.

---

2 *Beowulf,* l. 632.

3 An interesting analysis of this influence of ballad meters on modern technique of verse is made in George R. Stewart, Jr., *Modern Metrical Technique as Illustrated by Ballad Meter (1700–1900)* (New York, 1922).

4 *A Study of Metre* (London, repub. 1920).

In connection with this entire question it is interesting to observe that Whitman obviously intended his lines to be read aloud; that he wrote for the ear and not for the eye. This, of course, should be true of all poetry. Yet one observes in English poetry through the ages that the more "popular" it is, or the more closely connected with an oral tradition, the more prevalent is the tendency to discard the counting of syllables and to regulate rhythm by the interval of elapsed time between stresses—what Mr. Omond conveniently calls the "period." The first evidence of Whitman's determination to appeal to the ear rather than to the eye, lies in his discarding the verse or line whose length was arbitrarily fixed by predetermined metrical[442] pattern and writing in the unit of the logical clause or sentence. He realized, as Mr. Erskine pointed out, that English readers in oral reading had in large measure ceased to observe line-ends or terminal caesurae in verse unless they represented logical pauses. In his desire to be as natural as possible, therefore, Whitman usually constructed his lines as logical units. It is obvious, however, that the rhythm of such lines is clearly self-conscious, and that, both in respect to rhythm and to length, these verses generally conform to the organic principle as expressed by Coleridge—"such as the life is, such is the form."[443] . . .

In his feeling for naturalness of rhythm Whitman also developed another principle already inherent from early times in English poetry and speech. It becomes apparent to the attentive reader of Whitman, especially when reading aloud, that in a great many cases the stress does not fall sharply on a single vowel, but is distributed along the word, or a pair of words, or even a short phrase. This is the familiar phenomenon of the hovering accent . . . Mr. Fred N. Scott called attention to this characteristic in Whitman years ago, but he erroneously supposed that what he calls the "pitch-glide" of prose was the only source for such a practice, when as a matter of fact the phenomenon is inherent in the nature of our English speech, whether prose or verse.

It is difficult to read *Leaves of Grass* without the employment of the hovering accent; it is interesting to note how a sense of naturalness and colloquial ease immediately results when this phenomenon[444] of our speech is allowed to function. A typical example is found in the four-stress couplet:[5]

> Which of the young men does she like the best?
> Ah the homeliest of them is beautiful to her.

If one reads that second line without the "glide," and with strong vocalic accent on the words "them" and "her" the quality and emotional sense are changed, and the line, indeed, becomes jocose instead of pathetic.[445] . . .

It is a fact, of course, that the reading of Whitman's lines, or of any meter not based on syllable-counting, requires a greater degree of

---

5 "Song of Myself," Sec. II, ll. 6–7, Inclusive ed., p. 32.

participation on the part of the reader than does the reading of syllabic verse. That fact did not trouble the poet—on the contrary, such participation by the reader was precisely what he wished to achieve. Once the conception is established of the rhythm as a succession of equal time-intervals marked *either* by vocalic stress or by hovering accent, the reading becomes a natural and simple process. For example, De Selincourt, whose work has much to recommend it, failed[6] to grasp the basic rhythmical principle. He scans the following pair of lines[7] as of six and four stresses. Actually, they constitute a pair in seven stresses, a favorite length with Whitman; and each line is divided by a caesura into two sections of three and four stresses respectively:

A child said what is the grass? fetching it to me with full hands;
How could I answer the child? I do not know what it is any more than he.

The passage above when scanned by periods reveals a highly developed meter. Each line of a couplet of seven-stress verse is broken by medial caesura at precisely the same point, after the third stress. The rhythmic equivalence between the two lines is striking, and it is not caused by either logical recurrence or the iteration of identical phrases. This purely rhythmic patterning is quite as characteristic of Whitman's writing as the logical balance. . . .[446]

[Remainder of the article applies principles to longer units, including "Tears," "A Noiseless Patient Spider," etc.]

Whitman's Metrical Preferences

Arthur E. Briggs

FROM *Walt Whitman: Thinker and Artist* (New York: Philosophical Library, 1952). Reprinted by permission of the publisher.

In the first place, Whitman's fondness for trochaic movement distinguishes his poetry from the prevalent iambic movement of the English Bible, English poetry and English speech. In this respect English differs from classic Latin, French and Anglo-Saxon verse, in which the trochee predominated. More than 90 per cent of modern English poetry is iambic. This has come about through organic changes in our language. Our typical phrase, which begins with an article, preposition, or conjunction, merging into the word that follows it, gives the rising inflection of the iambic movement. Another influence has been the drop-

---

[6] *Op. cit.*, see, e.g., p. 71. [See Bibliography *s.v.* De Selincourt—Ed.]
[7] "Song of Myself," Sec. 6, Inclusive ed., p. 28.

ping of suffixes and grammatical endings that characterize other[318] European languages. Other grammatical peculiarities are the placing of the weaker adjective before the emphatic noun and the weaker auxiliary before the stronger verb, which tend to iambic stress.

Whitman is unusual therefore in his preference for trochaic and dactyllic rhythm. Why did he thus depart from customary usage? Canby conjectures that it may have been his obstinate desire for novelty, or (and I think this is much more likely) it was because trochaic verse is more emphatic, more in the oratorical style that Whitman fancied. Other advantages may also have weighed with him, for the trochee is a more sprightly and rapid rhythm than the iambic.

Another characteristic of Whitman's verse is a longer line than customary in the poetry that preceded him. . . . A longer line makes the trochee less distinctive unless it is emphasized by phrasing. Whitman was adept in phrasing, not as regular as supposed by Canby, for the patterns are many. Not so often a line of seven stresses balanced about a shifting caesura as to make one think of that as Whitman's style; as often some other number of stresses; and very often three major pauses in the line. And most frequently of all the racing recitative is an impressive feature of Whitman's rhythm.[319]

Whitman's Isosyntactic Patterning

Andrew Schiller

FROM "An Approach to Whitman's Metrics," *Emerson Society Quarterly,* No. 22 (I Quarter 1961), 23–25. Reprinted by permission of the publisher and the author.

. . . The most obvious mark of difference between Whitman's poetry and that to which his new reader is probably accustomed is the seeming looseness and irregularity. He is baffled by the absence of marching feet in regular rows, and is apt therefore to accept Walt's description of himself as a barbaric yawper—or even to dismiss him as no real poet at all.

The first step is to redefine and broaden our conception of metrics. The essence of the matter is *formalization of language.* The poet expresses his ideas in patterned language, in the same way that the composer patterns sounds, or the painter patterns shapes and colors. The patterns, or abstract forms, are in themselves satisfying, and when disassociated from the meaning-bearing portion of the artistic construct, represent the most primitive, non-philosophical stratum of the work, the non-sense level. Thus, a poem may have a certain appeal to a child, who gets little or no semantical sense from it, but who is moved by the pure formal sound of it. . . .

. . . Patterns are created by repetition and variation of linguistic features. Iambic pentameter lines repeat a ten-syllable unit; hence are isosyllabic. If they bear the same number of stresses they are also isoaccentual. (These are Harold Whitehall's terms.) But verses may be, for instance, isoaccentual without being isosyllabic. They may be isochronic—patterned in segments that require the same or related lengths of time to utter; or isosyntactic—patterned in segments that are syntactically parallel; or isomorphemic—a parallelism based upon the recurrence of morphemes; or isophonemic—rhyme, assonance, consonance, alliteration and the like are examples. Less probably in English, verse may be quantitative, as in Greek, or isotonic, as in Chinese.[23]

Such are the types of pattern formations, and a given poem may use any or all of them. Our students tend to think only of the first two, unfortunately for their appreciation of Whitman. He is almost never isosyllabic, and seldom (in the traditional sense of foot-counting) isoaccentual. The students, therefore, need to be shown how to look for, to them, strange rhythmic units in a Whitman poem.

For demonstration purposes here, I have chosen, chiefly for its brevity, "I Sit and Look Out."

I Sit and Look Out

I sit and look out upon all the sorrows of the world, and upon all
    oppression and shame,
I hear secret convulsive sobs from young men at anguish with them-
    selves, remorseful after deeds done,
I see in low life the mother misused by her children, dying, neglected,
    gaunt, desperate,
I see the wife misused by her husband, I see the treacherous seducer
    of young women,
I mark the ranklings of jealousy and unrequited love attempted to be
    hid, I see these sights on the earth,
I see the working of battle, pestilence, tyranny, I see martyrs and
    prisoners,
I observe a famine at sea, I observe the sailors casting lots who shall be
    kill'd to preserve the lives of the rest,
I observe the slights and degradations cast by arrogant persons upon
    laborers, the poor, and upon negroes, and the like;
All these—all the meanness and agony without end I sitting look out
    upon,
See, hear, and am silent.

Looking at the poem grossly, we note first that it is composed of ten lines, of which the first eight form one unit, the last two another. The contrast between the two unequal sections, as in a Shakespearian sonnet, is both formal and philosophical. The first part is a catalogue in parallel construction, the thesis; the second part, in different though related form, is the antithesis.

Turning to the first section, the most obvious patterning occurs at the beginning of each verse: I sit . . . , I hear . . . , I see . . . , etc. This is isosyntactic patterning. Putting it more abstractly, we can say that each verse commences with the structure NV. Looking more closely, we see that each line (we are still talking about the first eight only) develops a bit differently, but within a uniform formula. The NV is followed by a syntactical expansion group of some kind, ending in a terminal juncture, this followed in turn by another syntactical group, which also ends in a terminal juncture. Thus, each verse breaks into half-lines, set off by junctures. We may formulate it in this manner:

| NV | Group | # | Group | # |

My symbols are to be construed thus:

A—Adjective
Av—Adverb
N—Noun
NG—Noun Group: a noun expanded by markers, modifiers, phrases, or clauses.
P—Phrase
SG—Sentence Group
V—Verb
VG—Verb Group: a verb expanded by auxiliaries, modifiers, phrases, or clauses.
#—Precisely, falling juncture, but here used to indicate any terminal.

The frame remains rigid, but the variations within it are free. It is in the two Groups that the changes are rung, both syntactically and rhythmically. One way to demonstrate this is to schematize the first eight lines:

	NV	Group	#	Group	#
1	I sit	VG		AvP	
2	I hear	NG		AP	
3	I see	NG		AAAA	
4	I see	NG		SG	
5	I mark	NG		SG	
6	I see	NG		SG	
7	I observe	NG		SG	
8	I observe	NG ————————→			

The last two lines are summary and antithetical. Whitman preserves the large framework of two half-lines separated by terminal junctures. Thus, line 9 can be "scanned" syntactically:

N	NG	#	N	VG	#
All these—	all ...		I ...	look ...	

and line 10

V	V	#	VG	#
See,	hear		and am silent.	

Note that the patterning in the final two lines criss-crosses that of the preceding eight. That is, the first halves of lines 9 and 10 allude to the second halves of lines 1 to 8, and the second halves of lines 9 and 10 parallel the NV strings of lines 1 to 8. Moreover, the "All... all..." of line 9 binds with the "...all...all..." of the first line. This circular criss-crossing device reminds one of the Old English "ring-verse" formula.[24] . . .

What we have unfolded here is, as I carefully qualified earlier, but one aspect of Whitman's metrics, the isosyntactic. The language of poetry, like all language, must be analyzed in layers. Below this layer of syntax is the prosodic—the recurrence of stress patterns, for example, or, more properly, the interaction of stress, pitch and juncture in intonation contours. Also, I suspect that Whitman's prosody is largely isochronic. Each contour within a given pattern takes the same length of time to utter, or else the variants may be simple multiples of the basic contour length. This may be illustrated in the opening lines of "I Sit and Look Out."

> I sit and look out   #
> upon all the sorrows of the world,   #
> and upon all oppression and shame,   #
>
> I hear secret convulsive sobs   #
> from young men at anguish with themselves,   #
> remorseful after deeds done,   #

Each line breaks into three intonational contours, interjunctural spans bearing a single primary stress, and each contour occupies the same length of time. . . .[25]

8

WHITMAN'S STYLE AND LANGUAGE

Decadent Eccentricity

Barrett Wendell

FROM *A Literary History of America* (New York: Charles Scribner's Sons, 1900).

Here [section 6 of "Song of Myself"] is perhaps his best-known phrase, "The beautiful uncut hair of graves." Here are other good phrases, like "the faint red roofs of mouths." Here, too, is undoubtedly tender feeling. Here, into the bargain, is such rubbish as "I guess it is the handkerchief of the Lord,"—who incidentally uses perfumery,— and such jargon as "Kanuck, Tuckahoe, Congressman, Cuff." In an inextricable hodge-podge you find at once beautiful phrases and silly gabble, tender imagination and insolent commonplace,—pretty much everything, in short, but humour. In America this literary anarchy, this complete confusion of values, is especially eccentric; for America has generally displayed instinctive common-sense, and common-sense implies some notion of what things are worth. . . .[471]

[After quoting the final section of "Crossing Brooklyn Ferry":] The eight preceding stanzas are very like this,—confused, inarticulate, and surging in a mad kind of rhythm which sounds as if hexameters were trying to bubble through sewage. For all these faults, Whitman has here accomplished a wonder. Despite his eccentric insolence both of phrase and of temper you feel that in a region where another eye would have seen only unspeakable vileness, he has found impulses which prove it, like every other region on earth, a fragment of the divine eternities. The glories and beauties of the universe are really perceptible everywhere; and into what seemed utterly sordid Whitman has breathed ennobling imaginative fervour. . . .[473]

. . . The development of human expression seems like the growth of a tree. The same vital force which sends the trunk heavenward, puts forth branches, and from these in turn sends forth twigs and leaves; but the further they stray from the root, the weaker they prove. The trunk lives, and the greater branches; year by year, the lesser twigs and leaves wither. Now, eccentricity of manner, however unavoidable, is apt to indicate that art has strayed dangerously far from its vital origin. Oddity is no part of solid artistic development; however beautiful or impressive, it is rather an excrescent outgrowth, bound to prove abortive, and at the same time to sap life from a parent stock which without it might grow more loftily and strongly. Walt Whitman's style is of this excrescent, abortive kind. Like

Carlyle's or Browning's, it is something which nobody else can imitate with impunity; and so, like theirs, it is a style which in the history of literature suggests a familiar phase of[476] decline. That it was inevitable you will feel if you compare "Ethiopia Saluting the Colours" or "My Captain" with the unchecked perversities of Whitman's verse in general. The "Song of Myself," or "Crossing Brooklyn Ferry," which we may take as generally representative of his work, are so recklessly misshapen that you cannot tell whether their author was able to write with amenity. When you find him, however, as in those lesser pieces, attempting technical form, you at once feel that his eccentricity is a misfortune, for which he is no more to blame than a lame man for limping, or a deaf and dumb for expressing emotion by inarticulate cries. The alternative would have been silence; and Whitman was enough of a man to make one glad that he never dreamed of it.

In this decadent eccentricity of Whitman's style there is again something foreign to the spirit of this country. American men of letters have generally had deep artistic conscience. This trait has resulted, for one thing, in making the short story, an essentially organic form of composition, as characteristic of American literature as the straggling, inorganic three-volume novel is of English. . . .[477]

Whitman's Neologisms

Louise Pound

FROM "Walt Whitman's Neologisms," *American Mercury*, IV (February 1925), 199–201. Reprinted by permission of the publisher.

. . .

Walt Whitman took many liberties with the English tongue when he wished to reach certain effects. Along with his polyglot borrowings, such as *allons* and *ma femme* from the French, *cantabile* and *romanza* from the Italian, *libertad* and *Americano* from the Spanish, *rhythmus* from the Latin and *eidolons* from the Greek, he liked vernacular coinages or manipulations, or archaic revivals. When taken from their contexts these locutions often seem forced or absurd. But they are always clear, and, in their connection, read by those who are used to Whitman's verbal divagations, they seem appropriate and effective. They sound as he wished them to sound and they convey the meanings that he wished.

He was especially fond of launching agent-nouns: he had people constantly in mind. His poetry is thronged with human figures, types and classes and personifications. He had a special partiality for feminine abstract conceptions in -*ess*, some of which had book currency, some not. These he introduced characteristically in apostrophe:

Dispensatress, that by a word givest a thousand miles, a million farms,
 and missest nothing,
Thou *all-acceptress*—thou hospitable, (thou only art hospitable as God
 is hospitable).
—The Return of the Heroes

Approach strong *deliveress,*
When it is so, when thou hast taken them I joyously sing the dead.
—When Lilacs Last in the Dooryard Bloomed

Then courage, European revolter, *revoltress!*
For till all ceases neither must you cease.
—To a Foiled European Revolutionaire

. . .

These feminine formations (some, like *tailoress, protectress,* are
by no means peculiar to Whitman) may not seem very striking when
we think of our present-day ventures . . . ; but they were unusual for
the language of poetry when he wrote. . . .[199]

Whitman's coinages of abstract nouns show the suffixes *-ad, -ism,
-ion, -cy, -ness, -ship.* His *presidentiad* is more effective than the *presi-
dentship* of others. *Savantism* is the title of a poem. He refers to
scientism and to *partialisms,* but so have others. *Compaction,* which he
likes, is obsolete or rare. His neologisms among abstract nouns are as
many and as varied as his agent-nouns and personal nouns . . .[200]

Whitman writes *Grecia* to balance *Roma.* From the Latin he
coins *lumine* from *lumen,* a word which he used twice, and from the
French, with a Latin prefix, he makes *super-delicatesse.* His *formule*
and *apostroph* are either truncations of *formula* and *apostrophe,* or are
from the French. . . . *Pave,* a shortening of *pavement,* was perhaps a
current colloquialism in his day:

The blab of the *pave,* tires of carts,
Sluff of boot-soles, talk of the promenaders
—Song of Myself, 8

The name Canada, Whitman respells picturesquely with *k* . . .

This exhibit of coinages and manipulations or revivals is not,
perhaps, very formidable. Compared with the ventures of contemporary
journalists, they may seem few in number and conservative, and the
same is true of Whitman's slang expressions and colloquialisms. Nevertheless, for a serious poet, the array of his verbal novelties, when set
over against those of his contemporaries, looms large. The trend was
to be in his direction in the matter of informality and individuality in
language, as it also was to be for so many of his doctrines. He is our
contemporary in his democratic ideals, his international yearnings, his
desire to confront the world as a whole, his wish for a larger, freer life
for women, his advocacy of out-of-doors, his interest in eugenics, and
his outspokenness in sex matters. In vocabulary, too, except for his
peculiar reliance upon foreign loan-words, he better illustrates the
taste of the Twentieth Century than that of the Nineteenth.[201]

Evolution of Whitman's Diction

Rebecca Coy

FROM "A Study of Whitman's Diction," University of Texas *Studies in English,* XVI (1936), 115–124. Reprinted by permission of the publisher.

. . .

To the common stock of words serving alike the needs of literature and of colloquial speech, Whitman made additions from several sources. The most significant and far-reaching (strangely enough for a poet who made a creed of Americanism) are borrowings from foreign languages. . . .[116]

Colloquial American speech, as might be expected, supplied Whitman with many expressions. With regard to his colloquialisms, there is little to be said except that they are characteristic of his early period and not of his later. The chronological list showing the frequency of their introduction is sufficient evidence of their decline after 1860 or 1865. As a rule, they are short, forceful expressions which convey a shade of meaning and a freshness and vitality which Whitman could not find in their politer equivalents. They are indicative of his vigorous beginning.[117]

Like his colloquialisms, Whitman's Americanisms before 1865 are striking and numerous and are few and unimportant afterwards. . . .[118]

Whitman's use of technical and commercial terms undergoes the same decline at the same time as his use of colloquialisms and Americanisms.

In spite of theory, *Leaves of Grass* is studded with pedantic and archaic words. Several learned words which the poet uses are of Latin origin. The pseudo-science of phrenology supplied him with various terms. Still other terms are scientific in connotation. *Excrementitious,* which Whitman twice used, is a particularly striking example of his indiscriminate use of words.

Whitman's use of archaisms illuminates his development as a poet. Even at the beginning, when he was the avowed foe of the archaic, the poet employed such definitely poetic and archaic expressions as *anon, betimes, list* (for listen), *bussing, busses, ope, atwixt, erewhile, nay, ye, nigh, betwixt, lo, 'tis, 'twas.* . . . [After 1865] Such Elizabethan expressions as *jocund, obeisant, o'er, 'mid, methinks, beseems, vouchsafe, emprises, eterne, e'en, i'the* (without even the excuse of metrical necessity) thenceforward characterize his work. *Haply* occurs in almost every poem after 1870. . . .[121]

As important as the increase in archaisms after 1865 is their abrupt change in kind. Prior to 1865, the archaic terms used by Whit man were, for the most part, short, forceful words expressing a shade of meaning without a modern equivalent: *swags, busses, wrig, diminute,* etc. But with the magnificent threnody for President Lincoln, Whitman became deliberately conventional. Thenceforward his archaisms reflect a new spirit, a nostalgia for the past as definite as the tender passage on feudalism in "The Mystic Trumpeter" or the incongruous dryads and hamadryads of the California redwood. The poet of the modern had made his peace with the past.[123]

. . . [Whitman's innovations] are surprisingly few in number and relatively unimportant in view of the theories expressed by Whitman in the *Primer* at the outset of his career. Aside from the liberal introduction of technical and commercial terms, Whitman made no radical changes in conventional poetic diction. *Leaves of Grass* is not the rich depository of colloquial language and Americanisms which might reasonably have been expected. Even more significant is the alteration and evolution in Whitman's diction after 1865. At his best, unhampered by a theory, Whitman wrote poetry with a formal beauty of diction comparable only to the greatest in English poetry. At his worst, he produced, not the great representative American speech of which he dreamed, but only a Whitmanesque dialect which will remain forever personal and inimitable.[124]

Whitman's Verbal Strategies

Richard Chase

FROM *Walt Whitman Reconsidered* by Richard Chase (New York: William Sloane Associates, Inc., 1955), copyright © 1955 by Richard Chase. Reprinted by permission of William Sloane Associates.

Whitman was, of course, nothing like the modern poets in point of conscious technical sophistication. His practice was sometimes highly sophisticated, but his theory was either fragmentary and hesitating or nonexistent. One poetic device which did interest him and which he reflected on at length (doubtless with the encouragement of Emerson's essays on Nature and the Poet) was the use of words "indirectly"—that is, as "hieroglyphics," "symbols," or implied myths. Whitman conceived of language as he conceived of the universe. It was a flow—"that huge English flow," as he called it in the open letter to Emerson which he appended to the 1856 edition of *Leaves of Grass.* Words are "magical" or "spiritual" when they first emerge, as "identities," from the flow. All words, as[90] he had learned from Emerson, were originally poetic metaphors. And it is the business of the bard to speak words from which the sensuous poetic and "spiritual" quality has not been lost or to revivify words from which it has. This "real first-class poet," said Whitman, reviewing his own book in 1855, has hit upon a new scheme which is more "subtle" than the presentation of "acts and events" by Homer or of "characters" by Shakespeare. "Every sentence and every passage" of this poet "tells of an interior not always seen, and exudes an impalpable something which sticks to him that reads, and pervades and provokes him to tread the half-invisible road where the poet, like an apparition, is striding fearlessly before." This transcendentalist or prophetic illusion is to be created by using words still redolent of the essence of that universal flow of unconscious thought from which all words emerge. Words, poetic thoughts, thus originate as miraculously as do the leaves of grass. Indeed, the objects of nature, particularly phallic objects, are called, in "Spontaneous Me" (1856), "real poems." Like all natural things, "all words are spiritual..." he wrote in *An American Primer*. And like natural things they have a history, an evolution. "Whence are they? along how many thousand and tens of thousands of years have they come? those eluding, fluid, beautiful, fleshless, realities, Mother, Father, Water, Earth, Me, This, Soul, Tongue, House, Fire."

In Whitman's view of language (which is clear, it must be admitted, only in its general outlines), colloquial words best unite the "natural" and the "spiritual." Therefore the poet will use words in such a way as to give them the freshness, raciness, and mythic significance of colloquial speech. Such seems to be Whitman's argument in his "Slang in America," an essay of especial interest in relation to "Song of Myself." Slang he understands to be "the lawless germinal element below all words and sentences, and behind all poetry," which[91] provides "a certain perennial rankness and protestantism in speech." What he heard among the common people he took to be the genesis of poetry: "the wit—the rich flashes of humor and genius." The poet will use language as the earliest people did when colloquial words —the "living and buried speech," as he says in "Song of Myself"—were incipient myths, when they "gave the start to, and perfected, the whole immense tangle of the old mythologies." Characteristically Whitman thought of these incipient myths as having a comic element.

Thus in his ideas about words, as in his poetic practice, Whitman is paradoxically extremely civilized and extremely primitive. Both semanticist and bard, he is a kind of primitive I. A. Richards and a sophisticated Orpheus. As a poet who wishes to create a mythic poetry he is confronted with the dilemma (the democratic dilemma, Tocqueville would say) of a sensibility which quickens to mythic feeling only at opposite ends of the spectrum, either in spontaneous, inchoate, "germinal" experience or in abstractions such as Mother, Father, Equality, Love or Democracy. What he lacks, as compared with Homer, for example, or Dante or Milton, is a mediating body of mythic narrative and metaphor. All such mediating metaphors struck Whitman as "feudal" and therefore improper in democratic poetry. It was what he took to be the positive advantage of this attitude that led him to describe his poems as more "subtle" than Homer with his poetry of "acts and events" and Shakespeare with his poetry of "characters."

Having given up so much—so much more, indeed, than his democratic situation forced him to give up—Whitman is reduced to two principal stratagems of mediation—his use of words in a mythic-semantic manner, as if he were Adam naming the animals, and his one grand narrative and metaphorical image of the self with its dialectic powers and its eternal vitality and significance. Not, of course, that these stratagems[92] are his whole stock in trade; rather, he sets them triumphantly in opposition to the traditional techniques which remain in his poetry and which he always found necessary but which, nevertheless, he could never succeed with when he used them alone. When Whitman writes badly it is either because he is trying to get along without his own stratagems (as in "O Captain, my Captain") or because he is misusing them. Anyone who asks sheer words to do so much cannot help debasing the currency and sometimes producing mere lifeless lists of names. As Matthiessen pointed out, he also runs the risk of writing nonsense—for instance, such a line as

> O for you whoever you are your correlative body! O it, more than all else, you delighting,

where his word-adducing transcends all recognizable grammar and metaphor and becomes a sort of abortive verbal algebra. And the self cannot mediate between the concrete and the abstract when, as but too frequently happens, it is absorbed into the abstract. But in "Song of Myself" these errors are mostly avoided, and it is in this poem that Whitman's peculiar poetic devices work best.[93]

Some Lines from Whitman

Randall Jarrell

REPRINTED FROM *Poetry and the Age* by Randall Jarrell (pp. 112–132), by permission of Alfred A. Knopf, Inc. Copyright 1953 by Randall Jarrell.

. . .

To show Whitman for what he is one does not need to praise or explain or argue, one needs simply to quote. He himself said, "I and mine do not convince by arguments, similes, rhymes,/ We convince by our presence." Even a few of his phrases are enough to show us that Whitman was no sweeping rhetorician, but a poet of the greatest and oddest delicacy and originality and sensitivity, so far as words are concerned. This is, after all, the poet who said, "Blind loving wrestling touch, sheath'd hooded sharp-tooth'd touch"; who said, "Smartly attired, countenance smiling, form upright, death under the breast-bones, hell under the skull-bones"; who said, "Agonies are one of my changes of garments"; who saw grass as the "flag of my disposition," saw "the sharp-peak'd farmhouse, with its scallop'd scum and slender shoots from the gutters," heard a plane's "wild ascending lisp," and saw and heard how at the amputation "what is removed drops horribly in a pail." This is the poet for whom the sea was "howler and scooper of storms," reaching out to us with "crooked inviting fingers"; who went "leaping chasms with a pike-pointed staff, clinging to topples of brittle and blue"; who, a runaway slave, saw how "my gore dribs, thinn'd with the ooze of my skin"; who went "lithographing Kronos ... buying drafts of Osiris"; who stared out at the "little plentiful mannikins[114] skipping around in collars and tail'd coat,/ I am aware who they are, (they are positively not worms or fleas)." For he is, at his best, beautifully witty: he says gravely, "I find I incorporate gneiss, coals, long-threaded moss, fruits, grain, esculent roots,/ And am stucco'd with quadrupeds and birds all over"; and of these quadrupeds and birds "not one is respectable or unhappy over the whole earth." He calls advice: "Unscrew the locks from the doors! Unscrew the doors from their jambs!" He publishes the results of research: "Having pried through the strata, analyz'd to a hair, counsel'd with doctors and calculated close,/ I find no sweeter fat than sticks to my own bones." Everybody remembers how he told the Muse to "cross out please those immensely over-paid accounts,/ That matter of Troy and Achilles' wrath, and Aeneas', Odysseus' wanderings," but his account of the arrival of the "illustrious emigré" here in the New World is even better: "Bluff'd not a bit by drainpipe, gasometer, artificial fertilizers,/ Smiling and pleas'd with palpable intent to stay,/ She's here, install'd amid the kitchenware." Or he sees, like another Breughel, "the mechanic's wife with the babe at her nipple interceding for every person born,/ Three scythes at harvest whizzing in a row from three lusty angels with shirts bagg'd out at their waists,/ The snag-toothed hostler with red hair redeeming sins past and to come"—the passage has enough wit not only (in Johnson's phrase) to keep it sweet, but enough to make it believable. He says:

> *I project my hat, sit shame-faced, and beg.*
> *Enough! Enough! Enough!*
> *Somehow I have been stunn'd. Stand back!* [115]
> *Give me a little time beyond my cuff'd head, slumbers, dreams, gaping,*
> *I discover myself on the verge of a usual mistake.*

There is in such changes of tone as these the essence of wit. And Whitman is even more far-fetched than he is witty; he can say about Doubters, in the most improbable and explosive of juxtapositions: "I know every one of you, I know the sea of torment, doubt, despair and unbelief,/ How the flukes splash! How they contort rapid as lightning, with splashes and spouts of blood!" . . .[116] Not many poets have written better, in queerer and more convincing and more individual language, about the world's *gliding wonders:* the phrase seems particularly right for Whitman. He speaks of "those circling rivers the breath," of the "savage old mother incessantly crying,/ To the boy's soul's questions sullenly timing, some drown'd secret hissing"—ends a poem, once, "We have voided all but freedom and our own joy." How can one quote enough? If the reader thinks that all this is like Thomas Wolfe he *is* Thomas Wolfe; nothing else could explain it. Poetry like this is as far as possible from the work of any ordinary rhetorician, whose phrases cascade over us like suds of the oldest and most-advertised detergent.

The interesting thing about Whitman's worst language (for, just as few poets have ever written better, few poets have ever written worse) is how unusually absurd, how really ingeniously bad, such language is. I will quote none of the most famous examples; but even a line like *O culpable! I acknowledge. I exposé!* is not anything that you and I could do—only a man with the most extraordinary feel for language, or none whatsoever, could have cooked up Whitman's worst messes. For instance: what other man in all the history of this planet would have said, "I am a habitan of Vienna"? (One has an immediate vision of him as a sort of French-Canadian halfbreed to whom the Viennese are offering, with trepidation, through the bars of a zoological garden, little mounds of whipped cream.) And *enclaircise*—why, it's as bad as *explicate!* We are right to resent his having made up his own horrors, instead of sticking to the ones[117] that we ourselves employ. But when Whitman says, "I dote on myself, there is that lot of me and all so luscious," we should realize that we are not the only ones who are amused. And the queerly bad and merely queer and queerly good will often change into one another without warning: "Hefts of the moving world, at innocent gambols silently rising, freshly exuding,/ Scooting obliquely high and low"—not good, but *queer!*—suddenly becomes, "Something I cannot see puts up libidinous prongs,/ Seas of bright juice suffuse heaven," and it is sunrise.

But it is not in individual lines and phrases, but in passages of some length, that Whitman is at his best. . . .[118]

Whitman says once that the "look of the bay mare shames silliness out of me." This is true—sometimes it is true; but more often the silliness and affection and cant and exaggeration are there shamelessly, the Old Adam that was in Whitman from the beginning and the awful new one that he created to keep it company. But as he says, "I know perfectly well my own egotism,/ Know my omnivorous lines and must not write any less." He says over and over that there are in him good and bad, wise and foolish, anything at all and its antonym, and he is telling[125] the truth; there is in him almost everything in the world, so that one responds to him, willingly or unwillingly, almost as one does to the world, that world which makes the hairs of one's flesh stand up, which seems both evil beyond any rejection and wonderful beyond any acceptance. We cannot help seeing that there is something absurd about any judgment we make of its whole—for there is no "point of view" at which we can stand to make the judgment, and the moral categories that mean most to us seem no more to apply to its whole than our spatial or temporal or causal categories seem to apply to its beginning or its end. (But we need no arguments to make our judgments seem absurd—we feel their absurdity without argument.) In some like sense Whitman is a world, a waste with, here and there, systems blazing at random out of the darkness. Only an innocent and rigidly methodical mind will reject it for this disorganization, particularly since there are in it, here and there, little systems as beautifully and astonishingly organized as the rings and satellites of Saturn:

> I understand the large hearts of heroes,
> The courage of present times and all times,
> How the skipper saw the crowded and rudderless wreck of the steamship, and Death chasing it up and down the storm,
> How he knuckled tight and gave not back an inch, and was faithful of days and faithful of nights,
> And chalked in large letters on a board, Be of good cheer, we will not desert you;
> How he follow'd with them and tack'd with them three days and would not give it up,[126]
> How he saved the drifting company at last,
> How the lank loose-gown'd women looked when boated from the side of their prepared graves,
> How the silent old-faced infants and the lifted sick, and the sharp-lipp'd unshaved men;
> All this I swallow, it tastes good, I like it well, it becomes mine,
> I am the man, I suffered, I was there.

In the last lines of this quotation Whitman has reached—as great writers always reach—a point at which criticism seems not only unnecessary but absurd: these lines are so good that even admiration feels like insolence, and one is ashamed of anything that one can find to say about them. How anyone can dismiss or accept patronizingly the man who wrote them, I do not understand.

The enormous and apparent advantages of form, of omission and selection, of the highest degree of organization, are accompanied by important disadvantages—and there are far greater works than *Leaves of Grass* to make us realize this. But if we compare Whitman with that very beautiful poet Alfred Tennyson, the most skillful of all Whitman's contemporaries, we are at once aware of how limiting Tennyson's forms have been, of how much Tennyson has had to leave out, even in those discursive poems where he is trying to put everything in. Whitman's poems *represent* his world and himself much more satisfactorily than Tennyson's do his. In the past a few poets have both formed and represented, each in the highest degree; but in modern times what controlling, organizing, selecting poet has created a world with as much in it as Whitman's, a world that so[127] plainly *is* the world? Of all modern poets he has, quantitatively speaking, "the most comprehensive soul"—and, qualitatively, a most comprehensive and comprehending one, with charities and concessions and qualifications that are rare in any time.[128] . . .

Whitman and the Vernacular Tradition

Leo Marx

FROM "The Vernacular Tradition in American Literature." In *Studies in American Culture: Dominant Ideas and Images,* edited by Joseph J. Kwiat and Mary C. Turpie (Minneapolis: University of Minnesota Press, 1960), pp. 109–122. Copyright 1960 by the University of Minnesota. Reprinted by permission of the publisher and the author.

. . .

There is no need to insist that Whitman's language literally was the spoken language of his time. Indeed, we can be sure that it was not. What matters is that at his best he succeeds in creating the illusion that a certain kind of man is speaking. In his case the illusion probably stems from the cadence, and the absence of traditional meter and rhyme, rather than from the diction. In any event, his poetry is nearer to the spoken language of Americans than our poetry had ever got before. I do not mean to imply that there is any absolute value in using the spoken language in poetry. That depends upon the particular aims of the writer. But given Whitman's problem, his desire to convey ideas and emotions for which the standard manner of poetry was inappropriate, the vernacular was a source of immense vitality. To see this one only has to compare Whitman [section 10 of "Song of Myself"] with Longfellow ["The Slave in the Dismal Swamp"]:

> In dark fens of the Dismal Swamp
> The Hunted Negro lay;   [Longfellow]

> I heard his motions crackling the twigs of the woodpile,
> Through the swung half-door of the kitchen I saw him limpsy
>   and weak.   [Whitman]

What is most striking here is the extraordinary sense of immediacy that the vernacular mode conveys. We see Longfellow's subject through a murk of tired images: "like a wild beast in his lair"; to Whitman he is a man with "sweated body and bruis'd feet." Everyone knows that the more specific image is likely to be the more evocative. But why does one writer seize it while another avoids it? Longfellow says of the slave,[112] "great scars deformed his face." Whitman says, "And remember putting plasters on the galls of his neck and ankles." The fact is that Whitman imagines a completely different relation to the Negro, and it takes us back of language to something more fundamental, to the kind of persona Whitman felt impelled to employ. He is a man "hankering, gross, mystical, nude." He is aggressively ungenteel, and he thinks about the slave in a very different way than Longfellow does.

> In all people I see myself, none more and not one a barleycorn less,
> And the good or bad I say of myself I say of them.

Given this sort of hero, Whitman can introduce details once thought to lie outside the bounds of respectable poetry. Among other things, the vernacular made possible a long step forward in the candor of modern writing, as in Whitman's daring treatment of physical love.

There is another kind of immediacy that results from the use of the vernacular narrator. That is the way meaning comes to us here by what Whitman called "indirection" rather than by use of personification, abstraction, or, for that matter, direct statement. Longfellow finds it necessary to tell us of the slave, "on him alone the curse of Cain/ Fell ... " Whitman avoids comment. He describes the relations between his mythic hero and the slave, and then at the end he casually mentions the gun in the corner. The image *is* the meaning; it is a perfect expression of the democratic hero's relaxed but militant egalitarianism. Right here, incidentally, Whitman anticipates that mode of ironic understatement that was to become a dominant accent of twentieth-century American poetry.

But it must not be thought that a mere technical device enables Whitman to convey so much in so little. If he does not need to proclaim the solidarity between the two men, it is because he can describe it so vividly. That is, the style has been called forth as a fitting expression of something else, an ideal human situation, indeed a kind of model society. The slave and the hero exemplify the egalitarian community of Whitman's imagination. It is a society that stands in relation to the actual society as the vernacular language to the stock elevated language of poetry. All of Whitman's poetry exalts this conception. It is the same sort of community, as a matter of fact, that Mark Twain later sets up aboard a Mississippi raft. Here is the core of the American vernacular. It is not simply a style, but a style with a politics in view. The style is a vehicle for the affirmation of an egalitarian faith so radical that we can scarcely credit it[113] today. It sweeps aside received notions of class and status—and literature. In Whitman's mind all of these inherited forms are identified with Europe.

. . . To establish his identity the American is impelled to defy tradition:

> I too am not a bit tamed, I too am untranslatable,
> I sound my barbaric yawp over the roofs of the world.

Now granted that as a view of human experience there are serious limitations to this Whitmanian yawp, it does not seem to me that chauvinism is one of them. Whitman does not celebrate the vernacular hero because he is an American, but the other way around. It is because he is "untranslatable" that the American must be allowed to have his say in his own idiom. He is a new kind of man, and the social conditions which brought him into being may (at least theoretically) be reproduced anywhere. In reality the vernacular character is of an international cast. . . .

Curiously enough, Whitman represents that side of the vernacular tradition which drew its inspiration from Europe in the first place. We know that he was inspired by Emerson, who recognized what American[114] poets needed to do, even if he was not the man to do it. And behind Emerson, of course, we are led directly to England, and the revolution in poetry Wordsworth had announced fifty-five years before *Leaves of Grass* . . . Whitman went much further than Wordsworth, and he did so largely because American conditions imparted a special intensity to Wordsworthian doctrine. Was it a good thing for poets to escape the refinements of civilization, to catch impulses from the vernal wood? Then how lucky to be an American poet! . . .[115]

The vernacular style is a distinctive achievement of American culture. But this is not to say that it has served to convey anything like an adequate view of experience, or that it has yet given America a great literature. Its creativity came from the radical program of freedom it affirmed, but like any such program, it demands an exceptional discipline. The writer who works in the vernacular takes great risks. To see this we have only to recall those excesses of uncontrolled improvisation that mar the work of Whitman and Twain. This literary barbarism follows from the rejection of inherited forms and theories. It is of course a symptom[121] of primitivism, and along with it we get what is perhaps the chief defect of the vernacular mode—its unremitting anti-intellectualism. This seems to me a more valid point of attack than chauvinism. In defying the constraints and oppression identified with the European past, our writers also have tended to ignore the achievements of the trained intellect. This familiar primitivist bias has retained its affinity to the mode in our time. It seems to have followed the style from Walt Whitman to Carl Sandburg, from Mark Twain to Ernest Hemingway.[122] . . .

9

APPROACHES TO "PASSAGE TO INDIA"

A Dream of One World

Egbert S. Oliver

FROM " 'The Seas Are All Cross'd': Whitman on American and World Freedom," *Western Humanities Review*, IX (Autumn 1955), 303–312. Reprinted by permission of the publisher and the author. Reprinted also in *The American Review* (New Delhi), I (1956), 18–29.

. . .

As the arrival of the Japanese embassy in New York in 1860 stirred Whitman to the new vision of the Occident and the Orient being brought together across the Pacific Ocean and gave him glimpses of a harmonious world of democratic nations, so ten years later the concatenation of three dramatic events in the making of that new and more united world stimulated one of his greatest poetic expressions in "Passage to India." The Old World of Europe was united to the East by the Suez Canal; the new American continent was spanned by rail, when the Central Pacific and the Union Pacific met at Promontory, Utah, the last rails being laid in place by pigtailed emigrants from Old Cathay; and the "eloquent gentle wires," the Atlantic cable, was laid. Whitman was as always attracted by the pageantry inherent in such momentous occasions, the historic realization of the "unloos'd dreams," but in this great poem he had small use for contemporary spectacle. He saw the present world as but a growth out of the past and here his vision tried to encompass the unfolding past and project the future. It was a large and magnificent idea sweeping over the centuries and across continents, connecting the myths and fables of old Asia and Africa, the deep diving bibles and wise religions with the great achievements of engineers and light-bringing science.

From the gardens of Asia came Adam and Eve, their descendants moving across the world as mankind surged westward, even to our own day when the drive over the American plains toward the ancient lands[310] was bringing the circle of the world into one whole, thereby fulfilling what now seems to have been God's purpose from the beginning.

> After the seas are all cross'd, (as they seem already cross'd,)
> After the great captains and engineers have accomplished their
>   work, . . .
> Finally shall come the poet worthy that name,
> The true son of God shall come singing his songs.

This "true son of God" shall absolutely fuse Nature and man, until fragmentation shall be replaced by the fused, and the disjointed shall give way to the joined. The gifts and insight and splendor of old occult Brahma and the tender and junior Buddha, China's wisdom and the imaginative wonder of Persia and Arabia—all, all shall find their place when

> All these separations and gaps shall be taken up and hook'd and link'd together,
> The whole earth, this cold, impassive, voiceless earth, shall be completely justified.

This is the hope Whitman had, buoyantly optimistic and mystical, a generation before the Wright brothers and three generations before Willkie flew over the blue yonder into a dream of one world. Whitman's is the mystical, spiritual vision of the poet and not the practical blueprint of the diplomat. Like the saint and the religious prophet he saw how the world had come to the place in history where the westward thrust had carried around the whole globe, with the road between Europe and Asia crossing the western hemisphere. The United States on the highroad of the world furnished that essential and inevitable ingredient, the free individual. This has been God's intent. This is the course of history.

> Lo, soul, seest thou not God's purpose from the first?
> The earth to be spann'd, connected by network,
> The races, neighbors, to marry and be given in marriage,
> The oceans to be cross'd, the distant brought near,
> The lands to be welded together.

It was never a part of Whitman's nature to say, "Better fifty years of Europe than a cycle of Cathay." This mystical American democrat was a spokesman for the new day being born. He felt the American sense of destiny which was impelling it westward over the continent and confronting the Pacific, but more than his fellows he sensed the intangible value involved in the merging of cultures. He understood that there is something that does not like a wall—or an iron curtain, or a bamboo curtain—and tries to shake it down. He feared that the[311] era of worldwide wars might be upon man, and yet he pointed toward the balanced trinity, the free individual, in orderly society, under God, exemplifying freedom, law, and peace.

Man's passage is outward to more than India. The way may be hazardous and beset with dangers and be far from clear, but over the dark seas of tomorrow those shores are calling.

> Passage to you, your shores, ye aged fierce enigmas!
> Passage to you, to mastership of you, ye strangling problems!
> You, strew'd with the wreck of skeletons, that, living, never reached you.

Though there have been wrecks, and may yet be more wrecks, man can only go forward from where the world is, sailing outward. Whitman's final word, in this poem, and also in his word to the world, is to cease the cautious, fearsome fumbling and to sail forward. Hoist anchor! Cut the hawsers! Sail forth! Steer for the deep waters only.

"Are they not all the seas of God?"[312]

The Motion of the Circle

Stanley K. Coffman, Jr.

FROM "Form and Meaning in Whitman's 'Passage to India.' " *PMLA*, LXX (June 1955), 337–349. Reprinted by permission of the publisher and the author.

. . . "Passage to India" . . . shows two things of considerable importance in evaluating Whitman as a poet: that he could work, and with great success, within the traditional concept of form (insofar as imagery is concerned); and that the concept of organic form, as he understood it, is itself more traditional and orthodox than his use of the art-nature analogy would suggest.

. . . Stated broadly, the theme of the poem is that knowledge leads inevitably to faith, and we find this idea developed through stages marked by a series of declamatory phrases, the repeated chant, "Passage to India!" The "passage" refers first to the actual or physical passage made possible by the transcontinental railroad, the transatlantic cable, and the Suez Canal, linking West to East in a communication network that Whitman celebrates as indicative of his age's scientific achievement . . .[338]

. . . The actual passage is transformed into an intellectual one (or understanding) and then into a religious one (or faith) and finally into another "actual" one—the passage of the individual from life to death. Thus in the series of changes which provide the poem's organization, Whitman has caught some of the flowing of nature from lower to higher forms—it will be seen that, in one respect, the last passage is the highest—and has given a foundation for the emotion of joy and the sense of liberation that accompanies the process of natural or organic evolution. . . .

. . . For a study of the poem's imagery, the central passage occurs in Section 8 with the address to God, to the power which is the essence of nature, the life that manifests itself in the flux of shifting forms, of nature and poetry—in other words, the transcendent reality. This nameless entity is presented mainly through images of light and water: God is "Light of the light," and "fountain," affection's "source," "reservoir"—the basic idea being that He is the essence and origin of light and water. This, in fact, is the fundamental point that the passage emphasizes; God is also described[339] in terms that make Him the center of life as the scientist understands it; He is "fibre" (by which Whitman apparently intends a reference to an element in the blood), "Breath," and "pulse." . . .

. . . The impression given by the imagery is not only of the central nature of the single source but of its radiation outward through forms of increasing complexity and widening extent. And if Section 8 is followed to its close, this centrifugal motion is found to return upon itself, as the Younger Brother melts in fondness in the arms of the Elder, death as comradeship fulfilling itself . . .

. . . In Section 8, water is one way of representing the Source of life: God is "fountain,"[340] water rising and descending, but also "reservoir," defining a more or less still condition peculiar to this element at its source. . . .

This imagery is, though, countered by a pattern of images which suggest water in directional motion, as it is not in the quotations just cited. There are the "river Euphrates flowing," the "streams" of the Indus and Ganges and their "affluents"; thoughts move "like waters flowing," and literatures are described by the same term; a historical development is a "rivulet running." (Compare the image of the projectile in Section 1 and the references to the journey.) It is only when water appears in association with the more or less concrete, which channelizes it, that it is given some directional motion; as reservoir or fountain it lacks this, and thus the waters of space and the infinite reveal waves and ripples only, the directionless movement of "trackless" seas. What Whitman means by the contrast is suggested in his reference to the soul as a "thirst" unsatisfied: individuated and given identity by the body, it is thus separated from its source, to which it desires return. Its movement is therefore circular, but involves change, and therefore "direction" in one sense; and direction is evidently dependent upon the metamorphosis by which the spiritual expresses itself in terms that are the opposite of its own nature, and then returns to the source.[341] . . .

Descent characterizes Whitman's presentation of Adam and Eve in Section 5 . . . and it is not surprising to find that Whitman has borrowed the Christian myth because its meaning is closely allied to his own. . . . Without this descent, the divine could not express itself; even the motion of the circle would be impossible, and both spirit and matter would remain meaningless. As a result of it, individual man appears doomed to an inevitable sense of frustration and incompleteness; but this very sense is what leads him to seek an answer, and through the search humanity ultimately moves to completeness, individually or en masse.[342]

. . . The motion of descent is answered by a pattern of *ascending* imagery. . . .[343]

Along with ascent and descent, there is, in the manifestations of spiritual reality, a contrasting pattern of light and darkness. . . .[344]

One intent of the poem, then, is to convey a feeling for the apparently opposing forces or energies whose contradictory nature is inevitable and, in fact, essential to the emergence and evolution of meaning that the poem celebrates. A final group of images reinforces this by making explicit the dialectical union or merging of opposites and the progress that is the result of this. The railroad, cable, and canal, are, of course, variously described as "crossing" the earth, as "Bridging," "Tying": through them the earth is "spann'd, connected by network," the lands "welded together." This makes clear his celebration of technology, for it works out the purposes implicit in the principle of love that all "separations and gaps shall be taken up and hook'd and link'd together," that it shall, through the poet, "absolutely fuse" Nature and man. Thus the imagery of marriage, which symbolizes best for Whitman the whole process of opposites joining to produce better and more vigorous forms of life; the doge of Venice "wedding the Adriatic," the "lands, geographies, dancing before you, holding a festival garland,/As brides and bridegrooms hand in hand"; the "terraqueous globe, given and giving."

. . . The primary effect of the poem as image is of *motion* (and light may be considered a part of this), as should be evident from the discussion of the[345] kinds of imagery Whitman has used, and even from the most casual glance at his use of verbs. The motion is one of contending elements—the stationary and the directed, ascent and descent, light and darkness, constantly opposing one another, with the emphasis gradually or finally coming to rest upon light, ascent, and direction, as the closing lines show. And while the contention is not resolved, it is presented as recurring union of opposites in a marriage that produces new life, new forms; it is possible to say, in fact, that the marriage imagery is chosen because it assumes opposites for its existence. . . . These patterns condition or modify the ever-recurring circles of spirit manifesting itself and returning to its source; they reflect the consequences of the paradox of spirit become matter, and present the paradox as itself vital, contributing to evolution.[346] . . .

The Speechmaker

Richard Chase

FROM *Walt Whitman Reconsidered* by Richard Chase (New York: William Sloane Associates, Inc., 1955), copyright © 1955 by Richard Chase. Reprinted by permission of William Sloane Associates.

If pieces like "Passage to India" (1868), and "Song of the Universal" (1874), together with the large number of related poems, do not appeal to us very much, it is because Whitman has given up poetry and become a speechmaker. This seems clearly illustrated by the following three lines from "Passage to India":

> The Past—the dark unfathom'd retrospect!
> The teeming gulf—the sleepers and the shadows!
> The past—the infinite greatness of the past!

After an excellent (if derivative) first line, and a satisfactory second, the poet is tongue-tied and the orator takes over, declaiming vulgarly from his editorial chair or his public platform.

Toward the end of this poem Whitman exclaims:

> O sun and moon and all you stars! Sirius and Jupiter!
> Passage to you!
>
> Passage, immediate passage! the blood burns in my veins!
> Away O soul! hoist instantly the anchor!
> Cut the hawsers—haul out—shake out every sail!
> Have we not stood here like trees in the ground long enough?
> Have we not grovel'd here long enough, eating and drinking like
>   mere brutes?
> Have we not darken'd and dazed ourselves with books long enough?

The trouble here is that the answer is so insistent: No, not if the alternative is a merely vague spirituality, a hollow optimism, a sententious courting of immortality, a mystic identification[147] with the universe. Melville's comment on Goethe, in a letter to Hawthorne, might well apply as well to Whitman. "In reading some of Goethe's sayings, so worshiped by his votaries, I come across this, *Live in the All.* That is to say, your separate identity is but a wretched one,—good; but get out of yourself, spread and expand yourself, and bring to yourself the tinglings of life that are felt in the flowers and the woods, that are felt in the planets Saturn and Venus, and the Fixed Stars. What nonsense! Here is a fellow with a raging toothache. My dear boy, Goethe says to him, you are sorely afflicted with that tooth; but you must *live in the all,* and then you will be happy! As with all great genius, there is an immense deal of flummery in Goethe."

Whitman's later poetry[1] bespeaks a mind in which productive tensions have been relaxed, conflicts dissipated, particulars generalized, inequities equalized. Whitman has lost his intuition of what in *Democratic Vistas* he cogently described as those "developments either in Nature or human personality in which power (dearest of all to the

---

[1] Certain of Whitman's later poems have valuable qualities which I shall, however, not attempt to single out. I shall content myself with simply naming those poems which in any account of Whitman's work should not go unmentioned. These include "Tears," "A Noiseless, Patient Spider" (1862), "The Base of All Metaphysics," "Song of the Exposition," "Song of the Redwood Tree," "On the Beach, at Night," "Sparkles from the Wheel," "Prayer of Columbus," and "The Dalliance of Eagles."

sense of the artist), transacts itself." The musing, humorous, paradoxically indolent but unpredictably energetic satyr-poet of the early
1850's becomes the large, bland, gray personage with the vague, light
blue eyes and the circumambient beard. Dionysius becomes not Ap-
pollonian but positively Hellenistic—prematurely old, nerveless, sooth-
saying, spiritually universalized. The deft and flexible wit disappears
along with the contraries and disparities which once produced it. The
pathos,[148] once so moving when the poet contemplated the disintegra-
tion of the self or felt the loss which all living things know, is now
generalized out into a vague perception of the universal. The ocean,
which in "Out of the Cradle Endlessly Rocking" is felt as the source
of being and is said to be paradoxically fearful and infinitely delightful,
is, in the later poems, merely a featureless and homogeneous medium
in which the soul seeks its perfect equalization with all things.[149]

The World of Primal Thought

Gay Wilson Allen and Charles T. Davis

FROM "Critical Note." In *Walt Whitman's Poems: Selections with
Critical Aids,* edited by Gay Wilson Allen and Charles T. Davis (New
York: New York University Press, 1955), pp. 242–248. Reprinted by
permission of the publisher and the authors.

. . .

The form of "Passage to India" resembles the "ode" (the pseudo-
Pindaric type, the most free of all accepted English forms). The lines
vary in the number of strong stresses from three to eight generally,
with a tendency to return to the pentameter. The meter is roughly
iambic with much trochaic and anapestic substitution.

The poet's first general problem in "Passage to India" is determining the real significance of the "achievements of the present" (l. 2)
and singing of them properly. These "modern wonders" (l. 4) are the
Suez Canal, the "mighty railroad" (l. 6) in the New World, and the
Atlantic Cable, "eloquent gentle wires" (l. 7). Yet the poet, in celebrating present technology, would not neglect the past—the "dark unfathom'd retrospect" (l. 10) in favor of "strong light works" (l. 3) The
essence of the past is India . . . Passage to India, then, is a path
created anew by modern technology, which supplies a basis for new
and more harmonious social relationships and a new religion ("A
worship new I sing" [l. 36]).

The passive companion of the poet in his song is the soul, which
is able to evaluate and approve of the poet's speculation. The relationship between the "I" and the soul is neither perfunctory nor static,
even at the beginning of the poem. The poet anticipates objections

from the soul when there seems a chance for the past to be misunderstood and ignored ("Yet first to sound, and ever sound, the cry with thee O Soul" [l. 8]), and the soul accepts, after the poet has introduced them, the modern "tableaus" as rightful interests of its own . . .[244]

Passage to India means also a return to the world of "primal thought" (l. 165), the original Eden of man's childhood. It is here that man will recover his innocence and the purity of his intuitions. He will be able to re-establish a primitive and harmonious relationship with Nature, now sympathetic rather than impassive.[245] . . .

"Passage to India," it is true, has an overwhelming program, and Whitman's preoccupation with the idea does at times prevent the poem from being entirely satisfying as an artistic unit. There is strain upon the sensibility when the poet marshals his historical references to prove the existence, throughout man's life in the world, of the restless urge propelling him toward India. But there are many technical devices here that contribute to the unity and intensity of the poem, and make it finally one of his great works.

The figure of Columbus emerges as a compelling one in the poem. He appears first as the Genoese who dreams of India, becomes the failure who achieves ultimate justification long after death, and provides a permanent model for the poet—not for crossing the seas of[246] the earth but for sailing the eternal waters of time, space, and death.

There is a dramatic thread in the structure of the poem, too, though one not as colorful, perhaps, as that in "Song of Myself." It develops in the relationship of the poet and his soul. Soul is the passive partner in the association at first, accepting and approving the poet's explanation of the "passage" on its various levels. Revealing insight into this relationship comes from the appeal of the poet to the soul to see man's accomplishments: "Lo, soul, seest thou not God's purpose from the first?" (l. 31). The soul's function becomes more positive when the poet achieves his deepest understanding of "India," as the land of "primal thought." Here, the poet, anxious to complete his journey, speaks to the soul as an active associate, not one which must be invited or cajoled: "O soul, repressless, I with thee and thou with me" (l. 169). Finally, on the "trackless seas" of God, the poet turns to the soul and, in effect, disappears, and it is the soul that masters the orbs and comes to terms with time, space, and death. The invocation that concludes the poem is, significantly, to the soul:

O my brave soul!
O farther farther sail
O daring joy, but safe! are they not all the seas of God?
O farther, farther, farther sail! (ll. 252–255)

The symbol "India" has a rewarding richness in the poem. It begins by being simply the geographic East, east of Suez and west of the "mighty railroad." It becomes the past of religions, bibles, legends, fables, and the garden from which man commenced his feverish exploration. It terminates by being the rich land that will stay man's restless foot and the area of "primal thought" in which man can recover original innocence and live in harmony with Nature.

"Passage" itself has a rich elaboration. It is the formal procession in the Suez Canal and the railroad journey. It includes all the expeditions in history that strove toward the fabled land, and it extends to man's whole ceaseless exploration since departure from the Garden of Eden. It is the "retrospect brought forward," the Old and New World joined in happy marriage, and finally the voyage of the mind's return to innocence and primitive power.

In the diction water figures contribute much to the unity of the poem. Many of these are obvious—the voyages of the explorers, Columbus,[247] Vasco da Gama; others are less obvious and just as evocative— the earth itself "swimming in space," the "flowing literatures" (l. 134) of the East, the sailing of the poet and the soul upon uncharted seas, and finally the all-absorbing ocean of God, "spiritual fountain—affection's source—thou reservoir" (l. 198).[248]

The Soul's Circumnavigation

James E. Miller, Jr.

FROM "'India' and the Soul's Circumnavigation." Reprinted from *A Critical Guide to Leaves of Grass* by James E. Miller, Jr. (pp. 120–129), by permission of the author and The University of Chicago Press. Copyright 1957 by The University of Chicago.

. . .

The real subject of "Passage to India" is stated explicitly in section 8 of the poem:

> O soul thou pleasest me, I thee,
> Sailing these seas or on the hills, or waking in the night,
> Thoughts, silent thoughts, of Time and Space and Death, like waters
>   flowing,
> Bear me indeed as through the regions infinite.

"Passage to India" is created out of the poet's "silent thoughts" on time and space and death. But the poem is not about these large philosophical problems in some blurred, abstract sense. The structure of the poem reveals a dramatic progression. The nine sections of the poem may be grouped as follows: sections 1–3, space: the earth spanned; sections 4–6, time: the slopes of history; sections 7–9, death: the soul's circumnavigation. "Passage to India" is a dramatization of the poet's voyages through space and time until, at the end, he arrives at his destination outside both. The meditations on space and time lead to mystical insight into death and an affirmation similar to that in "Out of the Cradle Endlessly Rocking" and "When Lilacs Last in the Dooryard Bloom'd."[120]

I. Sections 1–3. Space: The Earth Spanned

Emphasis throughout sections 1 through 3 is placed on space as, paradoxically, the annihilator of time. The achievements of the present which the poet sings are man's contemporary achievements in spanning the globe and bringing the heretofore separated worlds together. . . . The tendency of the entire first section of the poem is, through the exploitation of the modern miracles that have diminished space, to diminish time, to connect closely and inseparably past and present. The section concludes with one of the most vivid of Whitman's metaphors:

> As a projectile form'd, impell'd, passing a certain line, still keeps on,
> So the present, utterly form'd, impell'd by the past.

The impact of this figure demolishes the differences between present and past: time is conceived as movement through space. What is present was once past and will be future: all are the projectile that carries within itself its impulse onward.

Section 2 of "Passage to India" continues the identification of time with space. The past, "the dark unfathom'd retrospect," eulogized in the opening section, turns out to be, in section 2, not a temporal but a geographical reference to Asia and Africa; but the reference is, ultimately, not really geographical but spiritual: the poet uses the past symbolically to mean "the far-darting beams of the spirit, the unloos'd dreams" of Asia and Africa. The refrain, which opens section 2 and, in variations, several subsequent sections and gives the poem its title, "Passage O soul to India," demonstrates the poet's achievement in identifying space with time, in merging the two and making them indistinguishable for the spirit.[121] . . .

Section 3 is devoted in its entirety to this "worship new," to the celebration of the achievements of the present through the depiction of "tableaus twain." But throughout these two elaborate pictures of material accomplishment the poet insists that their ultimate service is for the soul ("Lo soul for thee of tableaus twain"; "yet thine, all thine O soul, the same"). . . .[122]

II. Sections 4–6. Time: The Slopes of History

As the first part of "Passage to India" is devoted to the minimizing of space and uses time or the timelessness of time (the presence of the past) to that end, so the second part of the poem is devoted to the minimizing of time and uses a space now vastly reduced and under man's control to this end. Section 4 of the poem is transitional:

> Struggles of many a captain, tales of many a sailor dead,
> Over my mood stealing and spreading they come,
> Like clouds and cloudlets in the unreach'd sky.

These visions of history now stealing over the poet's mood are, significantly, linked by metaphor to space: events of time are like clouds of the "unreach'd sky." Time is equated with space not only in this figure but also in another that immediately follows:

> Along all history, down the slopes,
> As a rivulet running, sinking now, and now again to the surface rising,
> A ceaseless thought, a varied train—lo, soul, to thee, thy sight, they rise.

The ceaseless events of history are here envisioned as a rivulet running down the slopes of a mountain. Time is conceived in spatial images, and the events of time become visible outside time—to the soul. Time as a barrier is destroyed, once it is penetrated as the poet now spiritually penetrates it: all time is spread out before him as on a landscape. One should note that by implication the rivulet of time running down the slope of history must pour eventually into the sea of spirituality— the world of eidolons. . . .[123]

Sections 5 and 6 constitute the poet's spiritual view of the slopes of history. The first of these sections might be described as a poet's-eye view of history in contrast with the more orthodox historical view of section 6. . . .[124] . . .

III. *Sections 7–9. Death: The Soul's Circumnavigation*

After the triumph over space in Part I and the mastery of time in Part II, the poet and his soul are ready in Part III to launch a voyage both spaceless and timeless. Throughout section 7 there is the almost ecstatic realization of both the poet and his repressless soul that they may return, go "back, back to wisdom's birth." The highly charged metaphoric language of this section suggests several levels of meaning. That to which the poet and his soul may return might be any one of four—or all four—places. First, there may be a physical "return" to the East, the cradle of mankind. The material spanning of the globe has made such a return possible. Next, there may be a return in spirit to the time of civilization's birth in the Orient. This time, which coincides with the flourishing "realms of budding bibles," is historically valid. Again, there may be a return to "reason's early paradise," "back to wisdom's birth, to innocent intuitions." This time, the time of Adam and Eve, is not historically but mythically or imaginatively valid. Finally, there is the suggestion in such phrases as "the young maturity of brood and bloom" and "fair creation" that the poet and his soul may long to return, if[126] not to the womb, at least to the "time" before birth—a time of pure, innocent, spiritual existence, a world of spirit whence we come and to which we go. The poet and his soul long for the mystic's experience in his union with God—a union in life identical with the union before and after life.

Sections 8 and 9 represent the poet, in excited anticipation of imminent discoveries, exhorting his soul to begin the voyage. There is in these last two sections the fervency of the evangelist, almost a mystical ecstasy:

> O we can wait no longer,
> We too take ship O soul,
> Joyous we to launch out on trackless seas.

This note of urgency and joyousness that opens section 8 rises gradually to its highest emotional pitch at the close of the poem (a poetic technique Whitman has used elsewhere, particularly in "Starting from Paumanok" and "Song of the Open Road"). In section 8 comes the climax of "Passage to India." . . . This point in the poem might be recognized as the culmination of the poet's imaginative union with God. . . .[127]

The entire last section of the poem is given over to a dramatization of the poet's questioning, pleading with, and exhorting his soul. . . . As section[128] 9 progresses, the pleading becomes more fervent, the tone more ecstatic, and the poet cries out, "Passage, immediate passage! the blood burns in my veins!" But even in the ecstatic fervency there is order. The poet exclaims:

> Have we not stood here like trees in the ground long enough?
> Have we not grovel'd here long enough, eating and drinking like mere brutes?
> Have we not darken'd and dazed ourselves with books long enough?

The progression in this passage is not chaotic but systematic, from one end of the scale of life to the other, from plant to animal to man. As the poem closes, the exclamations become more frequent, the lines shorter, until, in the last, the hypnotically repeated words suggest complete ecstatic, but spiritual, abandonment: "O farther, farther, farther sail!"[129]

The Prophecy as Reality

John Lovell, Jr.

FROM "Appreciating Whitman: 'Passage to India.' " Reprinted, with permission, from the *Modern Language Quarterly,* XXI (June 1960), 131–141.

. . .

The reader can now fully appreciate the scope and thrill of this poem. Any man who is aware of his soul's potential is aware of this dazzling array of endless realistic accomplishment. Not in some gossamer way is he aware: "the blood burns" in his veins; he grovels no longer; he no longer eats and drinks like a mere brute. He captures and annihilates aged fierce enigmas—like inveterate problems, diseases, and worries of the human race. One by one the social and political problems that interfere with full democracy disappear.[1] And far in the evolutionary distance are positive victories which have not yet even come into perspective, beyond today's Indias—if only wings are plumed "for such far flights. . . ."

In addition to these realizations, the reader is further assured and invigorated by the appropriate music of the poem. He can believe the prophecy: it is reality itself. As Allen says, Whitman no longer questions; he affirms.[2] As Noel maintains, Whitman is more prophet than artist.[3] And as Daiches notes, Whitman carries a Bible accent on his prophecy.[4] [139]

There are two valid tests for the genuineness of "Passage to India." The first is to ask: looking backward, 1960 to 1869, has Whitman overstated the case? Has the dream of this poem come true under the hardest realistic scrutiny? The answer is certainly yes, and in most amazing particulars. The three great events which he memorialized in this poem—the three great monuments themselves—have more than realized the poetic potential he ascribed to them during a mere ninety years of development. And the prospect for the future of things corresponding to them (the more than India—things unseen when they were first sung) is greater than ever. Whitman thus opened the door not to mere celebration, but to cosmic awareness of progress and progressive reality.[5]

The second test is the analysis of Whitman's optimism. From all available evidence the same Whitman who conceived and wrote the caustic, devastating *Democratic Vistas* conceived and wrote what some call the ultra-optimistic "Passage to India." Out of his searing awareness of democracy's weakness and hypocrisy and incongruity and slow progress toward a great ideal, Whitman fashioned a poem which urged the reader not to lose his vision, but to continue to look at the sky, for he and the sky are real and belong together.[6]

---

[1] Whitman considered the development of the general population, not a select class, into a race of perfect men, women, and children, grandly developed in body, emotions, heroism, and intellect, more important than arts, literature, factories, architecture, ships, wharves, and bank-safes filled with coin or mints with bullion. [Gay Wilson Allen,] *Walt Whitman Handbook* [(Chicago, 1946)], p. 56.

[2] *Walt Whitman Handbook*, p. 198.

[3] [Roden B.] Noel [*Essays on Poetry and Poets* (London, 1886)], p. 305.

[4] [David] Daiches ["Walt Whitman: Impressionist Prophet," in Milton Hindus, ed., *Leaves of Grass One Hundred Years After* (Stanford, 1955)], p. 120.

[5] Bliss Perry says of "Passage to India": "The burden of it is evolution—the one thing escaping the other—the unfolding of cosmic purposes." *Walt Whitman: His Life and Work* (Boston, 1906), p. 195.

[6] See Floyd Stovall [*American Idealism* (Norman, Oklahoma, 1943)], p. 93, where the idea is expressed that, if there were no evil overleaping the divine function of the spirit of freedom, there could be no good.

One writer has said that Whitman was fighting the sweeping melancholy of his era.[7] Whether he was or not, it is important to note that "Passage to India" presents evidence to tone down Whitman's reputation as an unlimited and cockeyed optimist. Perhaps, psychologically, he was closer to pessimist, since, like Mark Twain, he seemed often to doubt man's ability ever to reach his potential; but, unlike Mark Twain, Whitman was determined to continue to beat against the door of the heart of mankind, demanding entrance for the faith that would glorify man if man would but open his heart.

An optimist would hardly need to convince himself by speaking over and over again such words of encouragement and reassurance to a failing partner in democratic idealism. In hundreds of poems and prose works Whitman showed that he knew the failings and the inherent dangers. But he never stopped warring against the doubt of democracy and the apathy.

"Passage to India" is an excellent poem for 1960 readers. First, it is a fine introduction to what is perhaps the most satisfying way to read Whitman, namely, to treat him not as an enthusiast of man's eternal glories, of indiscriminate love for all, or of undisciplined self-conceit, but as the promoter of hard work by skilled hands without which the divine dreams, which are the first stage in every man's[140] transformation, remain unfulfilled. Second, it is a chart of man's evolutionary growth over several periods: before 1492, 1492 to 1869, 1869 to 1960, and 1960 on. More than a chart of progressive civilization, it indicates the motive power of progress, man's insatiable passion for the next higher stage, and the reasons for the illimitability of that power, the constant urging from God. Third, it predicts and explains today's restless activity—even the international competition—in atomic energy, in space probing and underseas investigations, in plans for interplanetary travel, in driving ever deeper into the wilds of men's hearts and minds, and in that inexhaustible parade of invention and discovery which the coming years envision. "Are they not all the seas of God?" asks Whitman, eliminating much of the surprise (but none of the excitement) from whatever great successful endeavor. Fourth, it provides comfort to those who must find answers to uncommonly knotty problems, such as East-West coöperation, the growing pains of maverick new nations, the inscrutability of mental disease, and the fathoming of a saving balance as the world teeters between its greatest prospect and utter destruction. Finally, at a time when the tide rises against the democratic faith more threateningly than ever, from without and from within, this poem demonstrates how these dangers can be assessed at their proper value, and how man and soul can idealistically and realistically rise above them.[141]

---

7 [Standish] O'Grady [*Selected Essays and Passages* (Dublin, 1918)], p. 269.

10

EVOLUTION AND DESIGN OF
LEAVES OF GRASS

The Growth of *Leaves of Grass*

Oscar Lovell Triggs

IN *The Complete Writings of Walt Whitman,* Camden edition, X,
101–134.

Leaves of Grass has a marked tectonic quality. The author, like
an architect, drew his plans, and the poem, like a cathedral long in
building, slowly advanced to fulfilment. Each poem was designed and
written with reference to its place in an ideal edifice. The *Inscriptions*
form a façade, prophesying the content of the interior. The *Song of
Myself* is the main structure, with subsidiary and corroborating poems
of sex, comradeship, nationality, and nature. *Drum-Taps* occupies the
central position, looking both backward and forward, the unifying
dome. The later poems are like altars, burning incense; as through a
rosewindow the author looks Eastward to primal thought and realms
of Bibles, breathing prayer.

The symbol of a cathedral, however, does not exactly serve in
that it is too suggestive of mechanical production. The development
of the poem was more organic than the building of a formal structure.
The volume is better understood perhaps when[101] considered as a
growth and as related to the author's own life process. Its successive
stages have the vital rather than the mechanical connection. Whitman
himself always spoke of his poems as "leaves." There was, then, the
seed purport of 1855. Succeeding editions have the character of ex-
pansive growths, like the rings of a tree, or like a stag's antlers, or like
the evolution of one's own being. Each edition has identity with every
other edition, the same central heart, yet each is cumulative. The very
form is vital, like the fibres of growing things, admitting of substitution, adjustment, or extension. Lines and poems were added, sub-
tracted, or reshaped as the author's own life purpose was fulfilled. I
know of no other poem that exhibits such fidelity to the history of a
human soul. Langland's *Piers Plowman* has certain features of resemblance, but the experience of the earlier mystic was simple and cir-
cumscribed, while Whitman's was composite and universal. In *Leaves
of Grass* a human soul (Whitman's ostensibly, the race's in reality) is
urged to expression by resistless creative impulses from within. It
moves freely also among materials and absorbs and transmutes the
shows of outward nature into forms of its own life. By creation from

within and by absorption from without it attains identity and individuality, and attaining identity, puts on immortality and universality. It sings therefore the joys[102] of its individual existence, the songs of one's self, and the joys of its universal relationship, the songs democratic, the songs of sex, brotherhood, and immortality. It disciplines itself by undergoing special experiences in the guise of pain and evil. But with the full knowledge of death it joyfully meets its translation. Of such growths and translations no other book has equal record. . . .[103]

A study of the classification and rearrangement[119] of the poems through the seven editions [that is, through the 1881 edition] discloses the unitary ideas that determined the final grouping. The book as a whole is the bible of democracy—the term is Whitman's own. The content of democracy is two-fold—the idea of the one and the idea of the many. Its problem is to develop supreme individuals on the one hand and on the other to bind these separate sovereign selves into a social union. Socialization, however, follows upon individualization. Make great men, their unification is assured. *Leaves of Grass* has for its chief aim the stimulation of personality. The purpose of the first poems is to arouse, dilate, expand and greaten the reader. Consequently they radiate personal energy—they are proud, strenuous, joyful, optimistic. The function of the second group of poems is to provide for union. They show the identification of each with all, with Nature, and with God. The first stage of union is in sex—union in the natural. A higher, more spiritual identity is found in comradeship or union in the spiritual human. Other forms of union appear in the songs of occupations and in the chants of nature. The war was a war for union; the *Drum-Taps* inculcate, therefore, identity in nationality. The songs of death and parting declare the fusion of soul and body in a cosmic order. As Pride was the keyword of the first group, Love becomes the sign of the second series.[120] To sing the Great Idea, the transcendental Union—that, thought Whitman, must be the mission of poets. He himself was an absolute monist.

The poems of the annexes are like the eddies behind a great ship. . . . There is an Indian summer pause about them, a holding of the breath. The old poet seems to be passing over into the unknown region. Just on the borderland he turns, raises high the hand in sign that men are to remain in sight of him forever, and shouts the final farewell. The vision grows dim, the voice ceases, the book quietly closes. . . .[121] . . .

Whitman's Structural Pattern

Irving C. Story

FROM "The Structural Pattern of *Leaves of Grass*," *Pacific University Bulletin*, XXXVIII (January 1942), 2–12. Reprinted by permission of the author.

. . .

The 1881 *Leaves* contains 293 poems. All but five of these are members of some one of fifteen groups. Two of the groups are untitled. For the first of them, the sequence of poems from "Salut au Monde" through "A Song of the Rolling Earth," I have adopted, for purpose of reference, a title used by Whitman for a group in the 1860 edition, *Chants Democratic*. For the second, the sequence of five poems from "Proud Music of the Storm" through "To Think of Time," I have used the title of its key poem, "Passage to India." In addition, the pair of poems "Starting from Paumanok" and "Song of Myself" I have assumed to be sufficiently similar and inclusive in content to be considered as a group. I have named it, from an earlier title of "Song of Myself," *Songs of Walt Whitman*. The resulting sequence of fifteen groups outlines thus:

Inscriptions	24 poems
(*Songs of Walt Whitman*)	2 poems
Children of Adam	16 poems
Calamus	36 poems
(*Chants Democratic*)	11 poems[1]
Birds of Passage	7 poems
"A Broadway Pageant"	
Sea-Drift	11 poems
By the Roadside	29 poems
Drum-Taps	43 poems
Memories of President Lincoln	4 poems
"By Blue Ontario's Shore"	1
Autumn Rivulets	38 poems
(*Passage to India*)	5 poems[1]
Whispers of Heavenly Death	18 poems
"Thou Mother with Thy Equal Brood"	
From Noon to Starry Night	22 poems
Songs of Parting	17 poems[3]

. . .

This sequence [referring specifically to key poems in the groups] outlines the continuity of the *Leaves* as the story of the starting out

---

[1] I assume that the following poems were included in the 1881 *Leaves* primarily to fill out their respective pages: "Youth, Day, Old Age and Night," "Reversals," "Transpositions," "A Paumanok Picture."

from Paumanok of Walt Whitman, American, to discover the importance of his own individuality, to experience sex and comradeship, to identify himself with democratic America in its life on the "open road," to become a "pioneer" in the "westward movement" of the human race, and to listen to the whisperings of the sea concerning the mystery of death and the oneness of all life. Then to enter into the political world with its corruption, to know war and its suffering and comradeship, to discover the greatest American, Lincoln, and to come through the war with renewed acceptance of death and an intensified belief in America. Then to go on still further, into the spiritual world, to understand death as a part of the complete life and as a synonym for immortality, to see a new vision of the future America as a universal mother, and of human society as an all-inclusive democracy, and finally to understand fully the meaning to post-War America of "parting.". . .

A third analysis will further emphasize Whitman's intention to create a structural totality, and it will also emphasize the value of understanding this pattern as a means of understanding what Whitman wanted to say. It will disclose a third structural feature—a balance of the groups around a central section.

From this third point of view, the pattern of the *Leaves* separates into four sections. The first includes the *Songs of Walt Whitman* (as I have titled the first group) and its two supplements, *Children of Adam* and *Calamus,* the groups that are particularly poems of the individual or Songs of the Self. The balance in the pattern is worked out in what might be called the body of the *Leaves,* the part that presents Whitman's panorama of America—the sequence from *Chants Democratic* through *From Noon to Starry Night.*[10] . . .

The three-part structure of 1881 Whitman worked out apparently to suggest his concept of the complementary antithesis of Body or Life and Soul or Death and Immortality. In the sequence of poems from *Chants Democratic* through *Sea-Drift* he presents his Songs of Life; in the sequence from *Passage to India* through *From Noon to Starry Night,* his Songs of the Soul. Inspection of these two sequences discloses two four-part equivalent structures. Each is introduced by a group of major poems that is followed by two groups of minor lyrics separated the one by "A Broadway Pageant" and the other by "Thou Mother with Thy Equal Brood."

Analysis of these two structures demonstrates that each item in the second sequence is an intended balance or complement for an item in the first. . . .

By thus balancing his pattern around the War poems, Whitman emphasized not only the distinctiveness of the individual poems but also the intended unity of the structure. He desired, as he said, that his panorama of American life be considered for its totality.[11]

Whitman's Three Stages

Malcolm Cowley

FROM "Whitman: The Poet," *The New Republic,* CXVII (October 20, 1947), 27–30. Copyright 1947 by The New Republic. Reprinted by permission of the publisher and the author.

Dates are important in reading Whitman. There were three stages of his life—and, I think, only three—at which he wrote great poems.

The earliest stage, which lasted from 1855 to 1856, was the period of Whitman's miraculous flowering. It was the time when he wrote, or revised for publication, the 12 poems of the first edition and the 20 new poems that were added to his book the following year. Most of those in the first edition are among his best and all are examples of his boldest style, his freshest notations on the life he had always known. The "Song of Myself," which fills nearly half of this first volume, contains in germ almost everything else he would ever write. It is one of the great visionary poems of modern times. I don't know what to compare it with, except possibly Rimbaud's "Les Illuminations," though it also has qualities suggesting Blake in "The Marriage of Heaven and Hell" and others suggesting Nietzsche in "Thus Spake Zarathustra." There is nothing in American literature that in any way resembles it, except as a weak copy.

Some of the pure intensity of emotion that produced the first edition was carried over into the 20 new poems of the second, in 1856; but by then Whitman was less visionary and more calculating in his methods. If these new poems have one quality in common, it is that whether good or bad they are all inflated. . . . Some of the 1856 poems are masterpieces, notably "Crossing Brooklyn Ferry" and the "Song of the Open Road"; but all of them, even the best, are padded out with lists of things seen or done, things merely read about, anatomical details and geographical names. . . .

There are few inventories in the great poems of his second period, which coincided with his emotional crisis of the years 1859–60. That was the time when Whitman wrote the "Calamus" poems, some of which are mere statements of belief, to be read as if they were prose. Not all of them are prose, however; for others are tender and secret and, in their twisted way, his only real love poems. The same years produced his two great despairing chants, "As I Ebb'd with the Ocean of Life" and "Out of the Cradle Endlessly Rocking." These, for Whitman, were the end of a long search. . . .

At this ultimate point in exploring his mind, Whitman had found his two deepest longings, which were death and the womb of the mother-ocean; and he spoke of them in a tone of intense quiet, with a rightness that was lacking in his chants to democracy. The tone and the rightness were also lacking in the next poems he would publish [*Drum-Taps*]. . . .

The third period when he wrote great poems—but very few of them—was the years he spent in government service from 1865 to 1873. By then his style had become mannered and verbose and vague—Whitmanian in the worst sense—and he was losing his interest in daily scenes and occupations.[27] He was trying to present, as he said, "no more the puzzling hour or day," but rather the lasting reality behind it: an experiment noble in purpose that has produced whole libraries of bad poetry. In Whitman's case it produced bad poems, too, full of scorn for the humble details that had given its rich texture to the "Song of Myself"; he now dismissed the details in a barbarous phrase as "the ostent evanescent"—in other words, as fleeting appearances. But in compensation for losing his sharp images and exact phrases, he had acquired another gift, for symphonic form. And his few great poems of the third period, from his dirge for Abraham Lincoln (1865) through "Proud Music of the Storm" and "A Passage to India" to "The Prayer of Columbus" (1874), which was his last ambitious work and the epilogue to his poetic career—all these are to be read for their interweaving of themes, for their orchestral effects, for their elevation of tone, but not by any means for richness of style or immediate, fresh visions of the poet's world.[28] . . .

A Brief Revaluation

Richard P. Adams

FROM "Whitman: A Brief Revaluation," *Tulane Studies in English,* V (1955), 111–149. Reprinted by permission of the publisher and the author.

. . .

Inside the shifting, shimmering surfaces of Whitman's poems is a system of articulation that gives them strong, though not solid, shapes. This structural principle can be at least partially demonstrated, though we do not yet know it in all its details. It proceeds by the method of reconciling opposites which Coleridge recommended[118] and Hegel systematized. It begins with vast numbers of individual observations, or units of disconnected experience, and ties them together, dialectically, in a progressively tighter and more comprehensive synthesis. It is precisely the method advocated by Emerson in "The American Scholar," by which the intellect "finds how to join two things and see in them one nature; then three, then three thousand . . . discovering roots running under ground whereby contrary and remote things co here and flower out from one stem." Whether Whitman believes that the mind can go on, as Emerson hopefully says, "forever to animate the last fibre of organization, the outskirts of nature, by insight,"[1] is a difficult question, which we must postpone; but he handles the process, in his thinking, in his prose statements of theory, and especially in his poetry, with far more firmness, vigor, and subtlety than Emerson ever does.

The main lines on which he builds are those connecting the polar opposites of the individual and society, man and nature, body and soul, matter and spirit, the writer and the reader, and life and death. In each case, it is on the relation between the opposites, as relation, that he mainly focuses his attention, his thought, and his art. Ultimately, his aim is to suggest a complex of relations embracing all these elements and implying many more, not in a closed or completed system but in a progressively growing involvement of himself with his reader in an intellectual and esthetic contemplation of all things. But the word "contemplation" does not fully convey what happens. It is an activity which the reader is invited to share with Whitman, by which the relations aimed at are not so much examined, or defined, as they are created by the cooperative labor of both parties. Values are not established or communicated by Whitman; they are evoked in his reader's mind and feelings to the extent that the reader comes into relation with Whitman through the medium of the work. The object, then, is to integrate the universe in the reader's mind by persuading him to "see" (that is, to originate for himself) relationships—between himself as an individual and the mass of other individuals in society, between himself and nature, or the universe, between his body and his soul, between his own life and death—all through the means of the relationship established between himself as reader and Whitman as[119] writer by the formulas presented in the poems.[2] This is a difficult concept to understand, and one which seems impossible to state either clearly or accurately. But it leads, in Whitman, to a sound philosophy and to great poetry; therefore it is worth studying.[120]

. . . *Leaves of Grass* is to have the kind of unity the world has, or a man has. Therefore no important aspect of the world or of man can be omitted, or the completeness of the unity will be lost. Like Emerson, Whitman firmly believes that truth and beauty are attributes of the whole of man's experience of the whole universe. Anything seen by itself will be incomplete and therefore false and ugly. For that reason Whitman[127] identifies his book with himself and himself with the world, and for that reason he insists that no single poem can be

---

1 *The Complete Works of Ralph Waldo Emerson,* ed. E. W. Emerson (Boston, 1903–1904), I, 85, 86.

2 For related but somewhat different views on this problem, see H. B. Reed, "The Heraclitan Obsession of Walt Whitman," *Personalist,* XV (Spring, 1934), 132; L. Trilling, "Sermon on a Text from Whitman," *Nation,* CLX (Feb. 24, 1945), 215,

properly understood or valued except in relation to the whole book of which all the poems are conceived as integral, inseparable parts.

In general, critics agree, the book begins by celebrating the individual and then proceeds to indicate various ways of union between the individual and nature and between the one and the many in society. "Song of Myself" is of course the keynote of the first part, and of the celebration of individuality. *Children of Adam* concentrates on physical love, uniting men and women in families with children. *Calamus* describes the (to Whitman apparently) more spiritual love of comrades. Then comes a group of poems emphasizing general qualities of social, economic, and cultural unity, of which "Crossing Brooklyn Ferry" may be taken as typical. In *Sea-Drift,* however, and especially in "Out of the Cradle Endlessly Rocking," there is a return to the individual, whose development is completed by a realization, the result of some great sorrow and suffering, of the meaning of death. *Drum-Taps* generalizes this knowledge in the suffering of the nation at war, and expresses it in the companion poem to "Out of the Cradle," the elegy for Lincoln, "When Lilacs Last in the Dooryard Bloom'd." Then come the thoughts and feelings of declining years, the high point among which is the cosmic or metaphysical union of self and universe, or God, in "Passage to India."[3]

There are, we may say, two principles of organization in *Leaves of Grass,* closely related and simultaneously operative. The first is analogous to the organic process of thought or learning described above, by which individual facts or bits of experience are progressively united in larger and more complex integrations. The second is the process of organic growth seen as a pattern of death and rebirth. Both mean the same thing essentially, and they work together very well. The second suggests a stronger recognition of the principle that in order to register a change the organic structure must be totally reconstituted; it does not grow by addition but by emergent stages of complexity, each one radically different from the preceding one and radically unpredictable in terms of cause and effect. The assimilation of the fact of death, the transcendence of the feelings of fear and sorrow at the loss it involves, is one of[128] the greatest changes the growing organism of the human personality can undergo. Therefore the elegiac theme provides a most fitting climax for Whitman's book, and its resolution in the "Passage to India" formula leads to a highly satisfactory conclusion. The same formula is also the logical conclusion of the organic process of growth in knowledge and wisdom.[129]

"Passage to India" . . . marks a real advance. As Whitman explained in his 1876 Preface, he had originally intended, "after chanting

---

3 See *Handbook,* pp. 104–227. [Gay Wilson Allen, *Walt Whitman Handbook* (Chicago: Packard and Co., 1946).] One of the best surveys is in Sculley Bradley, "The Problem of a Variorum Edition of Whitman's *Leaves of Grass," English Institute Annual:* 1941 (New York, 1942), pp. 129–157.

in LEAVES OF GRASS the songs of the Body and Existence, to then compose a further, equally needed Volume, based on those convictions of perpetuity and conservation which, enveloping all precedents, make the unseen Soul govern absolutely at last."[4] The book was never completed, but "Passage to India," "with its cluster," was offered as a partial fulfillment of the same intention. Whitman's explanation may be taken to mean that "Passage to India" expresses the final unity toward which the assimilation of diverse experience is supposed to lead.

Its scope is universal. Beginning in that present moment with which Thoreau and Emerson were so much fascinated, it integrates the present with the past and future in a way that neither Emerson nor Thoreau was ever quite able to match. Whitman suggests a space-time continuum that includes all the lands and peoples of all time in a union with God, and God is apparently conceived as essentially identical with the total principle of organization in the universe. Thus "the strong light works of engineers," the achievements of materialistic science and technology, are seen first as means of reaching the (specifically Asiatic) past, second as means of bringing lands and people together in close, loving union in the present, and finally as vehicles of a new religious harmony between the immortal soul of man and the otherwise alien universe in the future. This aspect of the poem is illuminated by a remark in Whitman's 1872 Preface:

With Science, the Old Theology of the East, long in its dotage, begins evidently to die and disappear. But (to my mind) Science—and may be such will prove its principal service—as evidently prepares the way for One indescribably grander—Time's young but perfect offspring—the New Theology —heir of the West—lusty and loving, and wondrous beautiful.[5]

It is in this spirit that the speaker in "Passage to India" wishes to assimilate "the myths Asiatic," "The deep diving bibles and[141] legends,/ The daring plots of the poets," the "fables spurning the known, eluding the hold of the known, mounting to heaven!" These, fitfully glimmering out of the darkness of the past and man's subliminal consciousness, must mingle with the superficial clarities of science in the synthesis of the new religion. Only thus can man achieve his future;

For what is the present after all but a growth out of the past?
(As a projectile form'd, impell'd, passing a certain line, still keeps on,
So the present, utterly form'd, impell'd by the past.)

The dominant metaphor of the poem, in harmony with its title, is that of discovery. It uses the same combination of geographical and scientific exploration as Keats' sonnet "On First Looking into Chap-

---

4 *Leaves of Grass*, p. 513. [*Leaves of Grass*, Inclusive Ed., ed. E. Holloway (Garden City, 1948).]
5 *Ibid.*, p. 510. See also Whitman's longer statement to the same effect reprinted from the original version of "A Backward Glance on My Own Road," Barrus, p. 247 n. [Clara Barrus, *Whitman and Burroughs, Comrades.*]

man's Homer," but with a far larger reference. The goal is the meaning of life, which is ultimately to be discovered by the poet, who shall solve the problem of the whole relation of mankind to the earth, or the universe. By 1871 Whitman had become keenly aware of the central problem of naturalism: "What is this separate Nature so unnatural?/ What is this earth to our affections?" After the explorers and scientists "shall come the poet worthy that name,/ The true son of God," and answer the question.

[Quotes lines 106–115, end of § 5.]

The fusion, like the problem it has to solve, involves both the time and the space aspects of human life in the world, and throughout the universe and all eternity. The gaps are the discontinuities that existed in Western civilization during the latter half of the nineteenth century, and still exist, first between the "primitive" past, with its life-giving myths, and the "enlightened" present, with the sterile intellectuality that threatens to make a wasteland of the[142] world; and second between the human personality, conceived as an ideal entity, and the material world, conceived as a dead, rigidly regulated, impersonal machine. By concentrating on relationships rather than entities, Whitman suggests, we may be able to span these gaps and make ourselves immortal. There is nothing fanciful about either the problem or the proposed solution. Our civilization is being torn apart in precisely the way Whitman says, and, unless we can apply some such integrating force as he suggests, it, and most or all of us with it, will be destroyed.

"Passage to India," then, is the final and perfectly logical conclusion to which all of Whitman's art and all his thinking convergently lead. It is hard to imagine how the rest of the projected second volume of his poetic works could have added anything of fundamental importance to its message.[143]

A Century of Erosion by Time and Criticism

Mark Van Doren

FROM "The Poet." In *Walt Whitman: Man, Poet, Philosopher* (Washington, D.C.: Library of Congress, 1955), pp. 15–33. Reprinted by permission of the author. Reprinted also in *The Happy Critic and Other Essays* (New York: Hill and Wang, 1961).

. . .

Emerson of course did not have before him the bulky volume we now know as *Leaves of Grass* [when he wrote his congratulatory letter]. Including the preface, there were only 93 pages, though they were large ones, in the book he read [the 1855 edition], and there were only 12 poems, all without titles. The first of the 12, later to be called "Walt Whitman," and still later "Song of Myself," occupied more than half of the pages. It was and is one of Whitman's masterpieces, if not the chief[18] one; it had the right position in the book, for it said most of what Whitman had to say, at least until 1865, and it said it altogether personally, drawing its authority from Whitman's innermost being insofar as he could be conscious of that being. Emerson needed no more than this magnificent poem, so candid and yet so cryptic, so loose and yet so terse, so flowing and yet so broken, as evidence of the author's wit and wisdom. It still is the key to *Leaves of Grass,* however reluctantly it sometimes turns in the lock. It is not systematic; it is perhaps a series of notes, or better yet a collection of inspired sayings; it is not cluttered with transitions; it does not seek to explain itself; it simply and confidently, if arrogantly too, is what it is, to be taken or left as the reader desires. Emerson took it, and then went on, we may suppose, to take such further masterpieces, minor only by comparison, as "The Sleepers," "I Sing the Body Electric," and "There Was a Child Went Forth."

It was an excellent selection, an exciting selection, from the poems Whitman had been writing since his 30th year or thereabouts; since the day when he cut himself loose from his own past and from what he took to be the past of the human race. We can envy Emerson the experience he had with a lean book that was mostly nerves and muscle. *Leaves of Grass* in its ultimate state is a greater book because it contains further masterpieces then unwritten. But in one vital respect it is less attractive. It is stuffed with repetitions of statements that once were fresher and did not need to be made again. Its author is afflicted with the modern disease of rewriting: he is always tinkering with his text—sometimes, granted, for the better, but sometimes not so. He cuts and he inserts; he regroups and rearranges; he improvises sections, and provides transitions—dead connective tissue—between them. He composes "Inscriptions" which the reader shall find first, and at the end he keeps saying farewell to this same reader, bidding him take note and remember, assuring him of this or that meaning that he may not have expressed, hanging on for dear life to some image of his book as the rounded, systematic work which in fact it never was or could be, and indeed should never have tried to be. We do not require of a philosophical poet that he be systematic; we require only that he be always keen and convincing. Whitman dulls his final effect by laboring to convince us with something less than the best poetry he could write. For he is full of the notion that *Leaves of Grass* is a scripture, and that he is its editor as well as its maker. He is preserving it for posterity, he is altering it, coaxing it into shape, inserting things in it, taking things out, so that nothing will prevent its survival through the centuries ahead. Hence all the putty and the plastic wood. He is unwilling to let the individual poems stand free as their progenitors did in the original edition. It is as if he thought he had to keep on writing at a book he had not yet written, though in truth he had, for the best of his poems were that book. In his own words he was "garrulous to the very last;" and though we may love him for the admission, we are sorry that it has to be made.[19]

It has to be made because Whitman, strangely enough for one whose first appearance was in the role of the supremely satisfied person —satisfied with himself and with every portion of his world—has come to be a person so tentative, so unsure, that he irritates and tantalizes rather than reassures us. He seems uneasy as to whether he has said what he wanted to say, or whether he knows now what that was. He slips away into hints and approximations, and above all into promises that he will say it yet, or that if he never does, others coming after him will. But so far, he sometimes confesses, his subject has eluded him; it is not in the book after all.

> *For it is not for what I have put into it that I have written this book,*
> *Nor is it by reading it you will acquire it....*

The subject, then, is over and above the book, which merely suggests it, or if the subject is himself, he is forced to say:

> *Before all my arrogant poems the real Me stands yet untouch'd, untold,*
> *altogether unreach'd,*
> *Withdrawn far, mocking me with mock-congratulatory signs and bows,*
> *With peals of distant ironical laughter at every word I have*
> *written....*

The excuse he hopes he has, and keeps insisting he has, is the extreme difficulty of his assignment. Like Dante and Spenser he speaks of his book as a little bark that ventures in huge seas almost certain to overwhelm it. Like Milton he reaches after things unattempted yet in prose or rhyme. He must break new ground, and no wonder it is hard.

He remembers—or perhaps he does not remember—that the artist's business is nevertheless to find his subject and to finish the work which embodies it; to steer the bark into some port at last; to get there and make an end. He remembers—or perhaps he does not remember— that the great poet knows how to write his poem; he does not talk about the difficulty because he is occupied with conquering it; he does not promise to succeed tomorrow, he succeeds today. Homer did not discuss the problem of the epic; he wrote the *Iliad* and the *Odyssey.* Shakespeare did not write, at any rate in public, about whether or not it was impossible to write *Hamlet;* he wrote it, and made it seem easy. But Whitman, after his brave start, is forever doubting that he knows where to go or what to do. Which indeed is strange, considering that start. And which is why, for all the fine poems his book contains, it is not the finished thing, the effective scripture, the moving whole he presumably once desired that it should be. Even his retouchings, his nudgings, his inscriptions and farewells, do not accomplish the result. For they are done halfheartedly, as if he knew they would not succeed.

The answer he gave himself, and in many a place gives us, is that *Leaves of Grass* is not a work of art at all. "This is no book," he says. "No one will get at my verses who insists upon viewing them as a literary performance, or attempt at such performance, or as aiming mainly toward art."[20] *Leaves of Grass,* he seems to be saying, is so little like other books that perhaps it should be called something else. And if we ask again why it is that he expends so much effort in perfecting whatever he has between his hands, he says again that it is not a book as other books are books. If it is actually one, it is "a book separate, not link'd with the rest." Nor does it occur to him that this is a handicap rather than a help, since it means that he neither competes nor contributes, and so is lost, as it were, in literary space, with no masters for models, no company as he works. "The words of my book," he says, are "nothing, the drift of it everything." But in the long run, under the scrutiny of time and criticism, it is only the words that will count. The work of any poet is done with words. It is done with drift, too, but we must be the judges of that. And Whitman knew that this was so, or else he would not have denied it so vehemently. Somewhere in him was the consuming ambition of an artist. Somewhere in him too was the appalling suspicion that he had failed—not absolutely, in view of his masterpieces, but relatively to the vast vision of himself he once had had, and to the vaster vision he had had of the good world whose air he breathed.

He loved this world as a lover loves his mistress—loved all of it, including its alleged imperfections. And it is a fine thing to be able to do this, and to talk about it in the intense, free way we associate with no one more than we do with him. But much of his talk is not intense, not free, and therefore, by his own criterion, not good. *Leaves of Grass* is more often than not relaxed and flabby; it is uncertain of itself; on many of its pages it is, frankly, a bore. And this could be not alone because Whitman paid too little attention to his art; it could be as well because his theory, his thinking, failed at times to be first-rate. A philosophical poet must have examined at some stage the grounds of his thought, and made them as firm as possible. He has to be more than a thinker, but he had better think. He will always have a problem, of course, since that is the fate of philosophers. And Whitman's problem was an immemorial one: if the universe is to be accepted in all of its parts, if every part of it is to be loved and praised, how can one avoid monotony and unreality, how can one say more than the simple word "Yes"? For most men find the world both good and bad; they like some parts of it better than others, even when they don't know why. And this is likely to be true even of men like Whitman who do not want it to be true. For Whitman, as for Lucretius, all things were natural; and at least for Whitman all things were good. How then could he disapprove of anything—for instance, the piano poet, or the fool who corrupts, degrades, and defiles his body? Whitman regularly denounces this poet and this fool, and does so in the face of his insistence at other times that he accepts everything and everyone. But then he realizes what he has done, and makes amends by listing all the objects in the world for which he feels affection. Hence his famous catalogues which no one can read through. Every river makes the grade, every trade and occupation, every city, every valley, every individual, every class, every thought, every mountain, every man. Somehow the review is not impressive; it can even be ludicrous,[21] with its suggestion that if Whitman had not come along to love these things they would have felt neglected. He has a special license to approve of you and me, of democracy and sin, of India and Christ. It is something of a [j]umble before he has finished.

He embraces too much; he stretches himself thin; he becomes breathless with adoration. He sounds as if he were exaggerating—in art, a fatal weakness. Nor does he sound at these moments like one possessed, and therefore in some degree to be condoned. He makes his catalogues in cold blood; his theory tells him to. So there could be something wrong with the theory, or else with the thinker who holds it. And this could be summed up in his own phrase: "There is no evil." An artist, or at any rate a literary artist, is seriously handicapped if he has no theory of evil; for then his vision of good lacks definition; he does not know why he likes it. It is natural to love the good, but before that it is necessary to know how to recognize it, and to guess what its price is—or better yet, its pricelessness, which experience of evil defines. The vision of good which does not start from a sense of evil will be a watery vision, colorless and shapeless, indistinct and finally depressing. Whitman's vision of the good is at its best a sharp and wonderful thing; at its worst it is unconvincing because it lacks lines to limit it, and consequently lacks form. It is an ample vision, and for that it is to be admired, just as Whitman is to be admired for his all but incredible refusal ever to judge. He is like Christ in this, except that he has no such reason as Christ had, and incidentally no such capacity for anger in the presence of evil. The figure of Christ is always clear and firm: Whitman's figure is wavering, and sometimes it is timid—because he does not know what he thinks. He does not follow his thought even as far as Lucretius followed his; he is by no means so ruthless, so possessed, so on fire. Lucretius, with bad logic, denounced religion; if everything is a part of nature, then religion is too; but religion was in his way and he said so with his whole might. Whitman, who had his own religion, accepted all others too, though most of them were in his way. He was not sure he shouldn't. He was not sure of most things. He did not see his vision to the end. . . .[22]

There [the hymn to death in "When Lilacs Last in the Dooryard Bloom'd"] is the summit of Leaves of Grass. It has other eminences, and on the lower ground there are foothills—the great little poems—which time will find it hard to wash away. Time and criticism. Already they have eroded the mountain, as is the way with all such things—a good way, since it leaves what ought to be left, and shows it in interesting shapes. Probably they will cut still deeper in. But certain rocks will endure as granite does. That, at this moment in time, is criticism's guess.[33]

The Prototype Personality

James E. Miller, Jr.

REPRINTED FROM *A Critical Guide to Leaves of Grass* by James E. Miller, Jr., by permission of The University of Chicago Press. Copyright 1957 by The University of Chicago.

Once the evolution of *Leaves of Grass* is understood, it should be no surprise to find in the book a basic three-part structure. In its simplest terms the book may be said to be the creation of an individual, yet typical, personality for the New World. This creation or delineation first portrays an expanding awareness of the self and its relation to all else; next shows the impingement of a specific time and a particular place on self; and finally engages the self with the fundamental and all-encompassing "law" of spirituality. With the introductory and farewell poems, there are five major groups, as shown on page 186.

Whitman's own phrases appear as the titles for Groups II, III, and IV, the threefold division of theme. It should be stressed that these three groups are not mutually exclusive. Whitman's own description of the relation of the "Passage to India" poems to the rest of his work is highly revealing as to his method throughout: these poems, Whitman said, "are but freer vent and fuller expression to what . . . more or less lurks in my writings, underneath every page, every line, everywhere" ([Camden Edition,] V, 193). In reality this point could be made of each of his three major thematic groups. All these themes "lurk" beneath every page in the book. But, as Whitman put it, he "shifts the slides" so that primary attention is focused on an individual and distinct theme in each group. Moreover, though there is a definite correlation between the final structure of *Leaves of Grass* and the stages of its evolution as a volume of related poems, all of the poetry composed during one specified period was by no means confined to a single theme. Innumerable critics of *Leaves of Grass* have pointed out that the poems in it are not arranged chronologically, and some of the critics have implied that for this reason the order that does exist is defective. On the contrary, the very fact that Whitman chose not to leave his poems in the order of their writing confirms his assertion that he was throughout his life engaged in the task of developing a structure.

The question that remains, of course, concerns the nature, or perhaps even the validity, of the structure. In my examination of the[185] evolution of the structure, I have attempted to show that Whitman did not merely change, in arbitrary fashion, the character of his work each time he wanted to incorporate in it a new group of poems. The basic character of his work remained constant, but his concept of that character grew in dimension and complexity so that new poems and clusters of poems (written, after all, out of the same spirit and the same perspective on life) became organic parts of his total scheme.

Leaves of Grass: Prototype personality for the New World

I. Introduction to themes and greetings
   Inscriptions
   "Starting from Paumanok"

II. Gigantic embryo or skeleton of personality
   "Song of Myself" ⎫
   Children of Adam ⎬ the self and others
   Calamus   ⎭

   Songs (Eleven individual poems) ⎬ the self and the world
                                        (place)
   Birds of Passage   ⎫
   "A Broadway Pageant"   ⎪ the self and history
   Sea-Drift   ⎬   (time)
   By the Roadside   ⎭

III. This time and land we swim in
   Drum-Taps   ⎫
   Memories of President Lincoln   ⎬ national crisis
   "By Blue Ontario's Shore"   ⎫
   Autumn Rivulets   ⎬ rehabilitation

IV. The resistless gravitation of spirtual law
   "Proud Music of the Storm"
   "Passage to India"
   "Prayer of Columbus"
   "The Sleepers"
   "To Think of Time"
   Whispers of Heavenly Death

V. Review of themes and farewell
   "Thou Mother with Thy Equal Brood"
   From Noon to Starry Night
   Songs of Parting

Afterthoughts: the Annexes
   Sands at Seventy
   Good-Bye My Fancy
   Old Age Echoes[1] [186]

---

1 Brief poems such as "Reversals" at the end of "By Blue Ontario's Shore" and "Transpositions" following "The Sleepers" I have regarded as fillers only and not significant parts of the structure of *Leaves of Grass.*

Whitman's structure is not a mere grouping of poems in accordance with subject matter. It is, rather, an ordering of the poems and groups of poems in accordance with the shifting focus of the pervading theme. These groups are not separate entites, to be shuffled around at will, but exist in an appropriate order in which there is a complex network of relationships. It is necessary that the "gigantic embryo or skeleton of Personality" be first introduced, defined, and related to the world and time in general before it is plunged into this specific "Time & Land we swim in." And it is inevitable that this prototype personality be given birth, identity, and relationships with a certain century and country before primary attention is focused on his relation to death and immortality. There is not only a "poetic" sense to this order, but, throughout, sight is not lost of the basic poetic intent: the articulation of the prototype of the New World personality.[187]

Edifice or Mass?

Roger Asselineau

FROM *The Evolution of Walt Whitman: The Creation of a Personality,* translated by Richard P. Adams and the author (Cambridge, Massachusetts: The Belknap Press of Harvard University Press, 1960). Reprinted by permission of the publisher and the author.

What do these assertions [by Whitman concerning the design of *Leaves of Grass*] mean? At first glance they are at least surprising. The book gives the impression, not of having developed harmoniously over the years, but of having undergone a series of Protean metamorphoses. A quick look at the different editions is enough to show this. The text of 1855 is a river of lava. Some of the poems in it, particularly the one which later became "Song of Myself," are interminable. They are not differentiated by titles, they are all indiscriminately called "Leaves of Grass." In 1856 the work was enriched with a large number of short pieces, and this time all the poems had titles. But it is only in 1860 that we find the first attempt at organization; most of the short poems now are grouped in sections with titles, but within each section the poems lose their individuality; instead of titles they bear only numbers, as one numbers the panels of a frame house before taking it to pieces and moving it to another location. In 1867 the aspect of the book once more changed completely. Titles reappeared, each poem had its own, but now the sections in their turn lost their individuality. Except for "Children of Adam" and "Calamus" they were undifferentiated and all called "Leaves of Grass"; a partial return to the uniformity of the first edition. In 1871 the poems devoted to the Civil War were finally incorporated in the book. They formed three[7] groups interpolated among the existing sections, thus introducing an element of diversity and also giving the collection a sort of skeleton. The edition of 1876 consisted for its part of two volumes, but the first merely reproduced the edition of 1871. For the new poems were not yet part and parcel of *Leaves of Grass* proper. They were relegated to the second volume and mingled with pieces of prose. It was only in 1881 that they were allowed a place in the collection. Is it not altogether remarkable that from 1867, that is to say, precisely from the time Whitman tried to give his book a little order, he was unable immediately to incorporate the poems which he wrote? If he had really had a plan in mind, it would have been easy for him to find a place for each of them. Even if we concede that the Civil War surprised him and upset his projects, how can we explain his failure to include in *Leaves of Grass* the poems which in 1876 he was constrained to keep apart provisionally in the miscellaneous volume entitled *Two Rivulets?* Why, moreover, did he not announce his design in the 1855 preface? And, if he had a plan from the beginning, why is it that he continued until 1881 to change the order and the titles of the various poems? Why did his book begin to be organized only in 1860 (and even then not tightly)? As a matter of fact, in 1857, commenting in a letter on the 1860 edition which was almost ready, he made this very revealing statement:

It is, I know Well enough, that *that* must be the *true Leaves of Grass*—and I think it has an aspect of completeness, and makes its case clearer.—The old poems are all retained.—The difference is in the new character given to the mass, by the additions.

According to this, he had as early as 1857 the impression that the edifice was finished. But can we even speak of an edifice? He was so reluctant to give his work an architectural aspect that he used a word as little suggestive of order and harmony[8] as "mass" to describe the material of the volume to come. Besides, he made no allusion to any changes in structure; the difference he found between the two volumes was mainly quantitative; if the new edition was to produce a different impression, it would not be owing to a different arrangement, but to added material.[9]

11

THE WHITMAN PERSONA

Whitman's Comic Hero

Constance Rourke

FROM *American Humor: A Study of the National Character* (New York: Harcourt, Brace and Company, 1931). Copyright, 1931, by Harcourt, Brace & World, Inc.; renewed by Alice D. Fore. Reprinted by permission of the publishers.

Whitman stressed the personal intention, insisting that it belonged to all his poetry. *"Leaves of Grass* indeed (I cannot too often reiterate) has been mainly the outcropping of my own emotional and other personal nature—an attempt, from first to last, to put a *Person,* a human being (myself, in the latter half of the nineteenth century of America) freely, fully and truly on record." Yet Whitman's[168] emotion was rarely the personal emotion; it always included others who swiftly become the subject or even in a sense the singer. The "I" or "Me" of Whitman is no more personal in final content than was that of the rhapsodic backwoodsman: it has the urgency of many people. The gesture is open-handed, the framework that of autobiography: yet this poetry constantly slips into another realm. Once he acknowledged this escape or evasion.

> Before all my arrogant poems the real Me stands yet untouch'd, untold, altogether unreach'd.

In the end Whitman went far beyond that transcending of the merely personal which must occur if poetry is to be created. For the first time in American literature, perhaps for the first time in all literature, he created a generic and inclusive "I" who embraces many minds and many experiences

Passage after passage in his poems begins with the personal experience or mood only to drop these for the generic. In the first few lines of *Starting from Paumanok* Whitman is briefly himself: he then quickly becomes that being who was his great subject, that mythical American who had not only known Manhattan but had been a pioneer in Dakota and a miner in California, who had roamed the entire continent and had comprised all its typical experiences.

> I am of old and young, of the foolish as much as the wise,
> Regardless of others, ever regardful of others,
> Maternal as well as paternal, a child as well as a man,[169]
> Stuff'd with the stuff that is coarse and stuff'd with the stuff that is fine,

One of the Nation of many nations, the smallest the same and the
    largest the same,
A Southerner soon as a Northerner, a planter nonchalant and hospitable
    down by the Oconee I live,
A Yankee bound my own way ready for my trade, my joints the
    limberest joints on earth and the sternest joints on earth,
A Kentuckian walking the vale of the Elkhorn in my deerskin leggins,
    a Louisianian or Georgian,
A boatman over lakes and bays or along coasts, a Hoosier, a Badger, a
    Buckeye—

He was a Yankee sailor aboard a clipper; he was a farmer in a
country barn, among the dried grasses of harvest-time. Whitman was
not only full of this great theme but aware of queries which might arise
in relation to it, often humorously aware—

Do I contradict myself?
Very well then I contradict myself,
(I am large, I contain multitudes).

His inclusions might be grossly made: but by the scope of his view
and the urgency of his consideration he evoked a large and comprehensive figure not unlike that inclusive character toward which the types
of popular comedy had seemed to merge.

Often this figure went beyond the bounds of nationalism, as in
portions of the *Song of Myself* and in *Children of Adam*. Whitman
could leave the nationalistic for the purely[170] human. Yet the body
of his thought was nationalistic: his iterated theme was the American—
was the nation. . . .[171]

At times Whitman achieved a serene and ineffaceable and tender
strain of feeling which seemed a final residuum of humor; this
belonged to his finest poetry. At others he followed only the wildest of
western comic boastings—often with unconscious comedy. The rhapsodic, leaping, crowing backwoodsman had long since come into the
popular view, adopting the phrase "child of nature." Whitman in turn
celebrated "spontaneous me," or described himself as an acutely self-
conscious "child of nature" under the title *Me Imperturbe*—[173]

Me Imperturbe, standing at ease in Nature,
Master of all or mistress of all, aplomb in the midst of irrational things—

His famous "I sound my barbaric yawp over the roofs of the world"
might have been shouted by the gamecock of the wilderness, even
though the image belongs to the cities. . . .

In later years Whitman could fall into that rough-hewn grotes-
querie of language which the backwoodsman had exhibited in moments
of exhilarated comedy. "In fact, here I am these current years 1890
and '91 (each successive year getting stiffer and stuck deeper) much
like some dilapidated grim ancient shell-fish or time-banged conch
(no legs utterly non-locomotive) cast up high and dry on the shore

sands, hopeless to move anywhere—nothing left but to behave myself quiet." He noted the Negro dialect, and found there hints of "a modification of all words of the English language, for musical purposes, for a native grand opera in America." He theorized about language. "In America an immense number of new words are needed," he declared. "This subject of language interests me—interests me: I never get it out of my mind. I sometimes think the *Leaves* is only a language experiment—that it is an[174] attempt to give the spirit, the body, the man, new words, new potentialities of speech—an American, a cosmopolitan (the best of America is the best cosmopolitanism) range of expression. The new world, the new times, the new peoples, the new vista, need a tongue according—yes, what is more will have such a tongue—will not be satisfied until it is evolved." He freely used plain words, "farmer's words," "sea words," "the likes of you," and much of the jargon of the time. Whitman, in short, used language as a new and plastic and even comical medium, as it had long since been used in native folk-lore.

To enter the world of Whitman is to touch the spirit of American popular comedy, with its local prejudices, its national prepossessions, its fantastic beliefs; many phases of comic reaction are unfolded there. Nothing is complete, nothing closely wrought; often Whitman's sequences are incoherent, like sudden movements of undirected thought or feeling. "No one will get at my verses who insists upon viewing them as literary performances," he said. The scale was large; Whitman possessed that sense of a whole civilization which must belong to the epic; his sweeping cadences could have held the heroic form; and though he lacked the great theme of gods and men his awareness of the country had a stirring animism, and his prototypical American was of far greater than human stature. Yet Whitman did not achieve the heroic, or only rarely, in broken or partial passages. Like those popular story-tellers who had often seemed on the verge of wider expression, he failed to draw[175] his immeasurable gift into the realm of great and final poetry. For the most part he remained an improviser of immense genius, unearthing deep-lying materials in the native mind, in a sense "possessed" by the character of that mythical and many-sided American whom he often evoked. He was indeed the great improviser of modern literature. He had turned the native comic rhapsody, abundant in the backwoods, to broad poetic forms.[176] . . .

Whitman had circled from the generic and inclusive and nationalistic "I" to the realm of inner feeling; and the inner world which he discovered was that which had been opened by comedy; it was of the mind; that is, it was reflective rather than emotional . . .

In literature the scope was new and strange which could include the epical scale in free expression and at the same time reveal the conscious and indwelling mind. To these biases, which had belonged to American popular comedy, was added another, likewise of that province. Neither[178] Whitman—nor Thoreau—for all their inclusions of the outer world was primarily concerned with outer circumstance. Thoreau stood, as he said, at the meeting of two eternities; Whitman's true world was wholly visionary even when it included the touch and color of earth.[179] . . .

Whitman: Poseur

Esther Shephard

FROM *Walt Whitman's Pose* (New York: Harcourt, Brace and Company, 1938). Copyright, 1936, 1938, by Esther Shephard. Reprinted by permission of Harcourt, Brace & World, Inc., and the author.

Why Walt Whitman should have preferred to think of himself as Hebraic, Biblical, mystic, rather than George Sandian is another question. . . . In "There Was a Child Went Forth" he shows that he knows that he is a part of all that he has met. Why did he not admit that he had met the "Unknown" in *The Countess of Rudolstadt* [a novel by George Sand]? . . . He found excuse for writing his anonymous reviews by assuring himself in his private notes that "Leigh Hunt praised his own poems," and that Edmund Spenser praised his. Why did he not find a similar excuse for himself in expanding George Sand's suggestions for a poem of MAN by citing the precedents, much discussed, surely, in his time, that Chaucer owed much to his Italian and Provençal sources, that Shakespeare created his *Merchant of Venice* (as some say) on the model of Marlowe's *Jew of Malta,* forging his five-foot verse on the model of Marlowe's mighty line, . . . that George Sand herself borrowed the ideas of her lovers, one after the other? He admitted his great admiration for George Sand. In his imagination he must have felt a sort of intimacy with her or he would hardly, in speaking of her portrait, have brushed his hand across the hair on top of his head and said, "She wore her hair so." Why was he so secretive about the debt he owed her? Surely, if he had been willing to work as an artist, he could have argued with himself that the debt was not very great,[248] for, as has been observed before, it is a far cry from the bare outlines of the "most magnificent poem that can be conceived" to the fullness and completeness of *Leaves of Grass.* The poet in the book is after all only a fictional character; Walt Whitman, sauntering the pavements or loafing along the highways around Brooklyn, New York, and Washington, a-foot and light-hearted, would not have needed his pose but could have remained his real self; whether or not he was inclined to acknowledge his sources, he could have been a poet in the ordinary sense and not a "religious prophet" or "philosoph." No one except Walt Whitman himself requires that an artist shall be what his poem is. In one of his first anonymous reviews, we remember, he defined his theory: "First be yourself what you would show in your poems." For himself, he seems to have decided that, if he could not be an "average" human being, natural in the ordinary sense, he would pretend to be a "man," *natural* in his own extraordinary sense.

My conjecture as to the reason for Whitman's furtiveness is that he thought, in order to gain a reputation as a great and immortal poet, that he must be "original." It would never have done to acknowledge a literary source. . . .[249]

This raises another objection to this whole study of Walt Whitman's pose. What was it, after all, it may be asked, that Whitman did? Why shouldn't he find the inspiration for his poetry wherever he could find it. After all, another poem could be written on the pattern that George Sand suggested. Any number of poems could be written on the same pattern if there were artists great enough to produce such poems. *Leaves of Grass* itself, for that matter, might be used as an inspiration for a poem. One of Walt Whitman's disciples, Horace Traubel, did try to write poetry on the model of Walt Whitman's poems. Walt Whitman stole no poetry from George Sand, nor did he injure her reputation. Her reputation has gone down since 1855 but that is not because she has been overshadowed by Walt Whitman and his *Leaves of Grass;* and even if it were so, that would be merely what happens in the natural course of events in the world of art. What Whitman did cannot even be called plagiarism, unless we count that little scrap of poem he called "O Hymen! O Hymenee!" . . . Better poets than he (Walt would have said worse) as, for instance, Milton and Keats, have been guilty of such slight unconscious appropriations. And if Walt could produce better work by hiding the source of his inspiration, why wasn't he justified? The answer to that, it seems to me, is that perhaps he was. . . .[391] Certainly his successful hiding of the source of his inspiration allowed him an abandonment and naïveté which he could only have attained by a supreme power if he had been working in the open. The paradox of Walt Whitman is that while posing as an original and natural musician-poet of man he produced some original poems and some finely true natural lines and some beautiful word-music.

In so far as *Leaves of Grass,* then, is an expression in language of the blend of passion and pride that lay in the laboratory of Whitman's mind, we shall not be troubled at all about whether he did or did not reveal the source of his inspiration. But when Walt Whitman wants us to consider his poem an epic of man and tells us that the poem is himself and "himself" an epitome of mankind in America in the nineteenth century, then the fact that the whole fabric of his democratic message and his religious mysticism is nothing but shoddy becomes an indictment not only against Whitman as a person but against his poetry as well. . . . And his declared independence of books, i.e., his secretiveness about the inspiration of his poetry, was an even more fundamental failure in being what we hope we would mean by the word MANLY if we were writing an epic of MAN. We can only repeat Sidney Lanier's profound observation, that no one was ever more mistaken than Walt Whitman[392] in his belief as to what constitutes the true advance of art and man. It may be that the end, *Leaves of Grass,* with its many undeniable beauties among all the prosy banalities, justified the means which Whitman employed, his pose, in which, by pretending to obey what he called his inner light, he denied the inner truth of his mind. But Walt Whitman's way seems nevertheless despicable, if not pitiful.[393]

Whitman's Hero-Poet

Floyd Stovall

FROM "Walt Whitman and the American Tradition," *Virginia Quarterly Review,* XXXI (Autumn 1955), 540–557. Reprinted by permission of the author and The Virginia Quarterly Review, The University of Virginia.

. . .

In the identification of himself with Christ through a common experience, the hero-poet of "Leaves of Grass" does not lose his individuality. Some critics, citing Whitman's statement that he sometimes felt himself as two and noting the frequent occurrence of such duality in his poems, have concluded that he had an abnormally divided personality and was at war with himself. I think, on the contrary, that Whitman has merely accentuated in his hero a condition that exists in every individual. The sense of duality is merely a recognition of man's finite and infinite selves and of his consciousness of being both subject and object, the knower and the thing known. In short, it is simply the phenomenon of self-consciousness. When the knower looks into himself he may at rare moments have glimpses of a being more profound than he can compass, and this being, this "deep heart," as Emerson called it, is the infinite self that feeds his spirit from an inexhaustible fountain. Explain such an experience as you will—in terms of mysticism or in terms of imagination—it is equally close to the source of all poetry and all religion.

Of course this is Transcendentalism, but it is also akin to Evangelical religion as it was experienced in America. The mystery of conversion, the trance, the sense of purification and salvation, the consciousness of dying out of sin and being reborn to life and power— all these accompaniments of the revival meeting were implicit in the experience of Whitman's[551] hero-poet. It is true that the repentance of the revival-meeting convert did not always prove enduring; backsliding was all too common. But there is evidence of backsliding in Whitman's hero and his followers, and the devil is just as wily in "Leaves of Grass" as in any wavering human heart. "I know the sea of torment, doubt, despair and unbelief," the hero-poet confesses; "I take my place among you as much as among any." There is no unpardonable sin in these poems, but there is evil enough with its attendant torment. The development of the hero-poet from "Song of Myself" through "Passage to India" is that of a passionate and rebellious yet essentially religious person whose soul is purged by its own fires and stands at last tranquil and free.

This may be also, in general, the development of Whitman himself. Yet the critic must beware of the temptation to interpret "Leaves of Grass" as autobiography. The hero-poet is a mythical person and is no more identifiable with Whitman himself than with the American people, or even the human race. The end of the journey visualized in "Passage to India" is certainly not accomplished in his personal life, though doubtless he has come nearer the goal than most persons; otherwise he could not describe it so well. Even so we must give most of the credit to the poet's imagination. It is the passage of the soul from the dominant sense of physical life to the dominant sense of physical death. When the sense of life is strong, the spirit must content itself with mere moments of vision and freedom, but as the sense of death becomes dominant, the spirit sees more steadily and is less constrained. It is Christian's pilgrimage to the Celestial City seen not as Bunyan saw it but in the light of modern science and evolution. The journey image occurs in many of Whitman's poems, in some where it is not recognized at once. In "When Lilacs Last in the Dooryard Bloom'd" it is suggested in the fact that the poet-hero hears the hermit-thrush singing its song of death from the beginning of the poem but he is only gradually drawn to it away from the powerful hold of the symbolic star of life.[552]

In other terms, the journey theme is one from chaos to form, from diversity to unity, from freedom to law, and it is readily discernible in Whitman's increasing attention to poetic form in "Leaves of Grass" from 1855 to 1868. If there is a relapse in the later poems to the formlessness of some of the earlier ones, it proves merely that Whitman's power of execution, particularly after his paralysis, was inferior to his power of conception. It is also evident in the increasing certainty with which he foresees the triumph of man through the moral law. . . .[553]

QUESTIONS FOR STUDY
AND TOPICS FOR WRITING

1. Whitman's Prefaces

1. Whitman uses a dialectical method to present his claims for attention, contrasting his poetry with that of the past and/or that of other nations. Specifically, what claims does he make concerning America's (and especially his own) poetry? What does Whitman surrender that poets of the past have made use of? Why is Whitman's so willing a surrender?

2. Whitman claims in 1855 that his expression will be "indirect," rather than direct, descriptive, or epic. What does he mean by these terms? Is his claim valid?

3. What modifications occur in Whitman's theory of *Leaves of Grass?* Why, in the prefaces of the 1870's, did he assume that the *Leaves* were completed? Does that assumption discredit his later claims concerning the fully developed *Leaves?* Why?

4. In "Song of Myself" the poet vows to allow Nature to speak "without check with original energy." If Nature speaks through the poet, what is his role? (Read Ralph Waldo Emerson's essay "The Poet" for a further statement of this aesthetic point of view. Did Whitman seek to conform to the model of Emerson's essay?) What is the poet's intended relationship with the reader?

5. For a short paper, select some phase of the prefaces (the literary tone, for example) and trace its changes from 1855 to 1888. Or compare the more formal statements of purpose in the prefaces with the informal comments in section 4. For a longer paper, trace the relationships between Whitman's theory and practice of poetry throughout his career.

2. Whitman's Poems

1. The poems are arranged in the approximate order of composition, though Whitman revised most of his poems, some extensively, for each new edition. On the basis of this rough chronological arrangement, explain the difference between Whitman's earlier poems and his later. What are the poetic characteristics of each?

2. "Tears," "Out of the Cradle Endlessly Rocking," "Bardic Symbols," and "On the Beach at Night" were all finally placed in the section of *Leaves of Grass* called "Sea-Drift." On the basis of these four poems what can you infer about the unity of that section? Do the poems develop a consistent point of view? Write a short paper analyzing these four poems. Or, for a longer paper, read all the poems in "Sea-Drift" for your analysis.

3. Choose some particular phase of the poems for a short analysis—for example, the Columbus figure in "Passage to India" and

"Prayer of Columbus"; water imagery in Whitman's poems; the function of catalogues in the poems. Or choose a single poem for detailed
analysis.

4. T. S. Eliot has used the term "objective correlative" to des-
ignate "a set of objects, a situation, a chain of events which shall be
the formula of expressing that *particular* emotion [the poet seeks to
convey]; such that, when the external facts, which must terminate in
sensory experience, are given, the emotion is immediately evoked"
(*Selected Essays of T. S. Eliot,* new edition. New York: Harcourt, Brace
and Company, 1950, pp. 124–125). Analyze the figure of Columbus in
"Prayer of Columbus" as an adequate objective correlative for the
emotions of Whitman. For a longer paper, compare this figure with
the ocean and the redwood tree in two other late poems, "Song of the
Redwood Tree" and "With Husky-Haughty Lips, O Sea."

3. Revisions of "Bardic Symbols"

1. Which of the revisions were apparently made to improve the
rhythm of the poem? For what other purposes did Whitman revise?
Why did he change punctuation marks? Is the 1881 poem an improvement over earlier versions?

2. It is sometimes said that Whitman experienced a personal and
emotional crisis in the late 1850's which affected poems of the 1860
edition, and that Whitman later sought to conceal the effects of the
crisis through revisions and deletions. Do the revisions of "Bardic
Symbols" support or challenge that theory?

3. Write a short paper analyzing the changes in "Bardic
Symbols." For a longer paper, analyze the revisions in several poems
and generalize about Whitman's methods of revision. (Variant readings may be found in the Camden edition, in Emory Holloway's *Inclusive Edition,* in separate editions of *Leaves of Grass,* or, most conveniently and authoritatively, in the forthcoming Variorum edition
of the poems: see Bibliography.)

4. Obiter Dicta on Poetry and Language

1. For what literary characteristics does Whitman praise other
writers? For what does he withhold praise? Do Whitman's critical
opinions throw light on his own poetic theories? How do you explain
varying opinions of a single writer (e.g., Milton)?

2. The conversations with Traubel toward the end of Whitman's
life were contemporaneous with "A Backward Glance o'er Travel'd
Roads." Does Whitman appear as the same sort of spokesman in both
sources? Characterize the picture of Whitman that emerges from the
reported conversations.

3. To what extent does Whitman's poetry conform to the principles set forth in the "Notes" on *Leaves of Grass?* Are Whitman's most
successful poems notable for the stylistic and thematic characteristics
he seeks to attain?

4. For a short paper, take a phase of Whitman's critical theory
(such as the relationship between poetry and prose). For a longer

paper, use all the resources of this section for a paper on Whitman's poetic theories, his poems, and his practical criticism.

5. In one of his many notebook entries, Whitman cites precedents for the review and interpretation of one's own work (Edmund Spenser as "E.K.," Leigh Hunt, etc.). Is there a question of literary ethics or morality involved in anonymous reviews of one's own work?

6. Is Whitman's self-critique valuable as criticism? In other words, does he cite and illuminate the salient points of his own work? If his commentary is defective, explain why and how.

5. Contemporary Critical Estimates: 1855–1892

1. To the first reviewers of *Leaves of Grass* (Norton, Hale, and the anonymous reviewer of *The Christian Examiner*) what seemed to be the most revolutionary features of the book? For what did these reviewers admire the book? What did they deplore? Compare their reviews with Whitman's anonymous review of the 1855 *Leaves*. Consult a facsimile edition of the 1855 *Leaves*. Is its physical appearance revolutionary? Would reviewers have been likely to base their judgments on the form as well as the content of the first edition? Are form and content consistent?

2. Edith Wharton, in *A Backward Glance* (New York and London: D. Appleton-Century Company, 1934, p. 186), records that Henry James in later life shared her opinion that Whitman was America's greatest poet. How do you account for this apparent change in James's opinion?

3. What, specifically, does James object to in Whitman? He has the voice of intelligence say: "art requires, above all things, a suppression of one's self, a subordination of one's self to an idea." Would Whitman accept such theoretical requirements? Are twentieth-century critics of Whitman (those represented in this volume) concerned with his expression or suppression of the self?

4. Throughout the 1880's, 1890's, and early 1900's there were frequent skirmishes between Whitman's partisans and his adversaries. Judging from the writings of Lanier, Swinburne, Symonds, and Burroughs, what were the strategies of attack and defense? Is it significant that Lanier and Swinburne are poets whereas Symonds and Burroughs are not?

6. Whitman's Form and Technique

1. What does Bliss Perry's discussion of Whitman contribute to criticism of the poet? Compare *Leaves of Grass* with one of the sources cited by Perry.

2. Matthiessen discusses three of Whitman's analogies for his poetry. Choose some other analogies that Whitman uses and make a comparable analysis of these. Is a poet's or critic's judgment of the value of a work revealed by his choice of and response to certain metaphors or analogies for the work? Trace critical attitudes toward Whitman on this basis.

3. Both Matthiessen and Adams (section 10) comment on the debt of Whitman's poetry to Samuel Taylor Coleridge's principle of the reconciliation of opposites, but the two critics differ on Whitman's success at executing his poems according to this principle. Write a short paper in which you examine one of Whitman's poems as the reconciliation of opposites. If necessary, refer to Coleridge's *Biographia Literaria,* chapters 13 and 14, for a fuller understanding of the principle.

4. Both Fausset and Daiches examine Whitman's innovations of form in the context of the nineteenth-century literary situation. How do they agree about that situation? What does Daiches add to Fausset's analysis which makes it possible for him to accept Whitman's innovations more completely than Fausset can? Do such critics as Daiches and Adams satisfactorily deal with objections to Whitman's form of the sort raised by Raymond?

5. Using Wiley's terms and approach, analyze the reiterative devices in a poem by Whitman.

7. Whitman's Prosody

1. Choose a short poem or a section of a longer poem by Whitman for prosodic analysis according to (1) the traditional terminology employed by Briggs (also used by Perry and by Allen and Davis in other sections), (2) the approach and terminology of Bradley, and (3) the terminology of structural linguistics employed by Schiller. If this last approach is unfamiliar, you may want to consult Henry Allan Gleason, *An Introduction to Descriptive Linguistics* (New York: Holt, 1955). For an additional example of this approach to poetry, see Archibald A. Hill, "An Analysis of *The Windhover:* An Experiment in Structural Method," *PMLA,* LXX (December 1955), 968–978.

2. Many commentators on Whitman's verse refer to its kinship with prose. Ross, however, regards such an opinion as a misconception. Write a short paper on Whitman's verse, analyzing its relationship to prose or poetry. How shall it be classified?

3. Choose one or more of the approaches to Whitman's prosody and apply it to some crucial passages in "Passage to India." Does the prosodic analysis lead to critical judgments of other kinds?

4. Bradley writes: "Unfortunately for the reception of *Leaves of Grass,* most critics and prosodists have been of the classical school." Challenge or substantiate the sentence by reference to the critical premises among the critics of *Leaves of Grass* whose work you know.

8. Whitman's Style and Language

1. Pound cites "polyglot borrowings," "vernacular coinages," and "archaic revivals." From the poems by Whitman available to you for study, cite examples of each of these linguistic features. What is the poetic effect of the examples you cite? What poetic effect does Pound attribute to Whitman's neologisms? Does she assume other effects—for example, picturesqueness? How does Pound's *attitude* toward the neologisms differ from that of Wendell?

2. How does what Marx says challenge or confirm Chase's point concerning Whitman's dilemma of a sensibility quickening only at opposite ends of the spectrum? Do Chase's general points here provide the basis for his criticism of "Passage to India" and the later poetry? Do Coy's statistics (her substantiating examples are mostly omitted) support Chase's view of Whitman's achievement?

3. Why does Jarrell provide so many different quotations from Whitman? Jarrell seems at first to rely solely on impressionistic taste, but later he provides some critical principles that justify his estimate of Whitman. Formulate these as best you can and discuss their validity.

4. What is Jarrell's *attitude* toward Whitman's poetry? What is his attitude toward the reader? What does he assume the reader's attitude toward Whitman is? Explain how these attitudes and assumptions determine the kind of essay Jarrell has written.

5. According to the critics represented in this volume, did Whitman actually achieve what he claimed to achieve, in language? Was his actual achievement more or less revolutionary than he thought?

6. For a short paper, discuss the language of one or more poems by Whitman (using the approach or terminology of whichever critic you choose to follow). Or examine Whitman's language against the background of his theories of language (as given, for instance, in sections 1 and 4 of this volume). For a longer paper, read further in Whitman's essays on language: "An American Primer," "Slang in America," "The American Idiom" (see Bibliography: Hollis), etc.; and formulate his theories in as coherent a scheme as possible. Or, most ambitiously, discuss the relationship between the language and the poetic values of *Leaves of Grass*. (Do not overlook "A Song of the Rolling Earth" and other poems, Henry James's review of *Drum-Taps*, Whitman's comment that perhaps *Leaves of Grass* was "only a language experiment," and other evidence not localized in this or another section.)

7. For a short paper, contrast Whitman's poetic language with that of one of his contemporaries (Lanier or Tennyson, for example). For a longer paper, consider Whitman's linguistic theories and practice in the context of his times.

9. Approaches to "Passage to India"

1. Chase disparages "Passage to India" (and the later poetry generally) because "productive tensions have been relaxed." Do Coffman and Adams (see section 10) find productive tensions in the poem? What are these tensions, and in what sense are they productive? Compare "Passage to India" with one or more of the late poems admired by Chase or with one of the early poems in which the "satyr-poet of the early 1850's" appears. For an application to fiction of the theory of "productive tensions," see Chase's *The American Novel and Its Tradition* (Garden City: Doubleday and Company, 1957).

2. Lovell, Miller, and Chase all refer to the three lines beginning, "Have we not stood here . . ." What does each critic see as the most important literary feature of the lines? Which is most useful to your aesthetic response to the lines?

3. What different insights are provided by the background information (Oliver), analysis of the imagery (Coffman), structural analysis (Miller), and analysis of the dramatic character of the poem (Allen and Davis)? Are these insights compatible?

4. In view of Whitman's comments about the poem in the prefaces and elsewhere, which critic seems closest to interpreting the poem as Whitman intended it? Which seems furthest from doing so?

5. The oratorical or "declamatory" character of the poem is observed by several writers. Is this feature, per se, a weakness? What were Whitman's theories about poetry and eloquence?

6. Adams (section 10), Oliver, and Lovell all refer to the continuing relevance of Whitman's poem, and especially its relevance to our current situation. Within what context does each critic find the poem to be relevant? If a poem is judged relevant to a particular time and situation, is it thereby robbed of "universality"?

7. Elsewhere in his essay Lovell says: "It is unfair to judge Whitman's poetry by any standard other than that of Whitman the poet." Does he follow this standard himself? Which critic or critics seem most conscious of this standard? Comment on Lovell's analysis of Whitman's "optimism" and "pessimism."

8. In *The Explicator,* IX (December 1950), Q2, Richard E. Amacher asks why Whitman mentions three achievements of the present but elaborates on only two of these, omitting the Atlantic cable. Refer to his query and to the answer by Ruth Stauffer in *The Explicator,* IX (May 1951), item 50. Is the query satisfactorily answered? Has Amacher anticipated the answers and disposed of them in advance? For a classroom exercise, prepare a query on "Passage to India" or another poem, exchange the queries with your classmates, and prepare answers to them. How would you answer Mr. Amacher's query?

9. For a short paper, evaluate the various critical essays on "Passage to India"; or apply the critical approach of one of the essays to another poem by Whitman. For a longer paper, refer to Fredson Bowers' articles (see Bibliography, p. 180), in which he describes the earliest manuscript of the poem, an accompanying notebook kept by Whitman, and a later version of the poem. On the basis of the notebook, the variant texts, and the final version (and whatever secondary sources you need), write a paper on the composition of "Passage to India." Or, on the basis of Whitman's various remarks about the poem and the work of the critics, write your own analysis and interpretation of the poem.

10. Evolution and Design of *Leaves of Grass*

1. To what extent do Miller, Triggs, Adams, and Story agree about the design of *Leaves of Grass?* Is there a "consensus structure" to the book? Is this structure sufficiently meaningful to justify claims for Whitman of the sort made by Triggs? Do critics who see a design to the completed book take sufficiently into account such objections as those raised by Asselineau?

2. Compare the critics' analyses with Whitman's own comments on design. Which critic seems most in harmony with Whitman? Is Whitman or his critics more helpful concerning the design of the book? Is a poet's commentary on his own work valid? Can you distinguish between comment about the meaning of a poem and comment about an intended design? Are both open to suspicion according to the doctrine of the "intentional fallacy"? (See W. K. Wimsatt, Jr., *The Verbal Icon* [Lexington: University of Kentucky Press, 1954], pp. 3–18.)

3. Examine all the poems in one of the sections of the completed *Leaves of Grass*. In a short paper, explain the unity of the section (using other versions of the section in earlier editions of Whitman's poems, if available). For a long paper, examine all the poems of *Leaves of Grass* with a view to determining the structure of the book; use Whitman's comments and those of the critics for whatever guidance they provide.

4. Are Cowley's judgments about relative merits of Whitman's early and late poems sound? Do Cowley's judgments conflict with implied or stated judgments about the late poems in criticism of "Passage to India"? Critics disagree about the "best" edition of Whitman, some preferring the 1855, some the 1881. Compare these two editions. What impression does each one make? Could the 1881 edition have preceded the 1855 (leaving aside the quantity of poetry in each edition)? Why or why not?

5. On what points do Adams and Van Doren differ about Whitman? Do they start from different critical premises, or do they disagree about the poet's execution? (You may want to consult the full texts of both essays before you answer.)

11. The Whitman Persona

1. Is it easy or difficult to separate Whitman the author from Whitman the hero-poet of *Leaves of Grass*? Why? Is it important to do so? Again, why?

2. Whitman once claimed not to have read the work of Ralph Waldo Emerson before 1855. Does this claim seem consistent with the open letter to Emerson in 1856? Why would Whitman want to obscure his debt to Emerson, or, for that matter, to George Sand?

3. All three critics represented in this section recognize a discrepancy between the author and the persona, yet each one accounts for the discrepancy in a different way. For a short paper, analyze the different explanations of the Whitman persona provided by Rourke, Shephard, and Stovall (and others: Chase, for example, or Cowley or Fiedler—see Bibliography).

4. Malcolm Cowley (see Bibliography, p. 174) once differentiated three Whitmans: (1) the printer, small politician, and editor; (2) the persona, "one of the roughs," who became the Good Gray Poet; and (3) the poet, a man who had little to say after 1860, and who lapsed into silence in 1874. Whitman number two, he adds, lived until 1892. What does this formulation imply about the origin of Whitman's poetic talent, the relative value of early and late poems, the usefulness

of the hero-poet as a unifying device in *Leaves of Grass,* etc.? In what ways would Stovall disagree with Cowley's implications?

5. Read Edgar Allan Poe's essay "The Philosophy of Composition," in which Poe recounts steps in the composition of his poem "The Raven." Contrast Whitman's comparable accounts of the writing of *Leaves of Grass* with Poe's essay. What would each author have us believe about his art?

6. For a long paper, trace the evolution of Whitman's persona from the earliest editions of *Leaves of Grass* to the latest. Or consider Whitman's "pose" as the consequence of his poetic theories. Or broaden the perspective to take in Romantic poets in general: for example, how do Wordsworth's poems compare with the theories expressed in the preface to *Lyrical Ballads* (second edition, 1800), the "Essay Supplementary to the Preface of 'Lyrical Ballads,'" and the letter to Lady Beaumont. For further treatment of the Romantic "dilemma," see Perry Miller's "Introduction" to *Consciousness in Concord* (Boston: Houghton Mifflin Company, 1958). Is Miller's analysis of Thoreau valid? valid for Whitman? valid for Romantic writers generally?

Additional Questions for Study

1. Is there a significant difference between British criticism of Whitman (here represented by Daiches, Fausset, Swinburne, and Symonds) and American? For further study consult Blodgett and Willard (see Bibliography, pp. 183, 186).

2. Among critics of Whitman represented here, Lanier, Swinburne, Jarrell, and Van Doren are poets of distinction. Do these critics approach Whitman in a special way unlike that of others represented here?

3. Many poets have written poems about Whitman: Swinburne, "To Walt Whitman in America"; Edwin Arlington Robinson, "Walt Whitman"; Hart Crane, the "Cape Hatteras" section of *The Bridge;* Stephen Vincent Benét, "Ode to Walt Whitman"; Ezra Pound, "A Pact"; and others (George Meredith, Karl Shapiro, and Witter Bynner, to name a few). What has been the poets' view of Whitman? Is it substantially different from that of the critics?

4. Numerous studies have been made of Whitman's relationship to music. Examine the evidence available and discuss Whitman's debt to music, or prepare a musical analysis of a single poem (cf. Brown—see Bibliography, p. 180).

5. Use the *Concordance of Walt Whitman's Leaves of Grass . . . ,* ed. Edwin Harold Eby (Seattle: University of Washington Press, 1955), to study some specific phases of Whitman's poetic diction, such as use of slang, abstractions, or contractions.

6. On the basis of the essays in this book, write an analysis of the tendency of Whitman studies from 1855 to the present (using as many more essays listed in the Bibliography as possible). For a shorter paper, analyze Whitman criticism for its strategies of attack and defense, and explain why these have changed through the years.

SELECTED BIBLIOGRAPHY
FOR FURTHER READING

The critical and scholarly writing about Whitman is, of course, voluminous. Earlier annotated listings appear in *Walt Whitman: Representative Selections*, ed. Floyd Stovall (New York: American Book Company, 1939), pp. liii–lxiii; Gay W. Allen, *Walt Whitman Handbook* (Chicago: Packard and Company, 1946), *passim;* Willard Thorp, "Walt Whitman" in *Eight American Authors*, ed. Floyd Stovall (New York: Modern Language Association of America, 1956), pp. 271–318; Thomas H. Johnson, "Walt Whitman" in *Literary History of the United States*, 3 vols., ed. Robert E. Spiller *et al.* (New York: The Macmillan Company, 1948), III, 759–768; and the *Bibliography Supplement* (to the above-cited *Literary History*), ed. Richard M. Ludwig (New York: The Macmillan Company, 1959), pp. 203–207. These works list earlier, fuller bibliographies, such as those in the Camden edition and the *Cambridge History of American Literature*.

The principle governing selection and annotation for this bibliographical list has been relevance to issues raised earlier in this volume by the poet, his critics, or the editor, to guide the student in further investigation of specific topics. Up-to-date listings of Whitman studies may be found in the continuing bibliographies published in the periodicals *American Literature, PMLA,* and *Walt Whitman Review,* and in the abstracts that appear in *Abstracts of English Studies.*

Writings by Whitman

The now authoritative ten-volume Camden edition of Whitman's writings is to be superseded by a new edition (in about fourteen volumes) published by New York University Press and edited by Whitman specialists, under the general editorship of Gay Wilson Allen and Sculley Bradley. The first volumes of this edition to be published are two volumes of *The Correspondence of Walt Whitman,* ed. Edwin Haviland Miller (New York: New York University Press, 1961).

The NYU edition will also contain much of the uncollected Whitman material which has appeared variously in the past fifty or sixty years (e.g., Emory Holloway's *Uncollected Poetry and Prose*). For listings of these editions, consult the fuller bibliographical aids listed in the headnote to the bibliography.

Writings about Whitman

Writings about Whitman are separated into three groups for easy reference. Items from which excerpts appear in this volume are marked *. These are not annotated unless the excerpt above gives a misleading or inadequate impression of the complete essay or book. In addition to criticism listed here, the student should not overlook introductions to frequently reprinted editions of Whitman's work. To name only a few: *The Best of Whitman,* ed. Harold Blodgett (New York: Ronald Press, 1953); *The Portable Whitman,* ed. Mark Van Doren (New York: The Viking Press, 1945); and the Riverside edition of *Complete Poetry and Selected Prose,* ed. James E. Miller, Jr. (Boston: Houghton Mifflin Company, 1959).

General Studies of Whitman's Poetic Art

*Adams, Richard P. "Whitman: A Brief Revaluation," *Tulane Studies in English,* V (1955), 111–149.

Allen, Gay Wilson. *American Prosody.* New York: American Book Co., 1935. Chapter VIII: Whitman. A demonstration of Whitman's poetic devices, including parallelism, the enclosing "envelope," etc., concluding with analysis of the "Lilacs" poem.

——————. *The Solitary Singer: A Critical Biography of Walt Whitman.* New York: The Macmillan Co., 1955. The standard biography, with valuable information on all aspects of Whitman's life and poetry.

——————. *Walt Whitman Handbook.* Chicago: Packard and Co., 1946. The most valuable chapters in considering Whitman's poetry are II: "The Growth of *Leaves of Grass* and the *Prose Works*" and V: "Literary Technique in *Leaves of Grass.*" In the latter, Allen summarizes scholarship to 1946, including his own.

——————. "Walt Whitman's 'Long Journey' Motif," *Journal of English and Germanic Philology,* XXXVIII (January 1939), 76–95. The journey motif includes a scientific theory (evolution), a metaphysics, a religious faith, and personal philosophy; also Whitman's conception of the poet's role, style, etc.

——————, ed. *Walt Whitman Abroad.* Syracuse: Syracuse University Press, 1955. Translations of significant essays on Whitman by foreign scholars and critics.

*——————— and Charles T. Davis, eds. *Walt Whitman's Poems: Selections with Critical Aids.* New York: New York University Press, 1955. Introduction: pp. 1–51.

*Asselineau, Roger. *L'Évolution de Walt Whitman après la première Édition des Feuilles d'Herbe.* Paris: Didier, 1954. The first part of this work has been translated by the author, with the assistance of Richard P. Adams: *The Evolution of Walt Whitman.* Cambridge: The Belknap Press, 1960. A second volume will follow.

Austin, Mary. *The American Rhythm: Studies and Reëxpressions of Amerindian Songs,* new ed. Boston and New York: Houghton Mifflin Co., 1930. Since verse forms derive from the human being's rhythmic response to the land, it was inevitable that America should develop new forms resembling aboriginal forms. Whitman is important here but limited by adolescent intelligence and *relative* unfamiliarity with the land.

*Bradley, Sculley. "The Fundamental Metrical Principle in Whitman's Poetry," *American Literature,* X (January 1939), 437–459.

——————. "The Problem of a Variorum Edition of Whitman's *Leaves of Grass,*" *English Institute Annual: 1941,* ed. Rudolf Kirk. New York:

Columbia University Press, 1942. Pp. 129–157. On the revisions, growth, and unity of the work and editorial difficulties. Includes three versions of "On the Beach at Night, Alone."

*Briggs, Arthur E. *Walt Whitman: Thinker and Artist.* New York: Philosophical Library, 1952.

Buchanan, Robert. "Walt Whitman," in *David Gray and Other Essays, Chiefly on Poetry.* London: Sampson Low, Son, and Marston, 1868. Pp. 203–220. Despite "prodigious" faults Whitman is the clear forerunner of American poets with a genuine ministry to America.

*Burroughs, John. "Walt Whitman and His Recent Critics," in *In Re Walt Whitman,* ed. Horace L. Traubel, Richard M. Bucke, and Thomas B. Harned. Philadelphia: David McKay, 1893. Pp. 93–108.

*_____. *Whitman: A Study.* Boston and New York: Houghton Mifflin and Co., 1896.

Campbell, Killis. "The Evolution of Whitman as Artist," *American Literature,* VI (November 1934), 254–263. Through constant revisions Whitman's poetry gained in taste, in picturesqueness and comeliness of phrase, and in control of rhythm and cadence.

_____. "Miscellaneous Notes on Whitman," University of Texas *Studies in English,* XIV (1934), 116–122. Two of the five notes concern Whitman's language; one, his use of the figure *metanoia.*

Canby, Henry Seidel. "Walt Whitman," in *Literary History of the United States,* 3 vols., ed. Robert E. Spiller *et al.* New York: The Macmillan Co., 1948. I, 472–498. General survey of life and works, with detailed discussion of "Song of Myself" and a section on Whitman's prosody.

Carpenter, Edward. *Days with Walt Whitman: With Some Notes on His Life and Work.* London: George Allen and Unwin, Ltd., 1906. One note is on "The Poetic Form of 'Leaves of Grass,' " where it is argued that Whitman's form and content are inseparable, that his form and rhythms need no more justification than do those of Beethoven or Wagner.

Carpenter, Frederic I. "Walt Whitman's Eidólon," in *American Literature and the Dream.* New York: Philosophical Library, Inc., 1955. Pp. 40–50. The admitted discrepancy between poetic "Walt" and Walter Whitman can be interpreted not as "pose" but as an effort to realize an ideal, in poetry and in life. In "Passage to India" Whitman reconciles European tradition and the American dream, nature and man.

Catel, Jean. *Rythme et langage dans la 1re édition des "Leaves of Grass" (1855).* Paris: Les Editions Rieder, n.d. [1930]. A study of diction, phrasing, etc., in notes and drafts before 1855 and the poems of the first edition, stressing rhetoric.

*Chase, Richard. *Walt Whitman Reconsidered.* New York: William Sloane Associates, Inc., 1955.

Cheney, John Vance. *That Dome in Air.* Chicago: A. C. McClurg and Co., 1895. Although Whitman was "a giant of his shaggy, hearty kind," it is disheartening "that any man of culture can find Walt a great poet."

Colum, Padraic. "The Poetry of Walt Whitman," *The New Republic,* XIX (June 14, 1919), 213–215. Whitman is a master of language and of his special verse-norm; he is also an inspired rhapsodist and a tender poet of reconciliation and death.

Conner, Frederick W. *Cosmic Optimism: A Study of the Interpretation of Evolution by American Poets from Emerson to Robinson.* Gainesville: University of Florida Press, 1949. Chapter IV: "Whitman: High Tide." Examination of Whitman's quasi-Hegelian pantheistic animism and its embodiment in the poems, chiefly in their journeying character.

Cory, Robert E. "The Prosody of Walt Whitman," *North Dakota Quarterly,* XXVIII (Summer 1960), 74–79. Whitman's line is divisible into segments (usually four), consisting of sustained vowels and unstressed syllables clustered about these voiced elements. The segment comprises "one interval of a slow but regularly recurring beat in the time."

Cowley, Malcolm. "Walt Whitman's Buried Masterpiece," *Saturday Review,* XLII (October 31, 1959), 11–13, 32–34. The 1855 *Leaves* is the best, perhaps the only unified edition. "Song of Myself," Whitman's greatest work, is best in its unrevised state. It is a "buried masterpiece."

*_____. "Whitman: The Poet," *The New Republic,* CXVII (October 20, 1947), 27–30.

_____. "Whitman: The Poet and the Mask," Introduction to *The Complete Poetry and Prose of Walt Whitman,* 2 vols. New York: Farrar, Strauss, and Young, Inc., 1948. I, 3–39. (See above: Questions for Study *s.v.* "The Whitman Persona.")

*Coy, Rebecca. "A Study of Whitman's Diction," University of Texas *Studies in English,* XVI (1936), 115–124.

*Daiches, David. "Walt Whitman as Innovator," in *The Young Rebel in American Literature,* ed. Carl Bode. London: Heinemann, 1959. Pp. 25–48.

_____. "Walt Whitman: Impressionist Prophet," in *Leaves of Grass One Hundred Years After,* ed. Milton Hindus. Stanford: Stanford University Press, 1955. Pp. 109–122. Whitman was unique among poets of the English language in his combination of the prophetic and confessional—a poetic method with dangers, but one which manifested a complex vision.

De Selincourt, Basil. *Walt Whitman: A Critical Study.* London: Martin Secker, 1914. Includes discussion of form and style, as well as of the *Calamus* and *Children of Adam* clusters.

Ellis, Havelock. *The New Spirit,* 3rd ed. London: Walter Scott, 1892. Pp. 89–132: "Whitman." Self-revelation of human personality, for which all art searches, is precious and enduring. Herein is the might of *Leaves of Grass.*

*Erskine, John. "A Note on Whitman's Prosody," *Studies in Philology,* XX (July 1923), 336–344.

*Fausset, Hugh I'Anson. *Walt Whitman: Poet of Democracy.* New Haven: Yale University Press, 1942.

Fiedler, Leslie. "Images of Walt Whitman," in *Leaves of Grass One Hundred Years After* [see above *s.v.* Daiches]. Pp. 55–73. Whitman's effort to create an image has been disastrously successful. Four aspects of the image—prophet, faith healer, sexual emancipator, and democrat—have interfered with his availability as current inspiration. He must be recaptured as elegiac poet and artificer.

_____. "Walt Whitman Reconsidered," *New Leader*, XLII (March 2, 9, 1959), 20–22, 19–21. Through revision, expurgation, and rearrangement Whitman sought to make his book conform to the latest version of himself. But he is best remembered as a poet of love and death.

Foerster, Norman. *American Criticism: A Study in Literary Theory from Poe to the Present*. Boston and New York: Houghton Mifflin Co., 1928. Chapter IV: "Whitman." Whitman is called the foremost "prophetic" critic of his age, significant for speculation on the nature of poetry and expression of organic theory.

_____. *Nature in American Literature: Studies in the Modern View of Nature*. New York: The Macmillan Co., 1923. Chapter VI: "Whitman." Enthusiastic rather than exact in his nature lore, Whitman is pre-eminently the poet of the sea and of healthy joy in nature.

Gohdes, Clarence. "Democracy in Free Verse," in Arthur Hobson Quinn et al., *The Literature of the American People*. New York: Appleton-Century-Crofts, Inc., 1957. Pp. 598–621. A general survey of Whitman's life and work, concluding with an analysis of the arrangement of the 1881 edition.

*Hale, Edward Everett. *"Leaves of Grass,"* North American Review, LXXXII (January 1856), 275–277.

Harris, Lynn Harold. "Walt Whitman as Artist and Teacher," *South Atlantic Quarterly*, XX (April 1921), 120–136. Whitman is a master of phrasing and rhythm, but his poetry is disfigured by coarseness, lapses, and monotony. He is more notable as teacher than artist.

Hollis, C. Carroll. "Whitman and the American Idiom," *Quarterly Journal of Speech*, XLIII (December 1957), 408–420. Reconstructs Whitman's essay "The American Idiom" from manuscript fragments in the Feinberg collection.

Holloway, Emory. *Whitman: An Interpretation in Narrative*. New York and London: Alfred A. Knopf, 1926. Some incidental criticism in a predominantly biographical interpretation.

Howard, Leon. *Literature and the American Tradition*. Garden City: Doubleday and Co., Inc., 1960. Chapter 6: "The Time of Tension." Contrasts Melville and Whitman in that the latter found new symbolism but relaxed the tensions Melville found in old. Whitman's "I" is the poet, "natural" man, the American, and racial man. Most comprehensible as symbolic poet.

_____. "Walt Whitman and the American Language," *American Speech*, V (August 1930), 441–451. Summary and analysis of Whitman's comments on language in *An American Primer, Notes and Fragments*, and elsewhere, stressing remarks on place names, inclusiveness, and freedom of usage.

Jannacone, P. *La Poesia di Walt Whitman e l'evoluzione delle forme ritmiche*. Torino, 1898. The argument of this study is summarized in William Struthers, "An Italian Writer on Whitman," *The Conservator*, XI (April 1900), 21–22; (May 1900), 38–40; (June 1900), 53–54; (October 1900), 120–121; (November 1900), 135; and XII (March 1901), 7–9.

*Jarrell, Randall. "Some Lines from Whitman," in *Poetry and the Age*. New York: Alfred A. Knopf, 1953. Pp. 112–132.

Johnson, Maurice O. "Walt Whitman as a Critic of Literature," University of Nebraska *Studies in Language, Literature and Criticism*, XVI (1938), 1–73. "For great literature Whitman prescribed restraint, originality, purpose, optimism, universality, concern with Nature, concern with contemporary life, and emphasis on democracy" (p. 69).

Kennedy, William Sloane. *The Fight of a Book for the World*. West Yarmouth, Mass.: The Stonecroft Press, 1926. Part II contains observations on revisions and "Elucidations and Analyses of Difficult Poems."

——————. *Reminiscences of Walt Whitman: With Extracts from His Letters and Remarks on His Writings*. London: Alexander Gardner, 1896. Part II: "Drift and Cumulus." Explains *Leaves of Grass* as a trilogy celebrating the Body, Democracy, and Religion (also the structure of "Song of Myself"). Part III: "The Style of Leaves of Grass." Praises style for freedom and resemblance to nature, musicality (Whitman the "Wagner of poetry"), and resemblance to Oriental poetry.

*Lanier, Sidney. *The English Novel: A Study in the Development of Personality*, rev. ed. New York: Charles Scribner's Sons, 1897.

Lawrence, D. H. *Studies in Classic American Literature*. New York: Thomas Seltzer, 1923. Chapter 12: "Whitman." On the relationship between Whitman's conception of the self, death as a theme in his poetry, and confusions in his understanding of true sympathy.

*"Leaves of Grass," *The Christian Examiner*, LXI (November 1856), 471–473.

Lewis, R. W. B. *The American Adam: Innocence, Tragedy and Tradition in the Nineteenth Century*. Chicago: University of Chicago Press, 1955. Chapter 2: "The New Adam: Holmes and Whitman." Whitman, a member of the "party of hope," sought to re-establish natural unfallen man in the present. He characterizes Adam in his poems, which seem to come into being as into a new world.

Marks, Alfred H. "Whitman's Triadic Imagery," *American Literature*, XXIII (March 1951), 99–126. On Whitman's poetic use of Hegelian dialectic, with analyses of "Chanting the Square Deific," "Out of the Cradle . . . ," and other poems.

*Marx, Leo. "The Vernacular Tradition in American Literature," in *Studies in American Culture: Dominant Ideas and Images*, ed. Joseph J. Kwiat and Mary C. Turpie. Minneapolis: University of Minnesota Press, 1960. Pp. 109–122.

*Matthiessen, F. O. *American Renaissance: Art and Expression in the Age of Emerson and Whitman*. New York: Oxford University Press, 1941. Book Four: "Whitman," pp. 515–656.

Miller, James E., Jr. "Whitman and the Province of Poetry," *Arizona Quarterly*, XIV (Spring 1958), 5–19. Whitman's insistence that poetry mirror the realities, not the surface, of life accounts for the nature of his treatment of the past, and of myth, and his use of science.

More, Paul Elmer. *Shelburne Essays*, Fourth Series. Boston and New York: Houghton Mifflin Co., 1906. Pp. 180–211: "Walt Whitman." To get at Whitman one must overlook the disciples and read Whitman, who is often the preacher of poetry rather than the poet. Nevertheless, his verse is less lawless than supposed. Fond of dactylic measure and hexameter.

*Norton, Charles Eliot. "Whitman's *Leaves of Grass,*" *Putnam's Monthly,* VI (September 1855), 321–323.

Noyes, Carleton. *An Approach to Walt Whitman.* Boston and New York: Houghton Mifflin Co., 1910. Chapter 2: "Whitman's Art." "It is certain that Whitman has caught and registered something of the sinuous, mighty pulse of Nature."

Nuhn, Ferner. "*Leaves of Grass* Viewed as an Epic," *Arizona Quarterly,* VII (Winter 1951), 324–338. Like other epics, it comes at an early stage of the civilization it celebrates, is in verse of dignity and grandeur, and presents a hero overcoming tests: "an epic of the inner self . . . in its growth, struggle, and journey through the . . . universe."

O'Higgins, Harvey. "Alias Walt Whitman," *Harper's Magazine,* CLVIII (May 1929), 698–707. Whitman's petty deceptions and his lifelong "pose" discredit his poetic message and explain why he has remained unaccepted by America.

Pearce, Roy Harvey. "On the Continuity of American Poetry," *Hudson Review,* X (Winter 1957–58), 518–539. Strategies by which Poe, Emerson, Whitman, and Dickinson sought to universalize a poetry of the self in an anti-poetic culture. Pearce published a book of this title in 1961.

*Perry, Bliss. *Walt Whitman: His Life and Work.* Boston and New York: Houghton Mifflin and Co., 1906.

Pound, Louise. "Walt Whitman and the French Language," *American Speech,* I (May 1926), 421–430. A listing of French words borrowed by Whitman in his poetry and prose.

*————. "Walt Whitman's Neologisms," *American Mercury,* IV (February 1925), 199–201.

Powys, John Cowper. *Visions and Revisions: A Book of Literary Devotions.* New York: G. Arnold Shaw, 1915. Pp. 281–289: "Walt Whitman." Whitman's "free" poetry obeys the inflexible laws of his own creative instinct. A great poet, he is especially remarkable for intimations about love and the "magical *ugliness*" of parts of Nature.

Pritchard, John Paul. *Criticism in America.* Norman: University of Oklahoma Press, 1956. Chapter 6: On Whitman. Relates Whitman's theories and criticism to those of liberal New York group, Young America.

Rahv, Philip. "Paleface and Redskin," in *Image and Idea.* New York: New Directions, 1949. Pp. 1–10. Whitman, the Redskin, and Henry James, the Paleface, represent antipodes of the fragmented American literary imagination.

*Raymond, George L. *Art in Theory,* 2nd ed. New York and London: G. P. Putnam's Sons, 1909.

Reed, Harry B. "The Heraclitan Obsession of Walt Whitman," *The Personalist,* XV (April 1934), 125–138. Despite his monist metaphysics, Whitman was poetically and psychologically fascinated by diversity. Hence the sense of movement in Whitman. Portions of several poems are analyzed.

*Ross, E. C. "Whitman's Verse," *Modern Language Notes,* XLV (June 1930), 363–364.

Rountree, Thomas J. "Whitman's Indirect Expression and Its Application to 'Song of Myself,'" *PMLA,* LXXIII (December 1958), 549–555. On the necessity for a reciprocal relationship between poet and reader in Whitman's poems and its aesthetic results, illustrated by analysis of "Song of Myself."

Sandeen, Ernest. "Walt Whitman, 1819–1892: Ego in New Eden," in *American Classics Reconsidered: A Christian Appraisal,* ed. Harold C. Gardiner. New York: Charles Scribner's Sons, 1958. Pp. 229–263. The hero-ego is an image by which Whitman seeks his own salvation, necessitating rejection of orthodox moral standards. Contrasts Whitman with Kierkegaard, who regarded the self as ethical whereas Whitman's is pre-ethical.

Santayana, George. "The Poetry of Barbarism," in *Interpretations of Poetry and Religion.* New York: Charles Scribner's Sons, 1900. Pp. 166–216. Characterizes Whitman's poetry as sensuality touched with mysticism. "When the intellect is in abeyance . . . Walt Whitman is a welcome companion."

*Schiller, Andrew. "An Approach to Whitman's Metrics," *Emerson Society Quarterly,* No. 22 (I Quarter 1961), pp. 23–25.

Schyberg, Frederik. *Walt Whitman,* trans. Evie Allison Allen. New York: Columbia University Press, 1951. The longest chapter, "Leaves of Grass, *1855–89,*" is a detailed examination of successive editions, with a view to understanding Whitman, especially his sexual nature.

*Scott, Fred Newton. "A Note on Walt Whitman's Prosody," *Journal of English and Germanic Philology,* VII:2 (1907–8), 134–153.

——————. "The Most Fundamental Differentia of Poetry and Prose," *PMLA,* XIX (1904), 250–269. Concludes that "poetry is communication in language for expression's sake; prose is expression in language for communication's sake."

Shephard, Esther. "An Inquiry into Whitman's Method of Turning Prose into Poetry," *Modern Language Quarterly,* XIV (March 1953), 43–59. Comparison of a Whitman poem with its prose source (when one exists) usually results in devaluation of the poem because Whitman's method "is too often easy and so does not allow the reader to derive pleasure from the writer's artistry."

——————. "Possible Sources of Some of Whitman's Ideas and Symbols in *Hermes Mercurius Trismegistus* and Other Works," *Modern Language Quarterly,* XIV (March 1953), 60–81. Argues that Whitman was acquainted with esoteric sources, including the *Divine Pymander of Hermes Mercurius Trismegistus* (quoted in *The Dial,* 1844).

Shimizu, Haruo. "A Study of Whitman's Imagery," *Walt Whitman Review,* V (June 1959), 26–28. Summary of author's book in Japanese. Concludes that major images combined in journey of the soul toward eternal life.

Spiller, Robert E. *The Cycle of American Literature: An Essay in Historical Criticism.* New York: The Macmillan Co., 1955. Chapter V: "Romantic Crisis." Compares Whitman and Melville. *Leaves of Grass,* the growth of which is traced, is called an "heroic or racial epic."

Stedman, Edmund Clarence. *Poets of America.* Boston and New York: Houghton Mifflin and Co., 1885. Chapter X: "Whitman." Notable lyric poet. More original in style than versification.

Stewart, Randall. *American Literature and Christian Doctrine.* Baton Rouge: Louisiana State University Press, 1958. Pp. 60–65. Whitman's poems, especially the catalogues, express his democratic humanitarianism, but it is not the Christian equality of humility.

*Story, Irving C. "The Structural Pattern of *Leaves of Grass*," *Pacific University Bulletin,* XXXVIII (January 1942), 2–12.

Stovall, Floyd. "Main Drifts in Whitman's Poetry," *American Literature,* IV (March 1932), 3–21. The drifts are from individualism to nationalism and toward internationalism, from love of freedom toward love of law, from materialistic pantheism to highly spiritualized idealism.

―――――. "Walt Whitman: The Man and the Myth," *South Atlantic Quarterly,* LIV (October 1955), 538–551. The greatness of Whitman is the greatness of the completed *Leaves,* which matured like a human personality, not that of the "fragmentary and immature" first edition. The hero is the product of Whitman's imagination, as Hamlet was a product of Shakespeare's.

Sutton, Walter. "The Analysis of Free Verse Form, Illustrated by a Reading of Whitman," *Journal of Aesthetics and Art Criticism,* XVIII (December 1959), 241–254. Analysis of several poems by Whitman (especially "Out of the Cradle . . ."), under the headings of sound, syntax, image, and meaning, to illustrate their interrelationship in a complex poem.

Swayne, Mattie. "Whitman's Catalogue Rhetoric," *University of Texas Studies in English,* XXI (1941), 162–178. Catalogues in their concreteness, their primal quality, etc., are essential to Whitman's poetic theory and practice. To reject them is to reject virtually all of Whitman.

*Swinburne, Algernon Charles. "Whitmania," *Fortnightly Review,* XLVIII (August 1887), 170–176.

*Symonds, John Addington. *Walt Whitman: A Study.* London: John C. Nimmo, 1893.

Thomson, James ("B.V."). *Walt Whitman: The Man and the Poet.* London: Bertram Dobell, 1910. Reprinting of two essays of the 1870's, mostly biographical and polemical.

*Triggs, Oscar Lovell. "The Growth of 'Leaves of Grass,'" in *The Complete Writings of Walt Whitman,* Camden edition, 10 vols., ed. Richard Maurice Bucke, Thomas B. Harned, and Horace L. Traubel. New York and London: G. P. Putnam's Sons, 1902. X, 101–134.

*Van Doren, Mark. "The Poet," in *Walt Whitman: Man, Poet, Philosopher.* Washington, D.C.: Library of Congress, 1955. Pp. 15–33. Also included in the pamphlet: Gay Wilson Allen, "The Man," pp. 1–14; and David Daiches, "The Philosopher," pp. 35–53.

―――――. "Walt Whitman, Stranger," *American Mercury,* XXXV (July 1935), 277–285. Whitman, who may not have understood his own homosexual and erethistic nature, wrote poems about himself and about the man he wanted to be. The hero of *Leaves of Grass* is quite unlike the author.

Watts[-Dunton], Theodore. "Walt Whitman," *The Athenaeum* (April 2, 1892), pp. 436–437.

Weathers, Willie T. "Whitman's Poetic Translations of His 1855 Preface," *American Literature*, XIX (March 1947), 21–40. The preface, unreprinted until 1888, was the major source of four poems in 1856, especially the one later entitled "By Blue Ontario's Shore," and provided words and phrases for others. Whitman discontinued such use of preface after 1860.

Ware, Lois. "Poetic Conventions in *Leaves of Grass*," *Studies in Philology*, XXVI (January 1929), 47–57. Illustrates frequency of alliteration, assonance, parallelism, etc., in the poems.

Wells, Henry W. *The American Way of Poetry*. New York: Columbia University Press, 1943. Pp. 29–43. On the combination of objective and subjective in Whitman's work, with analysis of "Song of Myself."

*Wendell, Barrett. *A Literary History of America*. New York: Charles Scribner's Sons, 1900.

Criticism of Individual Poems

(Many of the general critical works listed above also contain discussions of individual poems.)

Adams, Richard P. "Whitman's 'Lilacs' and the Tradition of Pastoral Elegy," *PMLA*, LXXII (June 1957), 479–487. Of the recognized conventions of pastoral elegy Whitman rejects only the specifically *pastoral* and the personal. "Lilacs" is similar to "Adonais" in many respects—in the achievement of beauty out of death and suffering, in the context of Romantic belief.

Allen, Gay Wilson. "On the Trochaic Meter of 'Pioneers! O Pioneers!'" *American Literature*, XX (January 1949), 449–451. Reply to Fletcher (*q.v.*), arguing that poem can be scanned in trochaic meter.

————. "Whitman's 'When Lilacs Last in the Dooryard Bloom'd,'" *The Explicator*, X (June 1952), item 55. Reply to Jones (*q.v.*) on burial imagery of section 11, which Allen relates to Egyptology.

Bowers, Fredson. "The Earliest Manuscript of Whitman's 'Passage to India' and Its Notebook," *Bulletin of the New York Public Library*, LXI (July 1957), 319–352.

————, ed. *Whitman's Manuscripts: Leaves of Grass (1860)*. Chicago: University of Chicago Press, 1955. "Introduction," pp. xxiii–lxxiv. Description of manuscripts and discussion of growth of 1860 edition and its principal poems, "Starting from Paumanok" and the *Calamus* and *Enfans d'Adam* clusters.

————. "The Manuscript of Whitman's 'Passage to India,'" *Modern Philology*, LI (November 1953), 102–117. A reprint of the Harvard manuscript (which apparently derives from the "earliest": see above), a collation of it with extant proof sheets, and an analysis of their relationship to the first printed edition.

Brown, Calvin S. *Music and Literature: A Comparison of the Arts*. Athens: University of Georgia Press, 1948. Chapter XV: "The Musical Development of Symbols: Whitman." The exhibit for analysis is "When Lilacs Last in the Dooryard Bloom'd."

Burke, Kenneth. "Policy Made Personal: Whitman's Verse and Prose— Salient Traits" in *Leaves of Grass One Hundred Years After* [see above s.v. Daiches]. Pp. 74–108. An examination of the way in which the policy of *Democratic Vistas* is made personal in the language of *Leaves of Grass,* concluding with an exemplary analysis of "When Lilacs Last in the Dooryard Bloom'd."

Clarke, Helen A. "Passage to India," *The Conservator,* VI (March 1895), 7–10. Analysis of the poem stressing its religious character, providing "the most advanced anthropomorphic conception of God that has appeared in literature."

Coffman, Stanley K., Jr. " 'Crossing Brooklyn Ferry': A Note on the Catalogue Technique in Whitman's Poetry," *Modern Philology,* LI (May 1954), 225–232. Stresses artistic handling of catalogues in sections 3 and 9 to reveal structure and meaning of poem: statements and reconciliation of sympathy and pride.

✱_____. "Form and Meaning in Whitman's 'Passage to India,' " *PMLA,* LXX (June 1955), 337–349.

_____. "Whitman's 'Song of the Broad-Axe,' Stanza 1, Section 1," *The Explicator,* XII (April 1954), item 39. Interpretation of figurative language and rhythms of one of few examples of rhymed verse in *Leaves of Grass* as "an act of magic."

Cooke, Alice L. "A Note on Whitman's Symbolism in 'Song of Myself,' " *Modern Language Notes,* LXV (April 1950), 228–232. An interpretation of the opening lines of section 2 to show that Whitman approached knowledge through the concrete, as a scientist.

Feidelson, Charles N., Jr. *Symbolism and American Literature.* Chicago: University of Chicago Press, 1953. Pages 16–27 discuss "Starting from Paumanok" and "When Lilacs Last in the Dooryard Bloom'd" as enactments of the symbolic imagination, poems that came into being through realization, not perception.

Fletcher, Edward G. " 'Pioneers! O Pioneers!' " *American Literature,* XIX (November 1947), 259–261. A metrical analysis of one of Whitman's more regular poems, stressing its alliterative and accentual character. (See above s.v. Allen.)

Gohdes, Clarence. "A Comment on Section 5 of Whitman's 'Song of Myself,' " *Modern Language Notes,* LXIX (December 1954), 583–586. The uniqueness of Whitman's mysticism is its attendant sense of human ties (unlike solitariness of most mysticism).

_____. "Section 50 of Whitman's 'Song of Myself,' " *Modern Language Notes,* LXXV (December 1960), 654–656. Though ambiguous, the section seems to be concerned with mystical intuition.

Griffith, Clark. "Sex and Death: The Significance of Whitman's *Calamus* Themes," *Philological Quarterly,* XXXIX (January 1960), 18–38. Whitman's recognition of the incompatibility of his homosexual nature with the sexual program of 1855 and 1856 accounts for the character of

Calamus poems, "Out of the Cradle . . . ," etc., in the 1860 edition, and the apparent determination to cease writing poetry.

Huggard, William A. "Whitman's Poem of Personalism," *The Personalist,* XXVIII (July 1947), 273–278. Analysis of thought of "Song of Myself."

Jones, Joseph. "When Lilacs Last in the Dooryard Bloom'd," *The Explicator,* IX (April 1951), item 42. Comparison of language of sections 10 and 11 about decoration of tomb with that of Emerson in "The Poet" on emblems. (See above *s.v.* Allen.)

Kallsen, T. J. " 'Song of Myself': Logical Unity Through Analogy," West Virginia University *Philological Papers,* IX (June 1953), 32–40. On the grass symbol and the "short-journey" motif as unifying devices in the poem.

*Lovell, John, Jr. "Appreciating Whitman: 'Passage to India,' " *Modern Language Quarterly,* XXI (June 1960), 131–141.

McElderry, B. R., Jr. "The Inception of 'Passage to India,' " *PMLA,* LXXI (September 1956), 837–839. Inferences about Whitman's interest in Western railroad based on notebook described by Bowers (see above).

*Miller, James E., Jr. *A Critical Guide to Leaves of Grass.* Chicago: University of Chicago Press, 1957. Part I contains analyses of major poems; Part II, a discussion of the structure of *Leaves of Grass.*

——————. "Whitman and Eliot: The Poetry of Mysticism," *Southwest Review,* XLIII (Spring 1958), 113–123. On the similarities between "Song of Myself" and *Four Quartets:* form, musical analogies, mystical insight, poet as seer, etc., separated chiefly by divergent ideals of happiness and humility.

Miner, Earl Roy. "The Background, Date, and Composition of Whitman's 'A Broadway Pageant,' " *American Literature,* XXVII (November 1955), 403–405. On changes of emphasis through revisions of the poem.

*Oliver, Egbert S. " 'The Seas Are All Cross'd': Whitman on American and World Freedom," *Western Humanities Review,* IX (Autumn 1955), 303–312. Reprinted in *American Review* (New Delhi), I (1956), 18–29.

Pearce, Roy Harvey. "Toward an American Epic," *Hudson Review,* XII (Autumn 1959), 362–377. Three examples of American epic—Joel Barlow's *Columbiad,* Ezra Pound's *Cantos,* and "Song of Myself"—each of which seeks to create, rather than memorialize, a hero. Whitman's poem is in four parts, ending with sections 5, 16, 25, and 52, and proceeds rhythmically or dialectically.

Sixbey, George L. " 'Chanting the Square Deific'—A Study in Whitman's Religion," *American Literature,* IX (May 1937), 171–195. A detailed interpretation of the poem as "an intensely subjective statement of Whitman's theological tenets."

Smith, Henry Nash. *Virgin Land: The American West as Symbol and Myth.* Cambridge: Harvard University Press, 1950. Chapter 4: "Walt Whitman and Manifest Destiny" of Book I: "Passage to India." Whitman's "Passage to India" and kindred poems gave imaginative expression to an American political and cultural ideal.

Spitzer, Leo. *"Explication De Texte* Applied to Walt Whitman's Poem 'Out of the Cradle Endlessly Rocking,' " *ELH: A Journal of English Literary History,* XVI (September 1949), 229–249. Detailed treatment of Whitman's poem in the context of European literature.

Stovall, Floyd. *American Idealism.* Norman: University of Oklahoma Press, 1943. Pages 79–96, on Whitman, include detailed analysis of "Chanting the Square Deific."

Strauch, Carl F. "The Structure of Walt Whitman's Song of Myself," *English Journal,* XXVII (1938), 597–607. Divides poem into five parts, ending with sections 18, 25, 38, 41, and 52. First two sections comprise half of poem. Topics: the Self, definition of Self, life flowing in upon Self, the Superman, larger questions of life and mystic affirmation.

Walcutt, Charles Child. "Whitman's 'Out of the Cradle Endlessly Rocking,' " *College English,* X (February 1949), 277–279. On the unifying of three levels in the poem—childhood memory, mature passion, and philosophical speculation—and the meaning of the sea's answer.

Warfel, Harry R. " 'Out of the Cradle Endlessly Rocking,' " *Tennessee Studies in Literature,* III (1958), 83–87. Analysis of structure, figurative language, and meaning of the poem.

_____. "The Structure of 'Eidólons,' " *Walt Whitman Newsletter,* IV (December 1958), 103–105. In five parts, culminating in prophet-bard's responsibility for interpreting reality as spokesman of God.

Werner, W. L. "Whitman's 'The Mystic Trumpeter' as Autobiography," *American Literature,* VII (January 1936), 455–458. Interpretation of poem as treating phases of Whitman's career.

Whicher, Stephen. "Whitman's 'Out of the Cradle Endlessly Rocking,' " *The Explicator,* V (February 1947), item 28. Poem reconciles love and death in a Romantic treatment of fall from innocence to experience with compensatory deepened spiritual and poetic life.

Origins and Connections of Whitman's Poetry

Allen, Gay Wilson. "Biblical Echoes in Whitman's Works," *American Literature,* VI (November 1934), 302–315. A tabulation of the numerous allusions with some inferences on the origins of Whitman's style and approach.

Beaver, Joseph. *Walt Whitman—Poet of Science.* New York: King's Crown Press, 1951. Science is woven into Whitman's poetry. Numerous separate passages elucidated.

Blodgett, Harold. *Walt Whitman in England,* Cornell Studies in English, Vol. XXIV. Ithaca: Cornell University Press, 1934. A survey of Whitman's English reputation, with separate chapters on the work of W. M. Rossetti, Edward Dowden, John Addington Symonds, etc.

Brown, Clarence A. "Walt Whitman and the 'New Poetry,' " *American Literature,* XXXIII (March 1961), 33–45. Whitman's spirit, more than his technique or subject matter, was influential upon younger poets of the early twentieth century.

Canby, Henry Seidel. *Walt Whitman: An American.* Boston: Houghton Mifflin Co., 1943. Chapter 28: "I hear America singing." Treats the

Whitman style, stressing its origins in the Bible, Shakespeare, oratory, and Italian opera. Other criticism *passim*.

Carpenter, Frederic I. "The Vogue of Ossian in America: A Study in Taste," *American Literature*, II (January 1931), 405–417. Pages 413–417 treat Whitman's interest in Ossian and the Ossianic influence on Whitman's style.

Cooke, Alice Lovelace. "Whitman's Indebtedness to the Scientific Thought of His Day," University of Texas *Studies in English*, XIV (1934), 89–115. Elucidation of several poems by reference to contemporary astronomy, geology, and other sciences.

Faner, Robert D. *Walt Whitman and Opera*. Philadelphia: University of Pennsylvania Press, 1951. Survey of Whitman's acquaintance with opera and its effect on his poetry: subject matter, diction, etc.

Finkel, William L. "Walt Whitman's Manuscript Notes on Oratory," *American Literature*, XXII (March 1950), 29–53. Challenges originality of Whitman's notes and the presumption of influence of oratory on 1855 *Leaves of Grass*.

Gohdes, Clarence. "A Note on Whitman's Use of the Bible as a Model," *Modern Language Quarterly*, II (March 1941), 105–108. Three instances of imitation of the praise of charity in I Corinthians 13 from poems of 1856 edition support idea of Biblical influence, despite difficulty of making any general assertions about Whitman's versification.

_____. "Whitman and Emerson," *Sewanee Review*, XXXVII (January 1929), 79–93. On the twistings of the personal and intellectual relationship.

Goodale, David. "Some of Walt Whitman's Borrowings," *American Literature*, X (May 1938), 202–213. Stressed here are Whitman's borrowings from Frances Wright's *A Few Days in Athens* and C. F. Volney's *Ruins*. Whitman's indebtedness "is merely an interesting side light into his large proportions, and does not by any means account for his genius."

Jones, P. M. "Influence of Walt Whitman on the Origin of the 'Vers Libre,'" *Modern Language Review*, XI (April 1916), 186–194. Not an important influence. Whitman's "amorphous rhapsodies" are "much more unbridled than the freest French verses of that time."

Krouse, Sydney J. "Whitman, Music, and *Proud Music of the Storm*," *PMLA*, LXXII (September 1957), 705–721. Music provided Whitman with a subject, not a method, the chief interest of which was in its effect on the poet. Illustrated by analysis of "Proud Music of the Storm."

Lenhart, Charmenz S. *Musical Influence on American Poetry*. Athens: University of Georgia Press, 1956. Chapter on Whitman stresses parallels between his poetry and the Beethoven symphony.

Lowell, Amy. "Walt Whitman and the New Poetry," *Yale Review*, XVI (April 1927), 502–519. Modern writers of cadenced verse owe nothing, formally, to Whitman, who, though a genuine poet, had very little rhythmical sense and created his own form ignorantly, not consciously. Modern poets are indebted to Whitman for treating America as homeland, not colony.

Lowes, John Livingston. *Convention and Revolt in Poetry*. Boston and New York: Houghton Mifflin Co., 1919. Includes discussion of *vers libre* and of the borderland between poetry and prose, with brief mention of Whitman.

Miller, James E., Jr., Karl Shapiro, and Bernice Slote. *Start with the Sun: Studies in Cosmic Poetry*. Lincoln: University of Nebraska Press, 1960. Essays on the "Whitman tradition" in twentieth century, including such writers as D. H. Lawrence, Hart Crane, and Dylan Thomas.

Moore, John B. "The Master of Whitman," *Studies in Philology*, XXIII (January 1926), 77–89. Though he sought to minimize the debt, Whitman owed more to Emerson than to any other. Whitman finally came to undeviating allegiance to Emerson and Emersonianism.

Musgrove, S. *T. S. Eliot and Walt Whitman*. New York: Columbia University Press, 1953. On general relationship, similar literary devices, and echoes of some specific Whitman poems in Eliot's work. (See also above *s.v.* Daiches, "Whitman as Innovator.")

Pepper, Stephen C. *World Hypotheses: A Study in Evidence*. Berkeley and Los Angeles: University of California Press, 1957. Chapter XI: "Organicism," pp. 280–314. Gives philosophical background for much of Romantic aesthetic practice, including that of Whitman.

Pollak, Georgiana. "The Relationship of Music to 'Leaves of Grass,' " *College English*, XV (April 1954), 384–394. Resemblance of Whitman's rhythms is to semi-musical rhythm of recitative, not to that of pure music. Illustrated by comparison of Whitman passages with well-known recitatives.

Pound, Louise. "Walt Whitman and Italian Music," *American Mercury*, VI (September 1925), 58–63. Music inspired certain poems, affected Whitman's vocabulary, and may have colored his whole conception of poetry.

Romig, Edna Davis. "More Roots for *Leaves of Grass*," in *Elizabethan Studies and Other Essays in Honor of George F. Reynolds*. Boulder: University of Colorado Press, 1945. On some verbal similarities between Whitman and Emerson.

*Rourke, Constance. *American Humor: A Study of the National Character*. New York: Harcourt, Brace and Co., 1931. A characterization of three native comic figures (the Yankee, the backwoodsman, and the Negro), their similarities (masks, language, wandering propensities, etc.), and the way in which American literature rests on this comic groundwork.

Schumann, Detley W. "Enumerative Style and Its Significance in Whitman, Rilke, Werfel," *Modern Language Quarterly*, III (June 1942), 171–204. Catalogue style is technical equivalent of mystical faith in the oneness of existence.

*Shephard, Esther, *Walt Whitman's Pose*. New York: Harcourt, Brace and Co., 1938.

Smith, Fred Manning. "Whitman's Debt to Carlyle's *Sartor Resartus*," *Modern Language Quarterly*, III (March 1942), 51–65. Ideas and phraseology in poems of the first two editions of *Leaves of Grass* resemble those of Thomas Carlyle's book.

_____. "Whitman's Poet-Prophet and Carlyle's Hero," *PMLA,* LV (December 1940), 1146–1164. Clarification of Whitman's hero by reference to Carlyle's, whom he resembles in attitude, behavior, opinion, and linguistic habits.

Spiegelman, Julia. "Walt Whitman and Music," *South Atlantic Quarterly,* XLI (April 1942), 167–176. Survey of Whitman's relationship to music, inferences about its effect on his poetry, and information on Whitman's poems which have been set to music.

Stovall, Floyd. "Notes on Whitman's Reading," *American Literature,* XXVI (November 1954), 337–362. Identifies sources of 112 notes printed in Vols. IX and X of *Complete Writings.*

*_____. "Walt Whitman and the American Tradition," *Virginia Quarterly Review,* XXXI (Autumn 1955), 540–557. On progress, individualism, and the moral law in American thought and in Whitman.

Willard, Charles B. *Whitman's American Fame: The Growth of His Reputation in America After 1892.* Providence: Brown University Press, 1950. Examines work of enthusiasts, journalists, academics, and creative writers before generalizing on Whitman's fame.

Williams, William Carlos. "An Essay on *Leaves of Grass*" in *Leaves of Grass One Hundred Years After,* ed. Milton Hindus. Stanford: Stanford University Press, 1955. Pp. 22–31. Though the success of T. S. Eliot has obscured the fact, Whitman's probing of the poetic line is in keeping with comparable developments in modern physics, psychology, or even petroleum engineering.

DATE DUE

OCT 12 '70			
APR 15 '71			
NOV 16 '71			
APR 25 '74			
DEC 12 '78			
MAR 1 '79			
OCT 27 '76			
GAYLORD			PRINTED IN U.S.A.